Acknowledgements

CW01501271

This book would not have been possible without these friends, seniors and organisations who shared their inputs without reservations.

- Indian Army
- Indian Air Force
- Lt. Gen (Retd) ML Chibber
- Brig (Retd) VN Channa
- Col (Retd) Narinder 'Bull' Kumar
- AVM (Retd) Manmohan Bahadur
- Lt Gen Sanjay Kulkarni
- Lt Gen KH Singh
- Maj Gen Shokin Chauhan
- Lt Gen (Retd) PC Katoch
- Brig Abhijit Bapat
- Air Com (Retd) Anil K. Sinha
- Group Capt (Retd) WV Rama Rao
- 'Capt' Joesph 'Sam' Samuel
- Col (Retd) Gopal Karunakaran
- Col (Retd) Danvir Singh
- Army Medical Corps
- Ketki Angre
- Mayank Singh
- JAK LI Regimental Centre

BEYOND NJ 9842
The SIACHEN Saga

BEYOND NJ 9842

The SIACHEN Saga

Nitin A. Gokhale

BLOOMSBURY
LONDON • NEW DELHI • NEW YORK • SYDNEY

BLOOMSBURY PUBLISHING INDIA PVT. LTD.
London   New Delhi   New York   Sydney

ISBN: 978-93-84052-05-8

10 9 8 7 6 5 4 3 2 1

Published by Bloomsbury Publishing India Pvt. Ltd.
Vishrut Building, DDA Complex, Building No. 3
Pocket C-6 & 7, Vasant Kunj
New Delhi 110 070

To
The Indian soldier
Who gives so much and
Asks for nothing but dignity and a
little understanding from his countrymen

Foreword

At the strategic level, one requires a long memory and a longer foresight and vision.

Boundaries are a manifestation of national identity. Disputed boundaries are often trip-wires of war. Siachen sits astride two disputed boundaries: with Pakistan and China. Nitin Gokhale's book '*Beyond NJ 9842: The Siachen Saga*' has motivated me to write about its strategic significance for India and the complexities that come in the way of resolving this dispute.

Siachen lies in the Karakoram Range (beyond the Ladakh Range) in the Northwest of India. The Glacier descends from a height of 23,000 to 12,000 feet. It is 75 km long and covers about 10,000 sq km uninhabited terrain. Along with other glaciers in this area, it is an important source of water for the Indus River which passes through Ladakh and Kargil, and then into Pakistan Occupied Kashmir (POK). The area is claimed by us on the basis of accession of J & K to India in October 1947 and the Karachi Agreement of 1949, which described the ceasefire line beyond NJ 9842 (Saltoro Ridge and beyond) to be '*running Northwards to the glaciers*'.

Pakistan's cartographic attempt to join NJ 9842 to Karakoram Pass on the India-China boundary (a straight line moving *Northeast* instead of North) sending mountaineering expeditions and preparations to occupy it with military was foiled when India launched '*Operation Meghdoot*' in April 1984. Indian army occupied the Soltoro Ridge to secure the glacier and the territory to its east. This deployment (a) dominates Pakistani positions in the valley west of Soltoro Ridge (b) blocks infiltration possibilities across the Soltoro Ridge passes into Ladakh (c) prevents Pakistani military adventurism in Turtuk and areas to its south. Its Northernmost position at Indira Col overlooks the Shaqsgam Valley (illegally ceded by Pakistan to China) and denies Pakistani access to the Karakoram Pass. Since then the line dividing the military forces of India and Pakistan in the area north of Point NJ 9842 has come to be known as the Actual Ground Position Line (AGPL).

Siachen has always been considered a military setback by the Pakistan Army. That the Indians dominate the area from the Saltoro Ridge and Pakistan troops are nowhere near Siachen Glacier is a fact never mentioned in public. The perceived humiliation manifests itself in many ways. When the Indian Army pre-empted Pakistan plans and occupied the Saltoro Ridge, Benazir Bhutto publicly taunted the Pakistani Army as 'fit only to fight its own citizens'. She did that again when in 1987, Indian troops led by Naib Subedar Bana Singh captured the 21,000-feet Quaid-e-Azam Post in the area and renamed it Bana Post.

In Pakistan, Siachen is a subject that hurts, just like a thorn in its flesh. It is a psychological drain on the Pakistani Army. Pervez Musharraf had once commanded the Special Services Group (SSG) in this area and made several futile attempts to capture Indian posts. One of the motivating factors, and one of the military objectives of the Pakistan Army during the Kargil war in 1999 was to 'recapture' part of the Siachen Glacier and cut off our vital communication links to this area. They failed and suffered heavy casualties.

And now to the Chinese involvement and the Sino-Pakistan strategic nexus!

Two years after occupying Tibet in 1950, China started construction of a strategic road connecting Tibet to Xinjiang (China National Highway 219) through Aksai Chin, considered a part of J & K state. The road completed by 1957, heralded Chinese occupation of Aksai Chin whose boundary with Tibet had several disputed records and versions. The disputed boundary and claims on the area became one of the triggers for the Sino-Indian war of 1962. Soon after the war, Pakistan and China signed the Sino-Pakistan Border Agreement in 1963 in which Pakistan unilaterally ceded Shaqsgam Valley (J & K territory under occupation of Pakistan, flanking the Saltoro Ridge) to China. This agreement described the eastern termination of the Sino-Pakistan boundary at Karakoram Pass. On the maps, Pakistan drew the line from NJ 9842 towards the North East to Karakoram Pass, ignoring *thence north to the glaciers* statement of the 1949 Karachi Agreement. The result: Karakoram Pass, till then on the boundary between India and China, now had Pakistani involvement.

It should be noted that the Chinese were willing to negotiate and settle the boundary issue of J&K (west of Karakoram Pass) with Pakistan.

But till date, they have refused to discuss that boundary with India on the ground of it being 'disputed'.

In 1987, China and Pakistan signed the protocol to formalise the demarcation of their boundary. Termination of this boundary at Karakoram Pass and Pakistani recognition of Chinese sovereignty over Aksai Chin clearly indicated an understanding between them.

In 1997, when I was Chief of the Army Staff, China agreed to send its military commander opposite Ladakh to meet his India counterpart in Leh as a confidence-building measure. Near the date, it proposed that the meeting be held in New Delhi instead of Leh. As that would have served no purpose, the meeting was called off. After the Kargil war, military attachés from all countries except Pakistan were invited for a conducted tour of the battle zone. The Chinese attaché declined that invitation.

Four years ago, China started issuing "stapled visas" to visitors from J&K, thus bringing into question its status as part of India. It refused a visa to the GOC-in-C, Northern Command, who was to make an official visit to China as part of ongoing military-level exchanges.

China has now increased its civil and military presence in the northern areas, purportedly to improve infrastructure there. Among the infrastructure reconstruction projects to be given priority are those related to the repair and upgradation of the Karakoram Highway, which was damaged in 2009. China also plans to construct railway tracks and oil pipelines from Kashgar in Xinjiang to Gwadar port in Pakistan.

Why has military withdrawal from Siachen become more complicated now?

Whenever India and Pakistan have discussed the Siachen glacier issue, Pakistan has refused to authenticate the AGPL and the existing troops' locations. Pakistan demands Indian troops' withdrawal to the pre-1972 position i.e. to the east of the line joining NJ 9842 and Karakoram Pass. The strategic consequences of a deal without formal authentication are obvious. Pakistan army will have comparatively easier access to the Saltoro Ridge and to the glacier. That will also ensure security of the Shaksgam Valley for China and put a final stamp on its political control.

In the initial stages, occupation of the Siachen glacier area undoubtedly led to some financial drain on Indian resources, apart from a military effort of Herculean proportions. However, over the years, with experience and improved technology, these difficulties have been overcome substantially.

The lack of trust between India and Pakistan (particularly with the latter's army) is well known. Without formal authentication of the AGPL, how does one detect any future encroachment into this area? It must be stated categorically that no amount of existing technology can have fool-proof surveillance and capability to detect small-scale infiltration, which is sufficient to hold and defend a tactical feature in this terrain. Can India afford to forego the strategic significance of the Soltoro position due to the financial cost-benefit ratio analyses or because not a blade of grass grows in the area? Then why put up the Indian flag at Gangotri in South Pole? Can India trust Pakistan to the extent of foregoing formal authentication of the AGPL after what its army did across the formally delineated LoC in Kargil? Our negotiators must keep all these points in mind in their discussions with Pakistani counterparts.

So far, only a few people have written a detailed story on Siachen, which became the highest battlefield in the world, and is now the highest conflict zone. Nitin Gokhale, son of an ex-soldier, and now author, teacher and an accomplished journalist, gives an extensively anecdotal account and deep insight in 'Beyond NJ 9842: The Siachen Saga'. His interviews with soldiers who participated in the initial launch of Operation Meghdoot and their first hand accounts add an extremely useful human touch to the story. The large number of high quality, rare and unseen photographs of the glacier operations bring the story alive and help appreciate the harsh terrain and the human endeavours involved to overcome its physical and biological impact.

Nitin Gokhale's thirty years' experience, hunger for news and diligence in research makes this book extremely interesting and informative.

March 2014   **General V P Malik**
Former Chief of Army Staff
251, Sector 6, Panchkula 134 109

Contents

Introduction

'Mountains and the military fascinate me in equal measure'

Maybe because between 1983 and 2006, living in and reporting from India's North-east, I dealt with them more frequently than with anything else.

And then there was the summer of 1999.

Paying a silent tribute to the Siachen warrior

At the Siachen War Memorial with my wife, Neha

That year, a combination of serendipity and a risk-taking editor of *Outlook* magazine took me to the mountains of Kargil. That is when I first heard of Siachen, but only in passing.

During that 45-day assignment, reporting the mini war between India and Pakistan, I did occasionally hear a comment, 'Pakistan's ultimate aim was to isolate and cut off Siachen,' but as a reporter concerned only with getting the next story right, one never gave enough thought at that time to the 'strategic' aspect of the Kargil conflict.

Shifting to Delhi in 2006 and taking up larger responsibilities in NDTV, was an opportunity to widen horizons.

Within the first couple of months, the Siachen question popped up again in the context of searching for a lasting peace between India and Pakistan. Diplomats looking for a quick solution to the half- a-century old problem between India and Pakistan, identified Siachen and Sir Creek as 'low hanging fruits' to be plucked, to initiate a larger peace process.

When negotiations failed to make much headway, a convenient

scapegoat was sought to be found in the then Army Chief, who had insisted that the respective deployments of the Indian and Pakistani troops be marked on a map before arriving at any 'solution' to Siachen, a position not acceptable to Pakistan. The 'peaceniks' accused the Indian military of exercising a veto on foreign policy; the military said it was only giving professional opinion.

The renewed focus on Siachen revived my passing interest in the area. As I started reading available material, and simultaneously talking to people who had served there, the glacier beckoned. In July 2007, grabbing the first opportunity to visit Siachen, I spent four days at the Base Camp, talking to soldiers and pilots, and observing their routine, the adjustments that they made physically and in their minds; the preparations that went into the three-month deployment at altitudes where humans are not supposed to stay for prolonged periods.

For the next six years, I kept going back to Ladakh, once for a fairly longish family holiday and at least half a dozen times on work, reporting the trouble on the Chinese border, a natural calamity and celebrating a decade of victory in Kargil. Through all this, Siachen remained a half mystery: I knew the official Indian position, the extent of deployment of the Indian Army in the area, and the stupendous jobs that the air

At the Siachen Battle School in October 2013

warriors were doing in sustaining the deployment at those forbidding heights. Personal stories were however missing. Which officers and men outsmarted the Pakistanis in occupying the key watershed of Saltoro to secure Siachen in the summer of 1984? Was it a political or a military decision? Or a combination of both? Who discovered Pakistan's cartographic aggression in the Karakorams?

They would have remained questions in my mind, but for a chance meeting with Suresh Gopal of Bloomsbury India at a function to launch a book written by former Central Army Commander, Lt. Gen VK Ahluwalia. Over dinner a week later, we got talking. When Suresh asked me what book would I be interested in writing, my instinctive answer was, "a comprehensive book on India's North-east." And I proceeded to tell him about my long association and affinity with the region. Sure, he said, but how about something on the Indian military?

And at that moment, without thinking, I said "What about a book on Siachen?"

I do not know why I said it. I was aware of at least four books on Siachen that been written previously; I had not done adequate

With Army Aviation pilots and other officers at the Base Camp

The Thoise Airfield: Life line for Siachen

research on the subject, and I was not even sure of getting access to the Siachen area. So, how was I to write a book? But, Bloomsbury was eager. And I thought the time was right. April 2014 I knew, would mark 30 years of *Operation Meghdoot*, the Indian military's longest continuous deployment. So in a way, a deadline was already set. If I had to write any book on Siachen, its release had to be timed with the 30th anniversary. That left me with less than six months to assemble the material and write the manuscript.

Prodded and cajoled by the publishers, I gradually began looking at the subject more closely. By October 2013, the Army came around and allowed me to visit the Siachen base camp, and meet up with those posted there. As I warmed up to the subject, and started tapping those who had formerly served on the glacier, the trickle of information became a torrent.

When word spread about my attempt to chronicle the Siachen saga— and saga it is, unparalleled for the bravery, commitment and sacrifice of Indian soldiers—many soldiers and air warriors who had left service got in touch to share their stories. Many officers from the Army, the Air Force and the Army Medical Corps volunteered information, personal anecdotes and unreservedly shared their fears and triumphs; everyone

5

On the way to Turtuk: With my wife Neha

went out of his way to rummage through forgotten albums to dig out old, frayed photographs, and details of their stay on what is easily the most inhospitable battlefield. Everyone spared valuable time to sit down and allow me to record conversations. It was as if all Siachen veterans I could reach out to, were undergoing a catharsis, unburdening themselves and unlocking their long suppressed memories.

Sifting through the material, it became clear to me what the book should not be: a dry, officious Sitrep (Situation Report) about a military operation. Instead, we decided to concentrate on the human element: the tragedies, the comradeship, the commitment and sheer bravery of soldiers on Siachen.

This book is not a definitive history of *Operation Meghdoot*. But, it certainly is a slice of history seen through the eyes of those who had the opportunity to serve at Siachen. I have no pretensions of being a military analyst either. I am a journalist who has had the privilege of being trusted by officers and men in the Indian military, a trust I value far more than anything else in my profession.

Beyond NJ 9842: The Siachen Saga is a product of collective efforts, bolstered by contributions from many, but the ultimate responsibility lies with me. Several friends, colleagues, senior military officers and diplomats have given me their time and insights, but had it not been the constant companionship of my wife Neha, I wouldn't have been able to write this book in less than six months. She cheerfully put up with my irritating habit of waking up at 4 am and working on the computer in our bedroom; my consistent refusal to give her adequate time because the deadline loomed, and my general lack of participation in family matters. She even braved the hardship of visiting the Siachen base camp with me. Each time I finish a book—this is my fourth—I promise her that I will not work on short deadlines. Hopefully, I will be able to keep my word next time I take up a project. Both our boys, Harsh and Utkarsh, in their twenties, on the other hand, are like my News Editors in my early years in journalism, constantly asking uncomfortable questions: "How far are you from finishing the manuscript? Why is it taking such a long time?" Their frank inputs and Neha's detached and constructive criticism continues to keep me rooted.

Many others have helped create this book. All those who can be named have been quoted in the succeeding pages. Those who can't be, are no less valuable. I remain indebted to them. I am also grateful to former Chief of the Army Staff, Gen VP Malik for writing the Foreword and putting Siachen in a strategic context.

A three-decade long operation like *Operation Meghdoot* will have many untold stories; I have tried to capture as many as possible, but the list can never be complete. That is my failing. But read it for whatever it is worth.

It will force you to stand up and just say "Salute."

March 2014   **Nitin A. Gokhale**
New Delhi

The War Memorial at the Base Camp

With one of the Commanding Officers at Siachen Base Camp

*OPERATION MEGHDOOT
– THE EARLY DAYS*

I

Waking Up To Siachen

'Apne mian ko mat jaane do Col Kumar ke saath!'

Had it not been for a German expedition wishing to go rafting on the Indus River in North-west India's Ladakh region in 1975, this book would not have been written!

Thanks to that expedition, Col Narinder 'Bull' Kumar, India's most famous military mountaineer got possession of maps that indicated 'cartographic aggression' by Pakistan on the Siachen glacier and the quiet alteration to the map of the Karakoram Range of mountains!

One discovery led to another, resulting in India pre-empting a Pakistani

Col. 'Bull' Kumar at his home in 2013 (left) and in his younger days

military operation by launching its own in April 1984, triggering a standoff at Siachen, inarguably the world's highest battlefield.

But I am getting ahead of the story.

In September 2013, as I sat down to have a chat with the legendary Col Kumar in his South Delhi apartment and switched on the voice recorder, the renowned mountaineer first asked me if I had ample time. Without waiting for my answer, he said "I am going to tell you a longggg story about how we stumbled upon the Pakistani plan to occupy Siachen."

I had plenty of time.

The story, according to Col Kumar, really begins in 1975.

In those days, Shiekh Abdullah was Chief Minister of Jammu and Kashmir and Col Kumar was on deputation to the National Ski School at Gulmarg, the famous tourist spot. 'One day, Sheikh saab sent for me.' Apparently, two Germans wanted to go rafting down the Indus river which they called the world's fifth largest. It had not been done before and they wanted to be the first team to achieve that feat. So Sheikh Saab told them, 'if anyone can help you in this it is Col. Kumar!' Somehow he had tremendous faith in me.

Mustafa Kamal, Sheikh Abdullah's other, not-so-famous-son, used to be based in Tanmarg. He told Col Kumar to urgently go and meet Sheikh Abdullah. As Col Kumar reached Srinagar and was ushered in to meet Sheikh Abdullah, the Chief Minister introduced him to the Germans and said, "Please help them in their project."

As the expedition took shape, Col Kumar was made the leader of the team. The rafting was to begin from Chumathang in south eastern Ladakh, not very far from Demchok where the Indus crosses over into India from Tibet. Permissions took time. Normally, in those days, as now, any presence of foreigners in Ladakh had to be first cleared by the Army, and then the Home Department of the state government which formally issued the 'inner line permit.' In this case, the Sheikh Saab directly ordered the permit to be issued without clearance from the Army!

12   The expedition, first known rafting effort on the Indus, went through

without a hitch. "It took us five days to raft down from Chumathang to Khalsi (just before the Indus makes its way into Pakistan)," Col Kumar told me showing the newspaper clippings of that time. The headlines varied from a predictable "Indo-German team tames the Indus" to a spicier "Spying down river Indus."

But Col Kumar was not aware that some trouble awaited him after the expedition was over. India was under Emergency at that point in time, and any involvement with foreigners was not viewed too kindly by the Army. And sure enough 'Bull' Kumar was pulled up by a Brigadier who later went on to become the Corps Commander at Srinagar, for having by-passed the Army and gone ahead with the rafting expedition without permission. But the Sheikh knew Mrs Indira Gandhi. He directly spoke to the Prime Minister and got Col Kumar off the hook!

As his stint at the National Ski School came to an end, Col Kumar reverted to the Army and went on to climb the Kanchenjunga besides a number of smaller peaks. By now it was late 1977. After successfully climbing Kanchenjunga, then Army Chief Gen TN Raina sent for Col Kumar. It helped that both belonged to the Kumaon Regiment. As a reward for his exploits, "Bull" Kumar was made Commandant of the High Altitude Warfare School (HAWS), located at Gulmarg and Sonmarg just short of the Zojila Pass that connects the Kashmir Valley to Ladakh.

As luck would have it, completely out of the blue, the same German group that had rafted down the Indus under Col. Kumar's leadership, came back to Kashmir and now wanted to attempt rafting down the Nubra river that drained out from the Siachen glacier. No one had done rafting on the Nubra before. The Germans brought with them some American maps. As Col Kumar sat down to plan yet another expedition, his eyes kept straying to the Eastern Karakoram and particularly the area between (map grid reference) NJ 9842 and Karakoram Pass.

"Those maps, to my surprise, had shown the ceasefire line (line of control—LoC now) being extended to the Karakoram Pass," Col Kumar reminisced. "I instantly realised there was something wrong," the veteran mountaineer told me and took me back to 1961.

"A year before the 1962 war, I had frost bite from a mountaineering expedition and was therefore put in hospital and later attached to the intelligence department so that I could continue to get medical treatment. That is the time I did a lot of staff work, read maps and helped in drafting and reading Sitreps (Situation Reports). I knew the area and its map backwards. The ceasefire line which is now called the Line of Control or LoC had ended at (map grid reference) NJ 9842. So when I saw the American maps in late 1977 with the line extended to the Karakoram Pass (north-east of NJ 9842), instead of going northwards along the natural ridgeline, alarm bells went off in my head. All the old training of reading maps and retaining information here (pointing to his head) instantly came back. I made

14

a mental note of the line and completed the expedition quietly," the veteran soldier recalled.

Why did the map upset Col Kumar? He says the alignment shown on the American map beyond NJ 9842 meant Pakistan was laying claim to new areas and the Siachen glacier.

Col Kumar does not remember if the maps with the Germans were

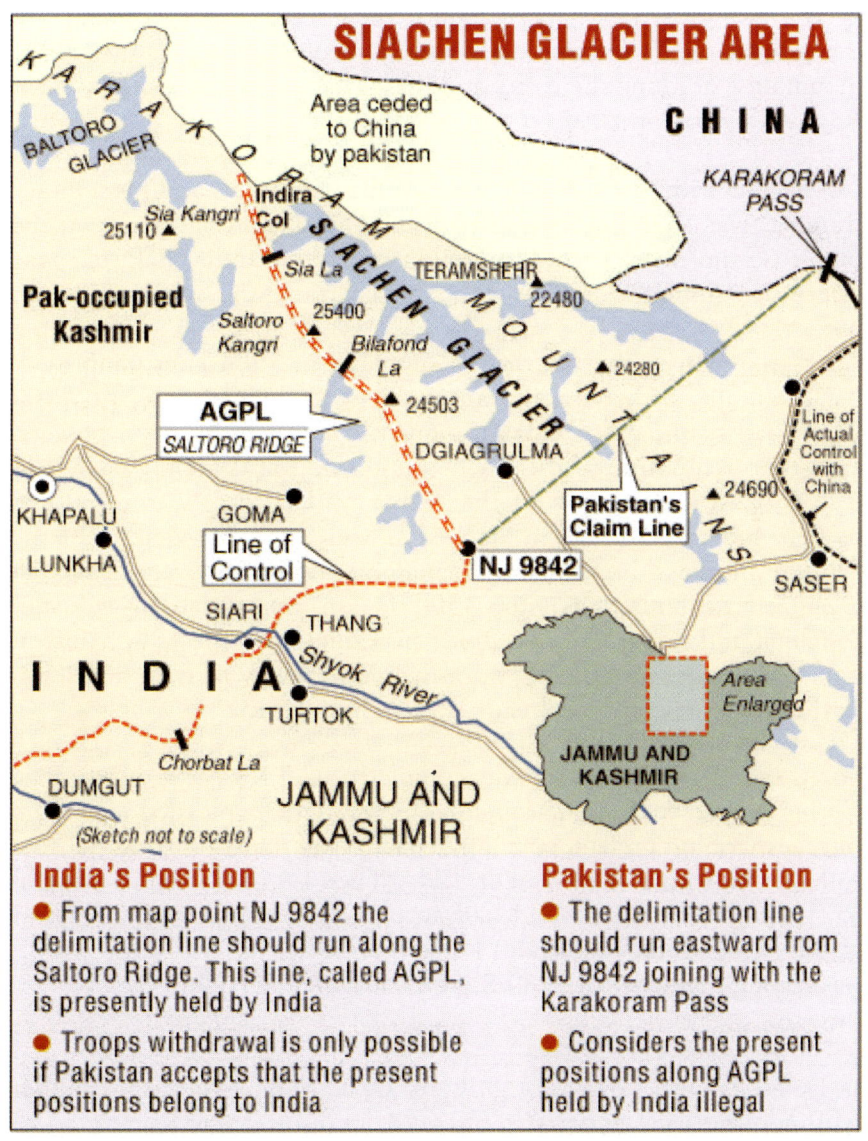

SIACHEN GLACIER AREA

India's Position
● From map point NJ 9842 the delimitation line should run along the Saltoro Ridge. This line, called AGPL, is presently held by India

● Troops withdrawal is only possible if Pakistan accepts that the present positions belong to India

Pakistan's Position
● The delimitation line should run eastward from NJ 9842 joining with the Karakoram Pass

● Considers the present positions along AGPL held by India illegal

the US Defence Mapping Agency's operational navigational charts but Lt Gen VR Raghavan, strategic thinker and former Director General Military Operations (DGMO) of the Indian Army in his path breaking book, *Siachen: Conflict without end*, says the 1974 edition of the US agency's map was the first to show an Air Defence Information Zone (ADIZ) separating India and Pakistan in the Karakoram region. "The line marking the separation was drawn straight from NJ 9842 to the Karakoram Pass, instead of following the international convention of marking boundaries along natural ridgelines. It could not have been a boundary since there cannot be a straight line boundary in the mountains. Boundaries are either formed along the watersheds of mountains, or along the rivers and the ADIZ was along neither," Gen Raghavan wrote in 2002.

Col Kumar with his vast experience of the mountains and his military training, was sharp enough to realise that Pakistan had redrawn the map to claim new areas. More dangerously for India, Pakistan was clearly attempting to link up with China through the Siachen glacier!

An assessment by the Northern Command in 1984 later confirmed: "With an all-weather Karakoram highway to the west and the Aksai Chin road to the east, Ladakh is open to a pincer by these powers. Pakistani occupation of the Siachen upto the Karakoram Pass would lead to their domination of the Nubra Valley and the route down to Leh. Indian positions in Siachen as well as in the vicinity of the Karakoram Pass are thus a formidable wedge between Pakistan Occupied Kashmir(POK), the 4500 sq km area ceded by Pakistan to China and Aksai Chin occupied by China after the 1962 conflict. Pakistani occupation of the region would in a way provide a cushion to the Chinese positions already present in the area."

So, as the 1977 expedition was completed, Col Kumar requested the Germans to leave the maps behind. "I cajoled them, pleaded with them but they wouldn't relent, so finally I had to pay them a substantial sum to keep the maps," Col Kumar said. "Then I took the maps straight to (Lt) Gen (ML) Chibber. I had an old association with him. I was in the MT (Military Training) Directorate when he was writing a lot of training manuals for HAWS. So I took the liberty of going to him directly."

In Delhi, as DMO (Director Military Operations), Maj Gen Chibber had more pressing matters to attend to than meet Col Kumar. So he sent Kumar to one of the Deputy Director Generals in the Operations Directorate, Brig Mehta and told him, "take this young fellow, my old officer, give him a cup of tea and listen to what bulls**t he has to share," almost dismissing Col Kumar!

But Col Kumar was nothing if not obdurate. He persuaded Brig Mehta to dig out all the old treaties from the time of Maharaja Ranjit Singh onwards, through the East India Company right up to the 1972 Shimla Agreement between Indira Gandhi and Zulfikar Ali Bhutto that converted the old ceasefire line into the LoC. After long deliberations, Brig Mehta saw Col Kumar's point about the new alignment shown on the American map and its dangerous implications.

"Brig Mehta was totally satisfied that I was right. He took me back to the DMO and asked him if we could take two minutes of his time," Col Kumar recalls. Brig Mehta then told the DMO that the line on the map was wrong and had security implications for India's defence in Ladakh. As the DMO took a second look at the American map, he was aghast. "*Badi halchal machi, DMO ke office mein* (there was a sense of disquiet)," Col Kumar still recalls that scene in the DMO's office.

"Looking at the map" Gen Chibber said, '*aare* Pakistan is occupying 10,000 sq km of land on their own and we know nothing!' This line was drawn in 1963. We were in 1978. For 15 years we knew nothing!"

After the initial shock, Gen Chibber asked Col Kumar: "What can you do for us?" "I said we will take an expedition there." That is how we launched the first expedition in 1978. As Gen Chibber recounted in an article after his retirement, "The matter (of increasing Pakistani forays into Siachen and the wrong depiction on some American maps) had to be handled with despatch and circumspection. I walked into the office of the Army Chief Gen TN Raina and explained the problem to him. By calling it an operational patrol it was possible to provide logistics support to Kumar. If he were to undertake a mountaineering expedition without official backing, it would cost somewhere in the region of Rs 8-10 lakhs. For example, if the party needed 100 high altitude porters, at a cost of Rs 50 per porter (this was the rate in 1978) per day, then the cost of porterage for about 60 days would amount to Rs 3 lakhs. The cost of special food, medical cover, insurance, air evacuation of casualties, air dropping of supplies,   **17** special clothing and equipment, all would add up to a prohibitive amount."

In Delhi, Gen Chibber and Army HQ took up the matter of wrong representation on American maps with the US government through the Ministry of Defence and the Ministry of External Affairs. But nothing came of it, since the maps were printed by a commercial firm! Kumar had in the meantime returned to HAWS and prepared to take his team to Siachen.

"Since I was the Commandant of the High Altitude Warfare School, I decided to take my own instructors and students of the advanced mountaineering course for the expedition," Col Kumar told me in 2013.

No officer or soldier was reluctant to join the expedition, but to Col Kumar's utter surprise, his wife brought an input that was quite revealing. "My wife overheard a wife telling another officer's wife *"apne mian ko mat jaane do Col Kumar ke saath! Woh Pakistan bhi jaa rahe hein or China bhi!"* referring to the supposedly ultra secret expedition that Col Kumar was to lead to the area, we now know as the Siachen glacier! "So much for our security," Col Kumar looks back and has a hearty laugh.

So off they went on a reconnaissance patrol in the guise of a civilian expedition!

As the expedition arrived on the glacier via Khardung La, Pullu, Khalsar, Sasoma and started showing Indian flags and presence up to Teram Kangri, which is half way up the Siachen glacier, Pakistani planes and helicopters came overhead and photographed the mountaineers. Apart from the memories of the climb, Col Kumar distinctly remembers that between Leh (then HQ of the 3 Infantry Division) and Partapur (the sector HQ) there were precisely three unarmed Ladakh Scouts soldiers basically keeping count of mules and convoys going to Daulat Beg Oldie or DBO!

Today, 35 years later, the defence of Ladakh is looked after by a full-fledged Corps. Beyond Khardung La (supposedly the world's highest motorable pass) by an independent brigade with six battalions under it (6,000 soldiers) is deployed to keep India's borders secure.

To return to Col Kumar's early forays into unexplored areas.

After completing the expedition, Col Kumar was back at HAWS. He gave a detailed report to the Army and suggested that another expedition, this time right up to the beginning of the Siachen glacier to Indira Col and Sia Kangri. Kumar also reported some "air activity" from the Pakistani side when a jet had overflown the expedition at one stage. However, that summer Kumar did not come across any Pakistani based expeditions moving in the Siachen area, but near the Bilafond La his team did find some signs of previous expeditions. They picked up some tin labels printed in Japanese. Col Kumar submitted his report and recommended establishing a post along the Saltoro ridge in the summer months to ensure the Pakistanis did not intrude onto the Siachen glacier.

At Army HQ and in the Northern Command, this recommendation was examined in depth, but it was felt that severe weather conditions and high altitudes precluded any possibility of permanent presence on the glacier. Gen Chibber recalled later: "It was decided that in addition to expeditions that went into this area now and then, the Siachen glacier should be regularly patrolled during the summer months. It was also decided to permit foreign expeditions and give wide publicity to such expeditions and their achievements in various mountaineering journals in order to discourage Pakistan-based expeditions from surreptitiously entering into this region."

In fact, Col Kumar wrote a detailed account of the expedition in the *Himalayan Journal* in the summer of 1979-80 (http://www. himalayanclub.org/journal/teram-kangri-ii-expedition/), without giving away the fact that the expedition had a military objective in mind! The only hint that this was an Army-supported effort was in one paragraph in the article authored by Col. Kumar. He wrote: "I needed administrative support of the kind we had received on the Kanchenjunga, if not more. So I called on the Chief of the Army Staff, General O.P. Malhotra (who had taken over from Gen Raina) and unfolded my plans. I was relieved to hear: 'Karakoram, an excellent idea.' So the sky was the limit as far as administrative backing was concerned." What Col Kumar doesn't say explicitly is that the Army spent over Rs 10 lakhs on the expedition and showed it as an Operational Reconnaissance Patrol on paper to avoid any uncomfortable queries from military auditors!

19

As 1980-81 dawned, Col Kumar was in 'been there, done that' kind of situation. After 28 years, his Army career was going nowhere. Many of his juniors had already become brigadiers. In mountaineering too, he had achieved much more than most people could dream of in a lifetime. So the veteran climber decided to hang up his army boots in early 1981, applying for voluntary retirement. The retirement date was set for 17 October 1981.

But unknown to him, another, perhaps the most difficult challenge of his already distinguished mountaineering career, was still to come.

Two days before Col Kumar was to go on six months leave prior to his eventual retirement, the Army decided to send another expedition to the eastern Karakoram, this time right up to Indira Col. "I thought to myself, *yaar meine yeh shuru kiya hai*, I should end it," Col Kumar remembers as we sipped coffee in his modest apartment in central Delhi in mid-September 2013. There was a catch: Col Kumar was on leave and was about to retire, and to top it all, his medical officer pointed out that the veteran was placed in medical category 'C' because of earlier frost bite injuries, which meant he wouldn't be permitted to climb beyond 7,000 ft! If he wanted to go, he would have to go at his own risk, Col Kumar was told by the Army doctor. There would be no medical cover provided!

Col Kumar (left) with Lt Gen S.P. Malhotra,
Northern Army Commander (1981)

"I was aghast, but had no alternative but to give an undertaking that I would go on the expedition at my own risk!"

Before going on the expedition, Col Kumar went to meet Army Chief Gen OP Malhotra, who was a month away from retirement. The Chief asked Col. Kumar what he needed the most. Col Kumar's simple answer: don't put the expedition on paper. "In the Army even a secret mission will go through six formations. I did not want anyone to know that this was a secret military expedition," Col Kumar said.

The Army Chief was only half convinced. But, he said the Northern Army Commander had to be on board, so Lt Gen SP Malhotra then heading the Northern Command was sent for and brought into the picture. The Army Chief told Lt Gen SP Malhotra of Col Kumar's request. Despite his own reservations, the Northern Army Commander agreed to the suggestion of keeping the expedition out of army records.

On the way back to Udhampur, which was the Northern Command HQ, Col Kumar hitched a ride on the Army Commander's plane. Lt Gen Malhotra was still not comfortable with the decision not to put anything down in writing.

Col Kumar recalls: "He was pacing up and down in the plane. Mid-way through the flight, the Army Commander remarked testily, 'Col. you don't want me to be your staff officer surely? Someone else must be in the loop apart from me.' So I said all right, can we take BGS (Brigadier,

Col Kumar's team on the Siachen glacier, circa 1978

21

General Staff) Brig. Dias, who later retired as Corps Commander, into confidence? Dias was six months junior to me and we had known each other earlier. The Army Commander agreed."

"I said tell Brig. Dias not to dub this expedition as a military mission. Let it be open. Since my background as a mountaineer was well known, I was certain if I led the expedition no one would give it a second glance," Col Kumar reasoned. He was bang on.

In all the photographs that the Pakistanis had taken of India's 1978 expedition on the glacier, there were no weapons to be seen. So, as the Indians began climbing the glacier again in 1981, there was no undue alarm among the Pakistanis. This was seen as just another mountaineering expedition.

And yet, as another member of the team, retired Major General BK Sharma, now a Distinguished Fellow at the United Services Institution (USI), then a young Captain remembers, a platoon of 9 Para Commandos and another of Ladakh Scouts were providing security to the mission. "We knew that we were on a high-risk, top secret mission", Maj Gen Sharma recalls. He also remembers there were Films Division and Survey of India teams as part of the expedition. "But we did not have any maps of the area," Maj Gen Sharma told me during an interview at the USI.

The team had been flown by an Avro aircraft from Srinagar to Thoise, an airstrip near the Sector HQ of Partapur. From there it went by truck to Sasoma, the last road head normally used as a staging point for missions to Daulat Beg Oldie. From Sasoma, the expedition walked for four days to the snout of the glacier, almost to the location where the current Siachen Base Camp is located, Maj Gen Sharma remembers.

Col Kumar came back from the mission and retired from service. He once again wrote an article (http://www.himalayanclub.org/ journal/the-indian-army-expedition-to-the-eastern-karakoram-1981) and prepared a secret report for the Army on the importance of the glacier and evidence of Japanese and other expeditions allowed by the Pakistanis onto the glacier.

Over the next two seasons, 1982 and 1983 (in those days it was believed you could climb the glacier only between May and October), India kept sending probing missions variously named Polar Bear I,

Polar Bear II, Ibex I, Ibex II, etc. The 26 Sector at Partapur was getting increasingly focused on the 'area beyond Sasoma,' as one former Commander put it. The area beyond Sasoma was to soon become better known as Siachen!

THE FIRST HELICOPTER LANDING ON SIACHEN

Like the Army, even the Indian Air Force had hardly flown beyond Sasoma. Helicopters used to cross Khardung La (a formidable obstacle at 18300 ft!), go up to Thoise, Turtuk, Tyagshi but rarely ventured over the glacier.

But in September 1978 all that changed.

AVM Manmohan Bahadur, fresh out of Helicopter Training School (HTS) was posted to the 114 Helicopter Unit—114 HU—then headquartered at Jammu. Commanded by a Squadron Leader, there were 10 other Squadron Leaders and two Flight Lieutenants already posted in the unit. With so many seniors, Flying Officer Bahadur—the junior most and youngest—thought he would hardly get any flying opportunities. In those years, helicopter pilots from Jammu used to go on monthly detachments to Leh. In September however, much to his surprise, Flying Officer Bahadur was asked to go on temporary duty to Leh. It was a dream come true for a young flier!

"The area was more beautiful than one could have ever imagined and flying was just out of this world," he recalls.

"Half way through the assignment, I was detailed to accompany the detachment commander Sqn Leader KDS Sambyal to the 3 Div (3 Infantry Division) HQ. We were briefed about the HAWS expedition led by Col. Narinder Kumar. Looking at the map, we realised we had never been there. We had in fact not thought about flying over those unknown areas. I remember the Colonel GS (General Staff) explaining to us the purpose of the mission: to show the flag on a territory, rightfully ours but opened to foreign mountaineering expeditions by Pakistanis. We were also told that Pakistanis and some western maps were now showing the area as belonging to Pakistan. We were told that the HAWS expedition was sent to the glacier to oppose Pakistan's 'cartographic aggression.' That is the time I first heard the word Siachen glacier! We, as helicopter pilots were supposed to supply fresh rations and carry mail for members of the expedition. My log book shows 20 September 1978 as the date when the first air sortie on Siachen was launched by 114 HU!"

As the Chetak flew over Siachen, the two pilots got their first glimpse of the magnificent glacier! "The black snout of the glacier was, to say the least, imposing and menacing, yet truly majestic. As we flew along, I looked left and right for any possible force landing sites. The glacier was full of ice. Or crevasses. A thought occurred to me: there were no skis on our machine! But the task had to be done, so we pressed on. As Camp I loomed ahead, the hepter was brought to a 'hover', the sliding door opened and out went the load. A little ahead was Camp II. The process was repeated.

"Back from our trip—in retrospect a historic one—we discussed that it may be a good idea to pick up mail from the soldiers for their folks back home. So when the next requisition for another sortie came on 23 September 1978, we were ready. Sqn Leader JK Kaushik had meanwhile taken over as detachment commander. Again over Camp I, the hepter was brought to a hover, Sqn Ldr Kaushik (fondly known as Chacha) opened the sliding window of the door and out went the main rotor tip cover at the end of a string. In the tip cover was a small note in Hindi which said, 'we will be back in 10 minutes. Please write your letters and put them in the bag.' As we drew away, 'Chacha' pulled the string up, as if drawing water from a well!"

At Camp II, Bahadur remembers repeating the same process.

On their return trip, the two pilots came back to Camp I, sure that the soldiers down below would have quickly scribbled something for their loved ones and send those letters back home. But they were in for a shock.

"As we again hovered over Camp I, out went the string with the tip cover and but instead of letters, the soldier put in a small object. I kept signalling for letters but to no avail. We were already running low on fuel. As the string was pulled up, out came a tattered tiny carton of an eye 'drop' medicine. Inside the carton was a crumpled piece of paper! On it was written (in Hindi) *Sahib hamare pas likhne ke liye kagaz nahin hai. Kripaya likhne ke liye kuch saman le aaiye* (we don't have paper to write, please bring some pen and paper to write on!)" After so many years, I vividly recall there was a lump in my as well as Sqn Leader Kaushik's throat! Luckily, there were some free issue inland letters meant only for armed forces personnel lying around in the helicopter. We gave those to the soldiers and thereafter on every trip, dropped and picked up mail for our gallant soldiers via the 'drawing water from well' method!"

As Air Force helicopter pilots learnt new tricks of flying at impossible heights with very little oxygen, little did Bahadur know that he and his senior Sqn Ldr SK Monga were about to enter history books in less than a month after the first sortie over Siachen.

As we sat sipping beer in his well-appointed house, I was taken back once again to 1978.

After doing two trips over the glacier in September, Bahadur was back in Jammu.

In early October, there was the requirement for an engine change in a Chetak helicopter located in Leh. So Bahadur, as the youngest pilot in the unit, was assigned to carry the engine to Leh along with Sqn Ldr Hoon. They flew out early morning from Jammu to Srinagar, refuelled at Srinagar and then made the two-hour flight to Leh. The idea was to come back to Jammu the same day. As the replacement engine was being offloaded, the base received a distress call for casualty evacuation (CASEVAC) from the glacier. A member of Col Kumar's expedition needed urgent medical treatment and had to be lifted out from the glacier.

As coincidence would have it, both the pilots on detachment in Leh that day—Sqn Leader Monga and Sqn Leader Dogra--had not done their run to the glacier. Bahadur was the only one—by a sheer stroke of luck—to have done at least two sorties to the glacier the previous month. So Sqn Ldr Monga asked him to be his co-pilot on what they presumed would be a quick run to the glacier.

"As a youngster, you are happy to do these adventures. Meanwhile, I had a cup of coffee as we prepared to fly to the glacier. This was about 10 am. Since the morning I only had an apple to eat. So after the mandatory checks, we were off. Now the Chetak, unlike the Cheetah, is an under-powered machine, not designed to fly at those altitudes. So we used to hug the hills and utilise the up drafts (wind that rises up along the cliffs in mountains) to power our engines to help the helicopter gain altitude and cross passes. That's the only way we could cross Khardung La and Chang La (two of the highest passes in Ladakh at 18,000 plus feet). Today no one believes that we used to fly Chetaks in the high mountains of Ladakh just as we couldn't believe that our predecessors used to operate Mi-4s in the 1960s. So the Chetaks would fly just 20 feet away from the hill side at 35 knots, one eye on the air speed indicator (should not drop below that), and the other looking at the getaway direction, in case the up draft did not materialise. The rotors used to claw their way in the thin rarified air and make a funny phut, phut, phut sound and use the 'up draft' to gain lift to cross the pass.

"Sometimes you didn't get the updraft so you turned sharply, down in to the valley, and came up again to attempt another crossing, courtesy another updraft! Anyway, that day we crossed Khardung La in the first attempt, carried on, went across Sasoma, crossed the base camp and flew further. I was on the map. I was supposed to know. We were given the Lat-Long (Latitude-Longitude reference) of the place so we went looking for the spot from where the casualty had to be evacuated. We crossed Camp I, Camp II and the spot where the Kumar Camp now stands, but there was no sign of the casualty. So we kept flying further. I am quite sure we went right up to Indira Col (the northern most tip of the glacier) and turned back. We had apparently missed a crucial turn. We kept looking for the spot from where we had to pick up the sick soldier. After some time, we spotted the group. Sqn Ldr Monga made the mandatory low recce to check whether we could land. And land we did. It was a tremendous feat of flying by Sqn Ldr Monga, I can assure you," Bahadur, remembers vividly even now, over 35 years later.

Over that beer session one Sunday afternoon at his Gurgaon residence, he in fact, fished out a log book page for that day (see pix – notice just 439 hours of total flying experience then!!).

It showed an entry for 6 October 1978 which read: Chetak Z-1410

Sqn Ldr (Squadron Leader) Monga/self—Leh-Siachen Adv Base Camp-Thoise, 2 hrs, 50 mins!

That, from all accounts, was the first landing ever on the Siachen glacier, then an unknown area.

The young Manmohan Bahadur

As CO, 114 HU

Air warriors line up at Leh to make a 'human' chain denoting 'IAF'

27

The historic logbook page showing the first landing on Siachen

But the adventure didn't end there for Bahadur, who went on to command the very same 114 HU in Leh, 16 years after he was first posted to the unit.

"As we landed on the soft snow, Sqn Ldr Monga got out, asked me to take controls. He got an officer and a soldier into the chopper, strapped them, and closed the door. All this while the rotors were still running. He was panting. Remember we were at an altitude above 18,000 feet. The lack of oxygen, without acclimatisation, makes movements very difficult at that altitude. Sqn Ldr Monga, entered the chopper, quickly took a few puffs of the oxygen (the oxygen used to be like a *hookah*, a bottle and a pipe attached to it) and we were ready to take off. One hair-raising take off it was! The weight had increased, we were at 18,000 feet plus. But the moment we were steady, he gave me controls though I was a rookie. The Sqn Ldr desperately needed oxygen since he had exerted himself in the process of getting the patients into the cabin. We needed to refuel so we decided to hop over the ridge to Thoise instead of heading for Leh.

"That's when something happened to me. I broke into a cold sweat, got a clammy feeling, there was suddenly a pit in my stomach. I was feeling desperately sick. But I was barely 23 years old. How do I tell an older guy that I was not feeling well? But there was no other way. Sqn Ldr Monga looked at me and asked: 'Have you had anything to eat since the morning?' I told him I just had an apple and a cup of coffee. He understood.

The moment we came in radio contact with Thoise, the first thing he told the base 'get something to eat on the helipad.' I was sick because my blood sugar had gone down drastically. As soon as we landed at Thoise, the first thing they did was to give me slices of handmade bread toasted over some fire and a slab of butter. The moment I wolfed down the bread everything was back to normal, as if by some instant magic. The biggest lesson I learnt that morning was: never fly in the hills on an empty stomach, especially at high altitudes! There has never been a day after that in my flying career when I hadn't eaten before starting to fly."

AVM Bahadur is candid enough to confess that a major part of this resolve was fulfilled by his wife Vinita, who ensured that even if it was 4 am, he never left the house without eating something!!

Since that first landing on 6 October 1978, helicopters have remained the most precious life line for those deployed on the Siachen glacier.

Col Kumar making a film on a 16 mm movie camera in 1978

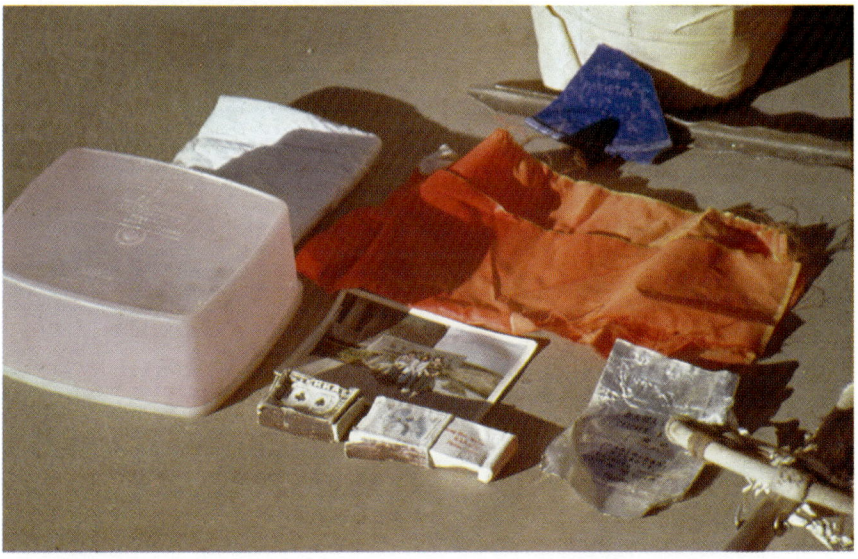

Items left behind by Japanese expeditions that had climbed to
Siachen through Pakistan

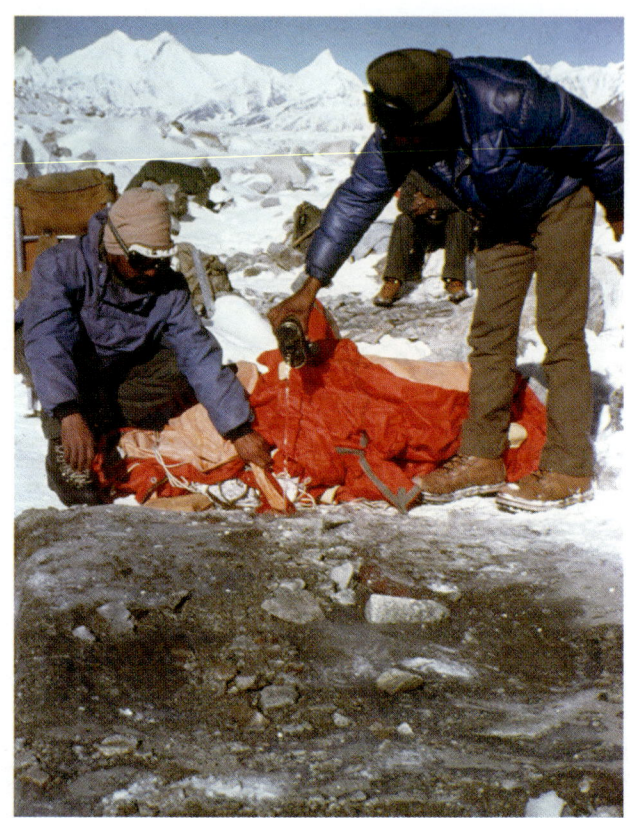

Col Kumar's team members trying to free the tents stuck in hard ice

Col Kumar with Gen T.N. Raina, Chief of Army Staff, 1978

II

Weighing the Options

"Pakistanis were not buying snow clothing for a picnic"

Col Kumar's expeditions in 1978 and 1981 and a couple of others in between, had given the Northern Command a fair idea about the civilian expeditions that were now increasingly coming into Siachen via Skardu and Gilgit. Clearly, Pakistan was throwing open the Karakorams for mountaineering expeditions. It began as an experiment to encourage tourism in the Northern Areas, but soon turned into

Col Kumar near the Base Camp in 1981

what Indian officials described as a bit of "mountain poaching", in which the Line of Control was extended to the Karakoram Pass from NJ 9842 showing the Siachen glacier as part of Pakistan!

Renowned mountaineer Harish Kapadia in his book, *Siachen Glacier: The Battle of Roses*, in fact claims that Pakistan had started permitting mountaineering expeditions onto Siachen glacier as early as 1974. "The first expedition to Siachen climbed the south ridge of Sherpi Kangri II. This was followed by an Austrian expedition, which climbed Sia Kangri from the southwest. A major expedition from Japan climbed Peak K12. Two climbers reached the summit and communicated this but they never returned to the base camp. They died during the descent. All three expeditions were in 1974 and on the rim of the Siachen glacier...it was not long before an expedition entered the main Siachen glacier. The Shizuka University team had applied to the Pakistani authorities for permission to climb peaks here every year between 1964 and 1969, but had always been denied. In fact, between 1961 and 1974, Pakistan had steadfastly refused permission to climb in the vicinity of the Siachen. Sometime in 1974, the Pakistani authorities informed the Japanese that their expeditions would now be permitted. The Japanese were offered a 50 per cent discount on peak fees as well as the assistance of the Pakistani Army. Their permit stated that the peak was located 'near the frontier of China and Pakistan.' Final permission was granted to them in January 1975. The 14-member expedition was accompanied by Capt Shaukat Nazir Hamdani of the Pakistani Army as the LO (Liaison Officer)."

Literature of the time also shows that Pakistan had launched a well-planned promotional campaign to attract mountaineers to come and climb some of the well known peaks in the region—According to one report, between 1975 and 1980, at least five Japanese and one American expedition were allowed to cross the Saltoro ridge via Sia La and Bilafond La to explore the Siachen glacier.

Harish Kapadia says the Pakistanis were testing waters. And waiting for Indian reaction. As he writes: " It is indeed surprising that Indian agencies showed no interest in the reports of mountaineering activities that were taking place right under their nose, even though details were published in many journals, including one from India. Was history repeating itself? The Indo-China war of 1962 had been triggered by a road that was being built in the Indian territory of Aksai Chin..."

A satellite picture of Siachen glacier

The Indians realised the importance of Pakistani activities only in 1978 (after Col Kumar's expedition returned) but did not take it seriously until the protest note from Pakistan laying claim to Siachen actually arrived in Northern Command in 1983, although three Army expeditions had been sent to the glacier in 1980, 1981 and 1982."

Gen Chibber, who had taken over as Northern Army Commander in 1982 after commanding a Corps in Punjab, was alerted to the Siachen issue again during one of the early briefings, when his staff showed him a protest note by Pakistan's Northern Sector Commander warning India to keep off the Siachen area, following India's expeditions in the previous three summers. Gen Chibber couldn't help recall the episode in 1978 when he, as Director General Military Operations, had permitted Col Kumar to launch the first operational reconnaissance patrol disguised as a civilian expedition to the Siachen glacier.

Gen Chibber, writing in a defence journal after his retirement, recalled: "To understand the origin of the Siachen conflict, it would be relevant here to look at the developments in the Gilgit region. In the mid-seventies, the Pakistani government adopted the policy of throwing open the Karakoram to international mountaineers. It was a step to promote tourism, and they simplified the procedure to clear expeditions. They even waived off the royalty for mountain peaks below 6100 metres. A well planned promotional campaign was launched to attract mountaineers to come and climb some of the well-known peaks in this region—Gasherbrum group, Mount Godwin Austin and Nanga Parbat. Travel facilities to Gilgit and Skardu were improved, as were hotel facilities in these towns. The response was really good. In clearing expeditions, a bit of 'mountain poaching' was undertaken!"[1]

By the summer of 1983, it was clear that India needed to keep a close watch on Siachen. Two patrols, Polar Bear I and Polar Bear II were sent between June and September 1983. The second patrol was tasked to build a small hut. A 'shelter of sorts' was put together by the end of September, 1983. It was good enough to protect the patrols from strong winds. To be fair, these patrols never came across any Pakistani ground patrols, although Pakistani helicopters did buzz them on a

Early days of *OP Meghdoot*: Brig Channa (extreme right) and
Gen Chibber (2nd from right)

couple of occasions. The troops came back to base by end September as the winter set in.

Northern Command HQ should have been satisfied with the feedback brought back by the patrols, but two protest notes by Pakistan in August 1983 were unusually strong and gave the first official indication of Pakistan's stand. The note sent on 21 August 1983 by the Northern Sector Commander for the first time claimed all areas northwest of the line joining NJ 9842 to Karakoram Pass as Pakistan's! It read:

"Request instruct your troops to withdraw beyond Line of Control south of line joining Point NJ 9842, Karakoram Pass NE 7410 immediately. I have instructed my troops to show maximum restraint. But any delay in vacating our territory will create a serious situation." Ironically the note ended on a conciliatory note: *"Assuring my fullest cooperation in maintaining peace and tranquillity along Line of Control."*

Northern Command was in no mood to accept the unilateral extension of the Line of Control. It sent a counter-protest note pointing out air violations.

But, Pakistan was not willing to accept India's protest. Another note received on 29 August was more explicit. It read:

"Your reply to our protest note of 21 August 1983 received.

A. Your troops have carried out intrusions across LC north of Point NJ 9842-Karakoram Pass-NE 7410. They intruded approximately 25 miles inside our territory in Siachen glacier, NJ 9797, NK 0689.
B. Last year also your troops had intruded into the same area for which protest had been lodged by our government.

This is a serious violation and unless stopped forthwith is likely to disturb the peaceful condition. Therefore please instruct your troops to remain south of the line Point NJ 9842-Karakoram Pass NE 7410."

Gen Chibber recalls: "We considered the protest note and took a view that such routine protests are a common feature of life in Jammu and Kashmir, where the armies of India and Pakistan are deployed against each other in a 'no-war-no-peace' confrontation. A suitable counter-protest was lodged and decision taken to continue our patrolling **37** during the summer 1983. It was during 1983 that the Pakistani side precipitated matters which developed into a conflict. In 1983, it became obvious to us that the Pakistani side was getting ready to physically come onto the Siachen glacier. Hence, we had to act swiftly in order to prevent them from doing so."

Northern Command kept the Army HQ in the loop and began its own assessment of the situation.

A detailed appreciation of the situation on Siachen and its importance as assessed at that time is buried in Indian Army files. A part of the assessment said:

"We had been launching expeditions and patrols onto the Siachen glacier since 1978. Pakistan launched protests against our activities in 1983 on the plea that our patrols have intruded into their territory. Their claim to the territory is part of their geostrategic scheme backed by the incorrect and unilateral marking of the imaginary extension of the LC on maps published in the USA. From the various intelligence reports received it was confirmed that Pak was sending an appropriately equipped force in the area to contest our patrol in 1984."

The assessment was based not only on the Army's own intelligence reports, since even RA&W (Research and Analysis Wing), India's external intelligence agency, had picked up information which suggested that the Pakistanis were shopping for Alpine clothing and equipment in thousands from Europe in the winter of 1983.

The former Chief of RA&W, Vikram Sood, was the agency's Srinagar station head in those years. He remembers walking into the 15 Corps Commander Lt Gen PN Hoon's office in the Badami Bagh Cantonment, and passing on this and other inputs about increased Pakistani activity in the area. "That time, we knew Pakistanis were sending more and more civilian expeditions into Siachen, but its importance was not so apparent until we put two and two together and realised Pakistan was up to something far more serious than just sending mountaineering

Vikram Sood

expeditions into the area. When we got reports of the large scale snow clothing and high altitude equipment purchase by Pakistan, there was enough urgency for me to go and share it with Prem (Lt Gen Hoon)," Vikram Sood recalled during an interview with me in 2013. "The Pakistanis were not buying all that for a picnic," he quipped.

In 2012, when the clamour for de-militarising Siachen following the death of 130 Pakistani soldiers in an avalanche accident was at its peak, Sood referred to the meeting with Lt Gen Hoon in an article.

"**The venue:** Badami Bagh, Srinagar, Headquarters of the Corps Commander 15 Corps, Lt Gen Prem Hoon

The year: 1983

The participants: The Corps Commander and the R&AW station chief.

The subject: Siachen and reported Pakistani activities in that region according to intelligence reports from across the LoC.

Mrs Gandhi with Gen P.N. Hoon (right); notice a young Col N.C. Vij, later Army Chief (left)

It would be untrue to suggest that this meeting led to the assault on the Soltoro Ridge which is actually west of the Siachen glacier, but the fact is, that the matter had assumed serious proportions and Indira Gandhi's government was deeply concerned.

The reports, that the Pakistanis were making probes ostensibly through tourism and mountaineering groups, were disturbing. The obvious aim of the Pakistanis appeared to be to cross the Saltoro heights and head for the Karakoram Pass on the Jammu and Kashmir border with Tibet (China)..."

Even Gen Chibber's note to Army HQ in 1983-84 justifying the need to launch an operation to occupy the passes on the Saltoro ridge had details of Pakistani activities and intentions in the area.

He told Army HQ: "Pakistan had inducted a column consisting of one Cdo(Commando) Coy (Company) and one NLI (Northern Light Infantry) Coy supported by a mor pl (mortar platoon) to Sia La. Pakistan build up of this column was apparently delayed due to the late arrival from abroad of snow clothing and equipment."

The note continued: "Whilst we were planning and preparing for *Operation Meghdoot*, there were intelligence reports that indicated Pak had designs of launching a military operation in the area. Some of the pertinent indicators were as follows:

(a) *Cancellation of leave:* In Jan 84, it was learnt that the turnover of troops/units, as also leave of persons in Force Commander Northern Area (FCNA) had been suspended till Sept 84.
(b) *Laying lines of communication:* In Dec 1983, intelligence reported laying of line of communications ahead of Skardu. Later in April 84, reports pertaining to establishment of an exchange at Khapalu were also received.
(c) *Procurement of high altitude equipment:* Reports in November 1983 had indicated Pak procuring approximately 1,000 sets of high altitude clothing and other related equipment."2

The assessment of the Indian Army's Northern Command was later borne out by Lt. Gen Jahandad Khan (then Commander of Rawalpindi-based X Corps) in his book.

40   *"When the SSG Company got across Bilafond La Pass (in 1983), the* *helicopter pilot reported an Indian location 1,000 yards ahead in the Siachen area. After seeing our helicopter, the Indian troops, comprising Ladakh Scouts, left their location in a great hurry abandoning all their rations and tentage. The SSG Company stayed in this area for 10 days but was ordered to withdraw in the first week of September 1983 as it had started snowing and the company did not have equipment for survival in the winter season under thirty to forty feet of snow, which is normal snow range.*

The withdrawal of the SSG Company was followed by many meetings in the GHQ to decide our plan of action for the summer of 1984 when the Indians were bound to come in greater numbers. Also taken into consideration was the fact that whoever succeeded in occupying the passes first would be able to hold them as it was impossible to dislodge them from these positions due to the terrain and the conditions. As Corps Commander, I gave the following assessment to the GHQ.

Next year (1984), India is most likely to pre-empt the occupation of the main passes of Saltoro Ridge with two battalion strength of occupation and a third battalion as reserve. It would need another brigade to provide them with logistics support. Maximum helicopter force will have to be utilised for logistics support. The Air Force will be available for air cover and also air drop of supplies and equipment.

We will need a brigade group with a battalion plus to occupy these passes and the rest of the force to provide relief and logistics support. We would also need maximum porter force to carry supplies and ammunition from Goma to the glacier positions. All our helicopter force, both Aloutte and Puma, will have to be mobilised for recce and logistics cover.. The PAF has to stand by to provide air cover. I had also cautioned GHQ that this operation will be very costly in logistics support. Our military intelligence must be alerted to keep us informed of all enemy movements beyond Leh to forestall their occupation of the glacier area.

A meeting was held in December 1983, in the GHQ Operation Room under the chairmanship of President Gen Zia ul- Haq. After listening to the 10 Corps Plan, the COAS thought that operations on both sides would be of a limited scale, involving not more than a brigade on the Indian side and a battalion on Pakistan side. The COAS had obviously underestimated the quantum of force required by both sides. He had also underestimated the logistics problem of this operation as presented **41** *to him by the logistics staff of the GHQ. In this meeting it was decided to incorporate the PAF in this operation and Maj Gen Pir Dad Khan (Commander of the Northern Areas) was given the task of pre-empting the occupation of the passes, reaching there not before May 1984, as weather conditions before that period would not allow the use of helicopters and the PAF. This decision was to be approved by the Defence Coordination Committee (DCC), attended by the Chairman, Joint Staffs Committee and all service chiefs. So preparatory work was started on procurement of high altitude equipment and clothing, improvement of roads and tracks, recruitment of porters etc. All these preparations were to be completed by April 1984.*

I handed over command of 10 Corps to Lt. Gen Zahid Ali Akbar Khan on 31 March 1984 after completing my tenure of four years. I gave him a detailed briefing about this operational plan and particularly stressed the importance of intelligence keeping a watch on Indian moves beyond Leh. However, I learned later that when our troops approached the SaltoroRidge passes during the third week of May 1984, the Indians were already in occupation of Gyong Pass in the south, strategically important because it could interfere with the enemy's line of logistics support. As it was impossible to dislodge the Indians, we had no option but to occupy the next highest feature opposite them. This was a great setback for Pakistan, although all plans, including the timing of the troop movement, had been laid down at the highest level. We had obviously failed to detect the movement of a brigade size force in this area. It was learnt that the Indians had moved up their troops from Leh in the second half of April 1984.

After the occupation of these positions by both sides, opposite each other, the border became active. Both sides started inducting heavy weapons including artillery guns, rocket launchers and anti-aircraft missiles. Fire duels, patrol clashes and engagement of helicopters through anti-aircraft guns became a daily affair. Both sides also brought up more troops to counter each other. Since then there has been no substantial change in the relative positions on both sides. It was in the winter of 1984 that the Pakistani troops first experienced operating at that altitude. But the troops were provided high altitude equipment and there was no abnormal loss of life due to weather conditions."

If further proof of Pakistani intentions in 1983-84 was required, it was provided in an article titled 'Geopolitics of the Siachen Glacier' published in the November 1985 issue of the *Asian Defence Journal*, written by Zulfikar A. Khan. It said, in parts: "To protect what it regards as its territory and prevent violation by Indian troops, Pakistan decided to establish a permanent picket at Siachen. To pre-empt this move, the Indians airlifted a Kumaon Battalion by helicopters..."

Of course it wasn't a battalion (1,000 men), but just a platoon plus strength (about 30 soldiers) of 4 Kumaon which commenced *Operation Meghdoot*!

Gen Chibber, who was associated with Siachen in one way or the other since 1978, was also aware of the possible violent reaction by Pakistan if Indian troops occupied Sia La and Bilafond La. "That our operation in the Siachen glacier could result in a local conflict which may further escalate was a distinct possibility. I was aware that *Operation Meghdoot* had the potential for escalation ranging from a conflict of a local nature, to one of major magnitude either along the LC in Kashmir, or along the whole of the international border with Pakistan," the then Northern Army Commander told Army HQ in an official note.

Despite the possibility of escalation, Army HQ in consultation with the Prime Minister's Office and particularly on the directive of Prime Minister Indira Gandhi decided to launch *Operation Meghdoot*. As Gen Chibber now recalls: "I gave an assessment to the highest quarters that if we were to prevent the Pakistani side from presenting us with a *fait accompli*, we had to act fast." He remembers telling Army HQ and the PMO: "If they (the Pakistanis) were to establish posts on the Siachen glacier it would be very costly to evict them. The probability that we may not be able to do so at all was also very high."

In retrospect, it can be safely said that intelligence provided by RA&W, Army's own assessment coupled with the tone and tenor of the Pakistani protest notes in 1983 hastened preparations for launching the operations on the glacier. They commenced soon after Patrol Polar Bear had returned in September 1983. According to official notes of the time, Gen Chibber had a number of discussions with Lt Gen PN Hoon and his staff between September and December 1983. He gave them broad guidelines to plan ahead for operations in a "deliberate and comprehensive manner".

Gen Chibber noted: "Our presence in this area till 1983 had been in   43 the form of expeditions and patrols, which were considered inadequate to meet possible Pakistani reaction. It was, therefore decided to launch a sizeable force suitably equipped to operate in the Siachen glacier during 1984."

Operation Meghdoot was now just months away!

The early camps on the glacier

The forbidding Saltoro ridge

The glacier and the peaks majestically rising above it

The mule convoys which travelled between Sasoma and DBO

III

Getting Ready

"Secure the Siachen glacier"

As January 1984 dawned, Northern Command and 15 Corps were furiously working towards launching assault teams atop the Saltoro ridge, the prominent watershed west of the Siachen glacier.

J&K, including Siachen and Karakoram

Fortunately for 15 Corps headquartered in Srinagar then—as now—insurgency in the Kashmir Valley was still some five years away. Most of its deployment was along the LoC stretching from Poonch right up to NJ 9842, running through Drass, Kargil, Batalik, Chorbatla and Turtuk. Unlike today, 15 Corps was also responsible for the defence of Eastern Ladakh bordering Tibet.

Raising another Corps to look after Ladakh or induction of another Division—the 8 Mountain Division in the Kargil-Drass-Batalik area—was not even on the horizon in 1984. The 3 Infantry Division with its HQ in Leh had two brigades (70 located at Kairi to hold south-eastern Ladakh, 114 to look after North-eastern Ladakh) and a Sector Headquarter (26, headquartered at Partapur for areas beyond Khardung La) under its command. The 3 Infantry Division was thus effectively in-charge of the area east of Zoji La right up to Sasoma.

Two years after Operation Meghdoot was launched, the 3 Infantry Division was stretched to its limits in defending both the Pakistan and China fronts. So one more formation—28 Division—was raised in 1986 at Nimu, not very far from Leh. In a peculiar arrangement, 28 Division was given charge of the Kargil-based 121 (Independent) Infantry brigade and the Siachen area.

This arrangement continued till 1991 when 28 Division was shifted to Kupwara in North Kashmir after full-fledged insurgency gripped the Kashmir Valley starting 1989. That is the time the Siachen Brigade reverted to 3 Infantry Division!

It was only after the 1999 Kargil conflict that the 8 Mountain Division was inducted into Kargil and 14 Corps was raised in Leh. 3 Infantry Division moved to Karu, an hour's drive from Leh and automatically came under the 14 Corps ORBAT (Order of Battle).

But back in 1984.

Apart from Gen Chibber, the officers involved in planning operations on the Siachen glacier were Lt Gen Hoon, GoC 15 Corps, Maj Gen S. Sharma, GoC 3 Inf Div and the man on the ground, Brig VN Channa, Commander 26 Sector.

The focus was on occupying Indira Col, Sia La and Bilafond La, the most prominent passes on the Saltoro ridge, as early as possible.

One for history books: Gen Chibber with his officers in 1984

As his Staff and Commanders on the ground prepared to launch operations, Gen Chibber wrote a detailed letter to Army Chief, Gen AS Vaidya, in January 1984 seeking his approval for the operation.

One of the highlights of the plan was to designate 79 Mountain Brigade Group in 15 Corps as the 'Himalayan Brigade' for operations in the snow bound regions. The force, according to the Northern Command plan, was to be equipped with specialised clothing and skiing equipment. Gen Chibber's note to Army HQ suggested that the type of equipment for the proposed Himalayan Brigade had to be on the lines of the ones that were being procured from abroad for troops who were to be involved in *Operation Meghdoot*.

"Besides organising and tailoring a specialised task force, it is essential to provide it a dedicated helicopter unit equipped with Mi-8 and Cheetah helicopters. Fire support from armed helicopters and air photos for areas of interest is also recommended. Logistics infrastructure in the form of air maintenance and road communications from Sasoma to base camp, construction of helipads at the Base Camp and Sasoma and construction of fibre glass shelters is also planned," the Northern Command note recommended.

Gen Chibber followed up his letter to the Army Chief with detailed discussions of the plan with Gen Vaidya and DGMO, Lt Gen Somanna at Army HQ on 9 February 1984.

FINALISATION OF PLANS

Five days later, the planning for *Operation Meghdoot* went into top gear.

As Gen Chibber returned to Northern Command HQ in Udhampur and called Lt Gen Hoon to firm up the plans. Gen Chibber's Chief of Staff (COS), Lt Gen NS Cheema and MGGS (Maj Gen, General Staff), Maj Gen Amarjit Singh and Brig. Channa were also present during the discussions. These five officers pretty much comprised the top brass of Northern Command in 1984. After day-long deliberations, punctuated only by a working lunch, major operational decisions were finalised.

Gen Chibber (pointer in hand) with Brig. Channa and Brig Jal Master

None of them would have anticipated that they were about to order a military action that would turn into India's longest running operation which had no precedent in military history!

Among the major decisions taken at the 14 February meeting in the Northern Command HQ was the proposed composition of the force for *Operation Meghdoot*. The brass earmarked one company plus a platoon of Ladakh Scouts and one company of 4 Kumaon with supporting elements as the basic force for the Operation.

Lt Col Pushkar Chand, Commanding Officer of 1 Vikas was appointed as the Task Force Commander for *Operation Meghdoot*. His location was to be at the Forward Logistics Base or FLB at about 16,000 feet. The Northern Command also designated a company of 19 Kumaon under its Commanding Officer to be located at Sasoma for any contingency.

There is an interesting aside here. The Vikas battalions—in 1984, there were two of them under 3 Infantry Division in Ladakh—are part of the ultra-secretive organisation now known as Special Frontier Force (SFF). Created in 1962 under code name 22 Establishment, the Special Frontier Force remains the subject of much speculation and little concrete information.

The SFF was supposed to keep an eye on Chinese military movements along the Indo-Tibet border, and gather as much intelligence as possible. In the event of war, operating in companies, the SFF was intended to be 'forward screens' for the Indian Army. It is trained in special operations, has the skills of paratroopers, and according to insiders is able to conduct conventional airborne assaults ahead of ground forces in areas such as the Aksai Chin.

The SFF recruits both ethnic Tibetans and Gorkhas. While Tibetans can, and do become officers, regular Indian army officers on deputation provide leadership. The Inspector General, head of the organisation based at Chakrata near Mussoorie, is usually a Major General rank officer of the Indian Army.

Currently, there are at least 2 Vikas battalions under the Leh-based 14 Corps deployed in Ladakh. Lt Col Pushkar Chand was commanding one of the two Vikas battalions in 1984, when he was designated Task Force Commander for *Operation Meghdoot*.

As the designated troops got down to training and equipping themselves for what looked like a formidable task, Army HQ gave its final go ahead for *Operation Meghdoot* vide letter No. A/35501/XM03 of 31 Mar 84. Tasks listed out in the directive were:

Tasks in General: Secure the Siachen glacier
Tasks in particular: Secure Bilafond La, Sia La, Siachen, Lolofond and Teram Sehar glacier.

51

Patrol up to Indira Col.
Prevent Pakistan sponsored infiltration in the area.

From the directive it was clear that Army HQ wasn't looking to launch any offensive against Pakistan, but was simply planning deployment to hold on to the heights on the Saltoro ridge. There were sound reasons for this directive.

The India of 1984 was much different from the country we see today. Mrs Indira Gandhi, after a spell out of power between 1977 and 1980 had once again become Prime Minister. Governing India has never been easy. But the 1980s were particularly bad.

Punjab was aflame with calls for a separate Khalistan; Assam was in turmoil because of the anti-foreigners agitation; insurgencies in Nagaland, Manipur and Mizoram were keeping a large number of Indian Army troops busy. India could not afford another war with Pakistan.

So, when Mrs Gandhi was briefed about Pakistani intentions beyond NJ 9842, her directive was simple: secure Siachen but prevent wider escalation with Pakistan.

Since the directive was limited, Northern Command too planned the operation on a limited scale. The brass was clear that the key to success would be the Indian Army's ability to occupy Sia La and Bilafond La in particular, before Pakistani columns could. The planners were also fully convinced that troops for the initial deployment in these locations had to be heli lifted and maintained by air. Significantly, Northern Command records of the time show that the initial plan was to withdraw troops from those altitudes around 31 Aug 1984 'unless the situation warranted otherwise.'

Now we indeed know that the situation did warrant troops staying on in these passes not only for the duration of that winter, but round the year for the past three decades!

There is another school of thought, which, with the benefit of hindsight, argues that India could have held on to three main passes on the Saltoro ridge instead of extending its deployment and widening the conflict. But Pakistan's counter-offensive—named Operation Ababeel—and two major attacks on Indian positions at Sia La and Bilafond La between

April and June 1984, forced India's hand. Northern Command records of the time have complete details of how it became necessary to station troops on those murderous altitudes after Pakistan made it a prestige issue to try and wrest back the Saltoro.

As Northern Command and 3 Infantry Division mulled over the likely date of launching the Operation, the task force under Lt. Col Pushkar Chand was busy acclimatising.

It moved to Sasoma by 28 March 1984. The task force concentrated at base camp by 3 April and commenced ice training. By that time, the infrastructure required for the launching of the operation was being steadily built, and high altitude huts to cater to essential accommodation at the base camp were nearing completion. The helipad for Mi-8 helicopters was also being constructed. Dumping of aviation turbine fuel (ATF) was among the top priorities, since helicopters would play a major role in sustaining deployment on the glacier.

According to records of the time, the Indian Air Force in the meantime was busy transporting supplies. It was tasked to lift 461 tonnes of material by fixed wing aircraft. Out of this, 73 tonnes was to be airlifted from Srinagar to Thoise between 19 March and 7 April. The remaining 389 tonnes was planned to be lifted from Srinagar to the Dropping Zone during April to August 1984.

An Mi-8 helicopter at the Base Camp in the early days of Op Meghdoot

Mi-8 on the glacier

Mi-8 helicopters were entrusted to airlift 74 tonnes of goods and drop them at the base camp in the period between April and August 1984.

The lighter Cheetahs were made responsible for lifting 30 tonnes from Sasoma to FLB and 79 tonnes from base camp to assault camp.

The logistics were getting organised systematically. For an operation that had no precedent in the world, every small decision had to be weighed carefully before being implemented. Supplies in place, everything seemed ready for *Operation Meghdoot*, except the specialised snow clothing for the first assault teams that were to be airdropped at Bilafond La and Sia La!

LADAKH SCOUTS

Ki Ki So So Lhargyalo (Victory to God)

The Ladakh Scouts are the Indian Army's youngest regiment but one of its oldest allies.

Raised in 1963, in the immediate aftermath of the 1962 war with China that witnessed some of the most intense fighting in Ladakh, the Ladakh Scouts was initially a para-military force that worked directly with the Indian Army in the high Himalayas. Nicknamed 'Snow Tigers' for their swiftness and bravery in the most inhospitable terrain, Ladakh Scouts are one of Indian Army's most decorated regiments with over 300 gallantry awards to their credit, including one Ashok Chakra (India's highest peace time gallantry award), 10 Mahavir Chakras and two Kirti Chakras.

In 1999, while reporting the Kargil conflict, I came across the gentle but hardy warriors of Ladakh Scouts for the first time in the Batalik sector. They were, I remember, in fact, one of the first units to successfully launch a counter strike against Pakistani incursions in the Kargil operations. Major Sonam Wangchuk, the handsome and soft-spoken officer became a household name for his heroics in the battle of Chorbatla in 1999. He won India's second highest award for bravery—the Mahavir Chakra—for his exploits. Now a Colonel, Sonam Wangchuk, a Buddhist from Ladakh, is originally a Short Service Commission Officer who was selected to join the Assam Regiment after year long training at the Officers' Training Academy. Later he was seconded to the Ladakh Scouts. His citation for Mahavir Chakra reads:

On 30 May 1999, Major Sonam Wangchuk was leading a column of The Indus Wing, Ladakh Scouts as a part of ongoing operations in Op VIJAY in the Batalik sector. The column was tasked to occupy Ridge Line on the Line of Control in a glaciated area at a height of about 5,500 metres. This was essential so as to pre-empt its occupation by the enemy and any subsequent infiltration.

While moving towards the Line of Control, the enemy ambushed the column by firing from a vantage position. In the process, one NCO of the Ladakh Scouts was killed. Major Sonam Wangchuk held his column together and in a daring counter ambush, led a raid on the enemy position from a flank, killing two enemy soldiers. The officer also recovered one heavy machine gun

Sonam Wangchuk

and one Universal machine gun, ammunition, controlled stores and three dead bodies of the enemy personnel.

Thereafter, the officer took stock of all forces along the Chorbatla axis in the Batalik sector and cleared the axis up to the Line of Control of all enemy intrusions at great risk to his life.

Major Sonam Wangchuk displayed exceptional bravery and gallantry of the highest order in the presence of enemy fire and in extreme climatic conditions in the glaciated area.

But Sonam Wangchuk is not the first hero from Ladakh. That honour goes to the legendary Col Chewang Rinchen, twice winner of Mahavir Chakra besides a Sena Medal for gallantry!

In fact, I can't think of anyone who can come close to Col Rinchen's exploits on the battlefield against extremely heavy odds. His heroics began as a 17 year old in 1947-48! In the first of the three wars between India and Pakistan over Kashmir, there was a determined Pakistani thrust to capture Ladakh. One attack came from the West. Well armed irregulars assembled by the Pakistanis, occupied the strategically located Zoji La to cut off Kargil and Ladakh from the Kashmir Valley. The other thrust was along the Shyok river towards Nubra. The irregulars crossed the Ladakh range, wedged between Shyok and Indus rivers and reached the Kargil-Leh road. They also put pressure on the Nubra Valley.

It was at that time when the 17 year old Chewang Rinchen became the first of the volunteers who raised a local militia force which was subsequently to be called Nubra Guards. Chewang Rinchen along with 28 local volunteers attacked a Pakistani post at Chumik La and captured it. This area was to later become the Central glacier.

In 1947-48, Rinchen and his colleagues held off a Pakistani offensive for a year and were involved in the capture of Lama House, Takkar hill, Tebedo hill and other operations to halt the intruders at Terche, just five km short of Thoise village in Sep 1947-48. For his contribution in the defence of Shyok valley in the 1947-48 Indo–Pak war, he was awarded the Mahavir Chakra and given the rank of Jamadar in the 7 J&K Militia.

As the 1971 war began, Rinchen was posted with 14 J&K Militia then located at Ferozepur in Punjab. He volunteered to join the

Ladakh Scouts and got posted to Ladakh as the deputy commander of Partapur sector under Col (later Brig) Udai Singh. After reaching Partapur, he immediately enlisted 550 volunteers into four companies of newly raised Nubra Guards known as the Dhal force. A short training of 15 days later, the Dhal force led by Maj Rinchen not only stopped Pakistani aggression, but also won back the Chalunka complex, Turtuk, Tyakshi and Pachathang.

By 15 December 1971, the Nubra Guards had liberated 800 sq km territory from Pakistan's grip. This in fact was the largest area captured by any unit on the Western/Northern front during the entire 1971 war. The entire operation was conducted without artillery or air support. For his contribution in recapturing the Turtuk-Tyagshi area, Maj Rinchen was awarded his second MVC.

Thirteen years after recapturing Turtuk, its importance became apparent, as the Indian Army prepared to deploy troops on the Saltoro ridge to prevent the Pakistanis from getting onto the Siachen glacier. Turtuk, south-west of the southern end of Saltoro ridge gives the Indian Army the necessary depth to hold off any flank attack by Pakistani troops. If Turtuk wasn't in India's possession, holding on to the Saltoro ridge would have become that much more difficult for India. Today, one full battalion under the 102 Infantry Brigade is deployed along the LoC ahead of Turtuk.

Maj Rinchen was promoted as Lt Col and retired in September 1986. On 26 January 1990, Lt Col Rinchen was given the rank of Hony Col in Nubra Guards!

Maj Chewang Rinchen (left); in his younger days

Weapon training classes for the volunteers

Just a year before *Operation Meghdoot* in1983, Ladakh Scouts were reorganised into a Headquarter and two wings, "Karakoram Wing" and the "Indus Wing". Troops of the Karakoram Wing were at the forefront of the exploratory expeditions to the Siachen glacier in 1981, 1982 and 1983.

In the immediate aftermath of the Kargil conflict, the Ladakh Scouts underwent another reorganisation in June 2000 when it was converted into a full-fledged regiment with four infantry battalions. This paved the way for raising more battalions. The fifth battalion was raised on July 31, 2002. Now, the Ladakh Scouts is a full-fledged regiment of the Indian Army.

Gen M.L. Chibber in 2013

Old Comrades-in-arms, 30 years later! Gen Chibber (left) and Brig Channa

The Nubra river in 1983

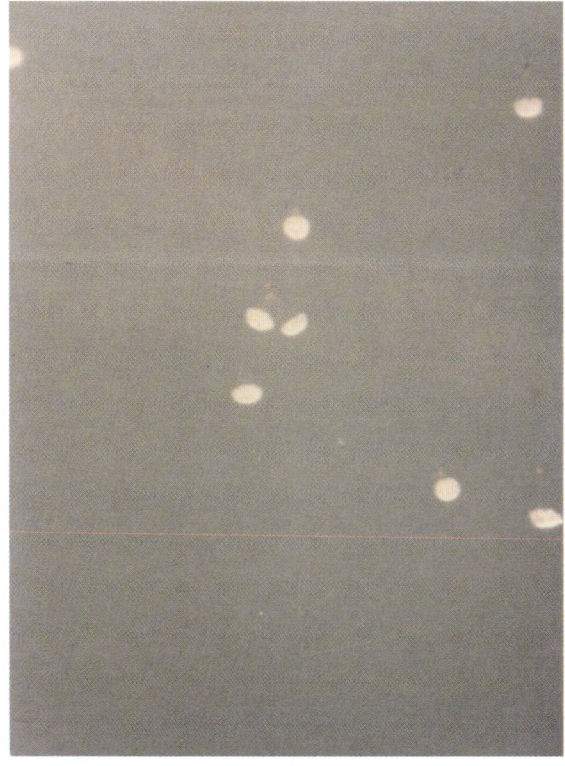

Supplies being air-dropped for Col Kumar's 1981 expedition

IV

Race to Bilafond La

"Pet mein roti, haat mein soti, chaal chhoti chhoti"

"That is the philosophy practiced by us, the Indian army soldiers deployed in the mountains and particularly in Siachen," Sanjay Kulkarni tells me in his cosy sitting room in Leh on a lazy Sunday afternoon in October 2013. "If your stomach is well filled, if you have a stick in hand for support and if you follow the basic rule of taking tiny steps during the climb and not get rushed, you have mastered the art of survival in the mountains," he says, explaining a routine that he and his mates have followed all their life in the army when deployed in the mountains.

I had specially flown to the capital of Ladakh to visit Siachen and more pertinently to meet Sanjay, then the Chief of Staff or the No. 2 man in the 14 Corps, the Indian Army formation that was raised post the Kargil conflict in 1999, which has the unique task of guarding disputed borders with both India's adversaries, China and Pakistan.

The ever smiling and weather beaten Sanjay, promoted as Lieutenant General in February 2014, has mostly served in the mountains guarding the frontiers with China

Photograph of (then) Capt
Sanjay Kulkarni
(Now) Lt Gen Sanjay Kulkarni

Lt Gen Sanjay Kulkarni; the man who launched *Op Meghdoot*

and Pakistan throughout his 35 year career in the army. Nathula, Tawang, Zakhama, Lekhapani, Leh—places in Sikkim, Arunachal Pradesh, Nagaland, Assam and Ladakh, that the average citizens don't know much about. That is where he has fought, stood guard and honed his soldiering skills. Mountains are almost like home for this soldier, like many of his contemporaries and juniors commissioned in the Indian Army, post the 1971 war. Delhi, Udhampur and other 'routine' places are but an interregnum in between postings to these far off places.

In retrospect, it's only befitting that on being commissioned, Sanjay Kulkarni was allotted to one of the oldest regiments of the Indian Army, and certainly one of the most decorated – the Kumaon regiment. The soldiers belong to the Kumaon hills of present day Uttarakhand state, a mountainous region in the lower Himalayas. But officers – who come from different parts of India and get commissioned into the Kumaon regiment – adapt quickly to the demands of the mountains.

So, when young Sanjay Kulkarni finished his training in the Indian Military Academy (IMA) in 1977, he was assigned to the 4 Kumaon battalion, a unit that had in the past produced two Chiefs of the Indian Army—Gen KM Srinagesh (1955-57) and Gen KS Thimayya (1959-1962). This battalion also has the distinction of winning the first Param Vir Chakra, India's highest gallantry award. Maj Somnath Sharma won it in 1948 for bravery in Kashmir.

But, learning the history of Kumaon regiment was far from my mind.

I was in Leh to understand the events of April 1984, when Sanjay Kulkarni as a young Captain, and his platoon of soldiers were airdropped at Bilafond La signalling the launch of *Operation Meghdoot* that has now lasted for three decades, and is easily India's longest running military deployment!

Even before 4 Kumaon moved to Leh in 1982, Sanjay had already done the basic and advance mountaineering courses in the High Altitude Warfare School (HAWS). In 1981, he had in fact climbed Stok Kangri in Leh, even as Col Kumar and his team were climbing Siachen that summer.

In 1982 and 1983, 4 Kumaon was part of the Long Range Patrols (LRPs) that India sent to the glacier in the summer months between May and August.

The unit was deployed at Turtuk, ahead of the 26 Sector HQ located at Partapur, then Commanded by Brig. Vijay Channa, a Guards Officer with the reputation of being a bold and unconventional strategist.

In 1984, the 26 Sector (equivalent to a brigade which normally has

The location of 26 Sector, now 102 Infantry Brigade at Partapur

three battalions under it) was in charge of the Chorbatla-Turtuk-Tyagshi-NJ 9842 portion of the LoC but was short of one battalion. The two battalions assigned to 26 Sector were concentrated in the Turtuk-Tyagshi area. In the summer months, a contingent would carry out the LRP, but would invariably return to base by the end of August, since heavy snow and dipping temperatures would make it impossible for the troops to stay on the glacier. Moreover, till then, there was no decision to permanently deploy troops at those forbidding heights.

The Ladakh Scouts, as mentioned earlier, used to be the common factor in every long range patrol that climbed the glacier. Unlike today, Ladakh Scouts only had a HQ and two wings—Karakoram and Indus—to speak of. Being local residents of Ladakh, soldiers of Ladakh Scouts had an inherent advantage. They did not need to acclimatise, nor did they have difficulty in climbing the formidable mountains. So, no matter which unit was deployed beyond the Khardung La, soldiers of Ladakh Scouts were always part of the long range patrols.

As the army turned its attention to the glacier, all incoming units were trained in the craft of mountaineering. "All of us were made to learn ice craft, rappelling, and mountaineering before going for the LRPs. In fact, some of us also learnt skiing," Gen Kulkarni remembers. Air support was provided by the Air Force helicopters. He remembers going right up to Bilafond La and Sia La during the summer deployments. The Air Force choppers used to drop soldiers at what is now known as Base Camp, and from there on the soldiers would climb to Camp I, Camp II and Camp III. Then they would walk up to what is now known as Kumar base, named after Col Kumar. From Kumar base, patrols went to Bilafond La and Sia La. But invariably by end-August or September, the patrols would return to base, Gen Kulkarni remembers.

As 1984 dawned, training was continuing apace, but no one except very senior officers had any inkling about the plan to go and occupy Bilafond La and Sia La. Then suddenly, by March, there was feverish activity in the 26 Sector.

OPERATION MEGHDOOT IS LAUNCHED

As Brig Channa returned from a meeting in Srinagar, he was instructed to launch the Operation only after thorough preparations. Even three decades later, he remembers the months in the run up to the launch of *Operation Meghdoot*. Sipping his favourite tea in a tall glass, Brig

Channa, now an active senior citizen in Delhi's Greater Kailash I locality, transports me back to those months and explains why the key to success in battle is planning and preparation.

"I would say 90 per cent of the battle is won if we are fully prepared for the task at hand. Personally, I would think that if you are administratively prepared it's a major start. Of course, the best way is to start living, eating, sleeping day in day out about your next operation. Especially, for an operation at those heights which had never been done before. No one had fought on the glacier at altitudes in excess of 18,000 feet. No one in the world had a clue how to fight a war on the glacier. So, everything that we did had to be beyond the conventional. Everything that we did had to be innovative.

"I had a hunch that something was going to happen 'up there'. Call it the soldier's hunch or instinct, I had this gut feeling since taking over as Sector Commander, but more so from the end of 1983. From then on, all that we were doing was to constantly think of the possible operation. Look, I had no executive orders yet (for an operation on the glacier), but one had to be prepared. That build up in the mind was there," he tells me and also explains why *Operation Meghdoot* was necessary.

"In my mind this occupation (of Saltoro ridge) was a must. Suppose whatever quantum of troops, even one company of Pakistan troops, had come in and fired on our Partapur HQ, can you imagine the reaction? It is like the whole body feeling the shock, when even a small pinprick troubles your finger. It would have been akin to that. Therefore, to my mind this occupation (of the Saltoro ridge) was a must, to prevent the Pakistanis from threatening the Nubra Valley.

"The decision wasn't taken in haste. It was a very deliberate, conscious decision taken at the highest level. The Prime Minister was involved in it. My only regret is that they only told me to hold the crest line. They didn't permit me to go down (towards Pakistani areas). One should have and closed the chapter once and for all. If we had gone down to Gyari, gone and held the area, you didn't need to occupy the glacier at all because all routes are blocked by you. But, of course those are all bigger political decisions. I remember pressing for it, though I was a small fry in the whole game. Had we done that, today's situation needn't have arisen. Siachen ensures that Pakistan and China don't link up on top of our head, but also makes sure that Pakistan alone does not create problems for us in the Nubra Valley. You have forestalled all that. Look at Siachen, look at Karakoram Pass and look at DBO," he points at the map and explains. "As it is, Pakistan has given Shagksham Valley to China. Why do you allow the two adversaries to encircle you," he asks.

After returning from Srinagar to his HQ in Partapur, Brig Channa got down to selecting his officers and men for the operation. Sanjay Kulkarni was asked to lead the platoon of 4 Kumaon to Bilafond La. Major AN Bahuguna (who retired as a Brigadier and now lives in Dehradun), then with the Ladakh Scouts, was to go and occupy Sia La. All these troops had first concentrated at Sasoma, and later moved to Base Camp under the Task Force Commander, Lt Col Pushkar Chand.

Brig Channa meanwhile had a major task ahead: Briefing the officers and men before they went on what looked like a high risk, if not downright suicidal, mission. He had to motivate the troops, not just by pep talk but also by action. "I had always led by example. What is motivation? Motivation is not only merely briefing. Motivation is also about establishing trust with troops and gaining their confidence, making them confident about your ability to lead them to victory. I will give you an example. Just prior to launching *Operation Meghdoot*, I was staying with 4 Kumaon (battalion). One morning the sentry outside my hut gave an exceptionally smart salute. I replied to his greetings, but simultaneously I kept that in mind. A day later, there was a *durbar*. I mentioned the smart soldier and his smart salute and as a reward I still remember, I gave them a crate of rum as reward in appreciation of the act. Troops remember these gestures."

There was another incident.

"In the same *durbar* the SM (Subedar Major) came up to me and said the unit was facing shortage of kerosene. In those days, kerosene used to be absolutely essential to keep the living quarters heated. He asked for an extra 5,000 litres of kerosene. Now, as Brigade Commander, I always kept additional stock in the HQ. I immediately called my staff in Partapur and asked them to despatch 10,000 litres of kerosene oil. My only condition: it should reach the battalion within seven days. Even as I was giving these instructions, the entire battalion was watching. It was important to deliver on the promise. So my staff ensured that the extra kerosene oil reached the battalion in four days. These are confidence building measures that go a long way in building trust with troops," Brig Channa told me explaining his leadership style, dubbed by many colleagues and subordinates as unconventional.

And sure enough, even in the final briefing before the launch of *Operation Meghdoot*, Brig Channa went beyond the rule book.

"I personally conducted the briefing, broken into three parts: Briefing for officers, the signallers and finally for the men. The officers will tell you how unconventional the briefing was. I had said there would be no time limit for briefing. I wanted all of them to absorb every small little detail of my planned operation. The briefing was in an informal setting. Officers were allowed to smoke, have tea, take off their cap, and take off their belt! I wanted them to be relaxed. When you are relaxed, you absorb more. It wasn't a one way talk. They were allowed to ask as many questions as possible. And they did. The briefing/interaction went on for three hours but at the end of it, I was absolutely certain that every officer had understood my Op(rational) orders. They had to, because I could not have been with them physically, and then there was to be total radio silence! With signallers, the briefing went on for an hour. We had decided to use the 'presser switch' on the radio set, only to convey that all was well, but there was to be no conversation. For the men, all that I had to tell them was: *'dekho yeh tumhare paltan ki aur desh ki izzat ka sawal hai. Jeetna zaroori hai.'*

Briefing over, the troops were now primed for action.

By 11 April 1984, 19 Kumaon (from 68 Brigade), the backup force for the operation concentrated at Leh. Ski troopers comprising 5 officers, 6 JCOs and 43 others from HAWS joined up with the task force at the base camp. Two Zu-23-2 guns, four grad P (multi barrel rocket launchers) and three detachments of SAM missiles were also at the base camp by then. The Air Force had positioned 6 Cheetah helicopters under Wg Cdr GS Sandhu, and two Mi-8 under Wing Cdr KK Sangar at Thoise for the operations.

Maj Gen Shiv Sharma, GoC, 3 Infantry Division and Brig Channa's immediate boss had by then established his tactical HQ at Partapur.

During discussions on the possible D-day and H-hour for the actual launch of troops, there were several suggestions. Of course, the operation had to be launched in the timeframe of 10-30 April, 1984 set by the Northern Command. The final day had to be chosen by the

Recalling those days: Gen Chibber and Brig Channa

Sector Commander, Brig Channa. He finalised 13 April. Why? Many have asked him for the rationale for choosing 13 April. Brig Channa has always kept mum. But talking to me in the winter of 2013, he finally revealed the reasons for deciding to launch *Operation Meghdoot* on 13 April 1984 although many had said the date '13' could be unlucky.

WHY 13 April?

Brig Channa says: "Well, what I say may sound controversial, but the fact is that both the Pakistani Army and us, follow the legacy left behind by the British. When the British planned, they used to be very cautious in their approach, very slow, erring on the side of caution. They were not prone to take risks. But, in such an operation I had to take a risk. And go up when they (the Pakistanis) least expected it. I was proved right.

"If you read Gen (Pervez) Musharraf's book, he says India pre-empted us. What does it indicate? That they (the Pakistanis) were preparing to occupy those passes too. I also know that when our team went abroad to buy snow clothing, the Pakistanis were already doing so; when we were collecting quotations, they had already bought the snow suits outright!

"So it was a race against time. You see the operating season on the glacier is generally end-May/early June when they say it is comparatively safe to operate. So, one had to choose that time frame. Pakistanis had a much shorter distance to cover, had lesser logistical problems. I would say no more. It was one of those intuitions where I said let's do it early. I was asked about it. When would I like to launch? I mulled over it and thought about *Baisakhi* (a harvest festival observed with much fanfare in North India, and even Pakistani Punjab). Now, *Baisakhi* is celebrated with equal fervour on both sides. People are in a joyous mood. Their guard is down. It was also the most unlikely date to launch a military operation. So there you are. 13 April it was. I would concede that it was risky. Some called it suicidal. But that is exactly why we had to do it that day. Rest is history!"

Once the date was set, Northern Command HQ was informed.

The Saltoro and the Cheetah helicopter

Reconnaissance of the area of operations by senior officers prior to the actual launching was considered essential. So on 12 April, Lt Gen Hoon, Air Marshal MSO Wollen, Commander-in-Chief, Western Air Command, AVM A Dayala, Air Officer Commanding of Jammu and Kashmir and Maj Gen Shiv Sharma visited the base camp, and carried out an aerial survey of Sia La and Bilafond La.

Meanwhile, a snow storm was building up. Fresh snowing had taken place in the higher reaches.

5.30 am, 13 April 1984: The first Cheetah helicopter, carrying Capt Sanjay Kulkarni and one soldier, takes off from the base camp. Then another follows. Then one more.

By noon, 17 such sorties are flown by Sqn Ldr Surinder S. Bains and Rohit Rai. Capt Sanjay Kulkarni, one JCO and 27 soldiers are heli-dropped at Bilafond La.

With this *OPERATION MEGHDOOT* WAS OFFICIALLY LAUNCHED.

Three decades after he jumped from the Cheetah at Bilafond La, to signal the beginning of *Operation Meghdoot*, Gen Kulkarni vividly remembers the scene. "Four of us jumped one by one, as the first two helicopters hovered just short of Bila around 6 am that day. I remember throwing a 25 kg *atta bori* (gunny sack full of flour) to test the depth and hardness of the snow. It was quite hard. We jumped and then constructed a helipad of sorts to allow the latter sorties to land for half a minute or so, and then return for another trip," he laughs and recalls now.

"The most abiding memory of that day is of course of extreme cold. It must have been minus 30 degrees Celsius. We were to be deployed by 'vertical envelopment' (heli-dropped) at Bilafond La and another platoon led by Maj. Bahuguna was to be dropped at Sia La, but they couldn't be sent until 17-18 April, because the weather turned bad and remained bad for the next three days. Extremely bad weather.

"Within three hours of landing, we had to evacuate our radio operator, one sepoy Mandal, who suffered HAPE (High Altitude Pulmonary Edema) despite being trained, acclimatised and being fit. So, we had a radio but no radio operator. Of course, it helped since we were supposed to maintain radio silence. So now 29 of us remained at Bilafond La. Within 48 hours, we were down to 28. Another boy died in two days. April, after all is winter on Siachen. Of this lot, 21 of us, I remember got severe frost bites.

"All this despite the fact that all these boys had come with me to the glacier in 1983, and were very familiar with the precautions that needed to be taken on the glacier. And this despite the fact that Gen Hoon had managed to get us imported snow clothing and equipment from abroad, just in the nick of time. I remember they arrived on the evening of 12 April, barely hours before we were being launched into *Operation Meghdoot*. Thermal coats, thermal pants, very nice balaclavas, excellent tents, ice axes, goggles, the works were bought from Europe. The weapons however remained the basic Indian Army 7.62 mm SLR. Of course, we had mortars, MMG, missiles, Grad P rockets. Some of the weapons came by air, some came through porters. I remember that at that time we were paying the porters princely sums. They were getting 50 rupees per porter per day, almost equivalent to the porter fee for expeditions to Mount Everest then. But we didn't mind since they were all local Ladakhis."

But, getting to Bilafond La turned out to be the easy part. As the day progressed, the "weather packed up," as military men would say in the mountains. The visibility was down to zero, it started snowing heavily, ruling out any further helicopter sorties.

Sanjay Kulkarni and his troop at Bilafond La, June 1984

"The blizzard hit us even as the two-man Pub tents were being set up. It was damn difficult. At that point of time, the higher authorities must have thought that this was a big mistake. We remained out of contact for three days," Gen Kulkarni recalls.

Amidst the blizzard however, the platoon led by Capt Sanjay Kulkarni planted the first Indian flag on Bilafond La on 13 April 1984!

Operation Meghdoot was now a reality.

But the job was far from done. The other passes had to be secured before the Pakistanis took counter measures, or tried to attack the small platoon level force at Bilafond La.

Down below, at the base camp, slight recriminations had started. The Staff in Northern Command and the Military Operations Directorate was sweating. Sending troops in winter on the glacier now seemed murderous.

Remembers Brig Channa, whose final call it was to send Capt Sanjay Kulkarni and party to Bilafond La on 13 April: "There were many who stared at me with the 'I-told-you-so' look. But to be frank, I was still confident that the storm would pass over. And it did. Three days later. The radio silence worked wonderfully. The Pakis came to know about the operation only after we had established and occupied the post at Bilafond La, that too because Sanjay opened the radio to tells us that one boy had died of hypoxia."

But, even as Sanjay Kulkarni and his platoon remained out of contact, the ground troops commenced their arduous move on foot from base camp and established Camp I on 13 April itself. Camp II and Camp III were established by 15 April along the route to Bilafond La. Lt Col Pushkar Chand, the Task Force Commander, pushed the Ladakhis and 19 Kumaon to Camp I and then to Camp II. Lt Col Pushkar Chand, who later retired as a Brigadier, was a para-commando and a renowned mountaineer. Speaking to me from his village in Uttarakhand where is settled now, he remembers walking to each and every post in the six months that he remained the Task Force Commander in the initial deployment of *Operation Meghdoot*.

"I was actually far away from this action as CO (Commanding Officer) of 1 Vikas regiment then stationed at Kiari. But the Corps Commander

The Cheetah in early days

Getting essential supplies to Bilafond La

(Lt Gen Hoon) personally called me and ordered me to take over as the Task Force Commander, possibly because I was the fittest CO in the area that time," Brig Pushkar Chand says. Many young officers and jawans who worked with him on the glacier remember him with fondness. "He kept the spirits high in the most difficult circumstances," remembers a young officer from that time.

Four days later, on 17 April when the weather improved, the Air Force flew a record number of 32 helicopter sorties with five available Cheetahs and two Mi-8 helicopters. That day, Sia La was occupied by a platoon of Ladakh Scouts under Maj Ajay Bahuguna. Troops had to be dropped approximately five km east of Sia La. They had to trudge up the treacherous slopes, which made movement extremely difficult because of heavy snowfall during the preceding days.

As the radio sets opened up—Sanjay Kulkarni had to tell base that one of the soldiers had died of hypoxia—and helicopters started flying again, the Bilafond La platoon had an unexpected visitor: A Pakistani helicopter overhead!

"When the Pakistanis saw us, they turned. If they had not seen us, they would have probably done exactly the same thing (heli-dropped at Bilafond La). Now they had no chance. They realised we were already at Bilafond La!" Sanjay Kulkarni remembers.

The improved weather meant that the follow up action to consolidate deployment all along the Saltoro ridge was speeded up.

Northern Command records of the time show that the link up force established the FLB (Forward Logistics Base) in the general area of Lolofond and Siachen glacier on 18 April and Camp IV on 22 April. Link up with Bilafond La post took place on 24 April, and on the same day Camp V was established. After establishing Camp VI on 26 April, the balance force was divided into two parties, one party established the assault camp for Indira Col and Turkestan La on 29 April, and the other party under Maj NS Salaria of Ladakh Scouts linked up with the Sia La post on the same day.

The top brass in Northern Command then took stock of the situation.

By now, Pakistani helicopters and even fighter planes were making reconnaissance sorties over the Saltoro ridge. Indian soldiers were surely visible to them on the key passes. The reaction at GHQ in Rawalpindi can only be imagined! India had beaten them to the top.

A backlash was inevitable.

As a first step, for providing air defence cover to counter the Pak air threat, two detachments each of SAM-7 (Strella) missiles were inducted at Sia La and Bilafond La on 22 and 24 April respectively. Simultaneously, two Zu-23-2 guns under 2/Lt Manoj Misra of 126 Lt AD Regiment were airlifted by Cheetah helicopters to the FLB. While these guns were being deployed on 23 April when in fact, Pakistani jet aircraft flew over Sia La, Indira Col and then along the glacier to the base camp. They were certainly on a photo reconnaissance mission.

Gen Chibber, meanwhile along with Maj Gen Sharma and Maj Gen Amarjit Singh, flew over Sia La and Bilafond La. He subsequently ordered deployment of four ZU-23 guns. Two guns were meant for protection of the Leh Airfield and the two others for the Thoise airfield. One detachment of Grad Peach was also inducted by air at Bilafond La. With the link up of ground troops and induction of AD (air defence) guns, the entire Siachen glacier had been secured.

Immediately after *Operation Meghdoot* was launched, Gen Chibber wrote in an official note: "The two main passes were sealed off. The

The early gunners

enemy was taken completely by surprise and an area of approximately 3,300 sq km, illegally shown as part of PoK on the maps published by Pak and the USA were now under our control. The enemy had been pre-empted in their attempt to occupy the area claimed by them."

No one, least of all Gen Chibber, would have imagined that the Operation would go down in India's history as the longest continuous deployment!

The early participants of *Op Meghdoot* (top and bottom)
in their basic clothing

Capt Sanjay Kulkarni flying out from Bilafond La

The early landings at Bilafond La

V

Staying Put

"We never thought we would stay there forever"

Pakistan, stung and surprised by India's pre-emptive action, launched *Operation Ababeel* (Swallow) in response to *Operation Meghdoot*. Its aim: to try and evict Indian troops from Bilafond La and Sia La.

The initial plans of *Operation Ababeel*, planned and war gamed in January 1984, envisaged launching operations through the proven and easier approaches via Bilafond La and Sia La to get on to the Siachen glacier.

But, once Bilafond La and Sia La were occupied by Indian troops, Pakistan began exploring other ingress routes along the Saltoro ridge, in the general area of Bilafond La and Sia La.

Indian intelligence reported the formation of the Burzil Force in the 80 Infantry Brigade sector, although the 62 Infantry Brigade was initially supposed to be responsible for conducting operations, since the Siachen glacier was within its operational responsibility. Incidentally, the Headquarters of the Task Force were reported to be located at Khapalu for controlling *Operation Ababeel*.

By 15 May, Northern Command had, with the help of the Indian Air Force photo reconnaissance missions and other intelligence assets, gathered enough information about Pakistan's build up in an attempt to wrest control of the Saltoro ridge. A Northern Command note of the time said:

"In our appreciation, Pak had formed several task forces to try and wrest back control from India. These were:

- *Hyder Force:* Approximately one company minus of SSG (Special Services Group) and one section of NLI (Northern Light Infantry) at location NJ 6299, approximately 10 km south-west of Sia La.
- *Baber Force:* One company of SSG and one platoon of NLI, located in Ali Brangsa.
- *Ashgar Force:* The force comprising one company of SSG and one platoon of NLI was operating on the Chumik glacier and also patrolling towards the Gyongla glacier at point NK 0069.
- *Hafeez Force:* This force of approximately one company was probably operating between the Hyder and Baber forces, with the view of exploiting any gaps/unoccupied dominating heights.
- *Kalander Force:* This force, probably trained for infiltration tasks, was inducted in the area in the first week of May 1984, to probably disrupt Indian lines of communications. However, detailed movement/deployment of this force could not be known.
- Our analysis showed that while SSG soldiers were being used for occupation of defences, NLI troops were used for administrative duties, occupation of base camps, and to act as reserves, or to be deployed for route opening and as combat porters.
- By the first week of May 1984, Pakistan build up opposite our glacial posts and in the area of Gyong La had increased considerably. There were also intelligence reports of Pakistan's likely intentions to infiltrate through the gap between the Kargil and Gallies sectors. Our forward troops in this area also reported reinforcement of some Pakistan posts opposite the Kargil sector."

INDIAN BUILDUP

Northern Command and 15 Corps was aware that it was essential to deny Pakistan troops any access across the Saltoro range to the Siachen glacier. With Sia La and Bilafond La under Indian control, Pakistan was making determined efforts to get across the watershed of Gyong La.

Gen Chibber visited the area of operations on 22 April 1984 and after an extensive aerial survey, gave the following directions:

A lonely post framed against the vast expanse of the glacier

(a) Patrolling of all southern glaciers, that is Gyong La, Lagongma, Layogma, Urdolep and Korisa to be carried out by our troops to counter infiltration attempts.
(b) Enemy will be prevented from establishing any hold on the Saltoro range or areas east of it.
(c) Patrolling of Teram Sehar glacier to be undertaken immediately.

Following these directives, Lt Gen Hoon issued instructions to expedite movement of troops to the Saltoro crest line, especially to Gyong La. He also ordered forward movement of back up platoons to the passes both at Sia La and Bilafond La, to dominate the heights astride the passes by regular patrolling. Lt Col Pushkar Chand moved to Forward Logistics Base (FLB) which was reinforced by a platoon each of Ladakh Scouts and 19 Kumaon. Maj Sujan Singh, Officer in-charge (OC), Ladakh Scouts (Karakoram Wing) was made responsible for organising a base camp with two companies of 19 Kumaon and one platoon of Ladakh Scouts, and was also tasked for ferrying stores from the base camp to Camps I, II and III. One company of 19 Kumaon was ordered to move to the crest line at Gyong La.

Movement of Guns

One 165 mm IFG Mk I gun sourced from the 108 Medium Regiment was test fired and became operational at the base camp on 10

May 1984. One 75/74 howitzer was dismantled and carried by the troops—a rare feat indeed to deploy a mountain gun at an altitude of approximately 16,000 feet after humping it over miles of rocky and snowy glacier. Two more IFG MK I guns were moved to the base camp and by 26 May, an array of guns had been deployed.

Occupation of Gyong La by 19 Kumaon

While the guns were being deployed, one company of 19 Kumaon under Lt Col DK Khanna advanced towards the crest line of Gyong La. The progress of this column was rather slow and by 20 May, after 14 days of marching from the base camp, the troops were still moving in the general area of the administrative base.

Brig Channa during his aerial reconnaissance of the ridge line had seen a small group of Pakistani personnel in khaki and dark clothing around Saddle 6646. No tents or field fortifications, were however seen. The enemy had apparently secured a foothold on Saddle. The Sector Commander directed CO 19 Kumaon to move towards the crest line at the earliest, and if possible, to engage the enemy by manoeuvring troops to a suitable vantage position, or by physical action. This column reached the line after 18 days of marching.

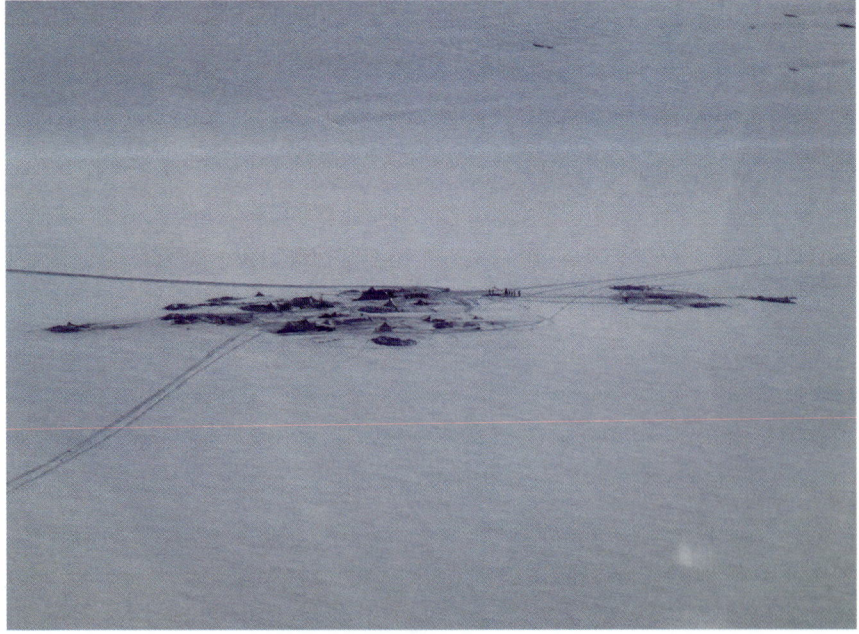

The wilderness of the glacier

Finally, by the first week of June 1984, one company of 19 Kumaon consolidated its position on Gyong La. The occupation of Point 5705, OP Hill, the Ring Countour and the eastern slopes of Point 5965 meant that, the complete area south and west of the crest line came under India's domination. It wasn't easy.

A Northern Command communication of the time noted: "Our maintenance route to Point 5705 lay over very difficult and a crevassed surface. To overcome this problem, troops of 1 Vikas were ordered to open a route through Zingrulma glacier. Namgyal Sangpo gallantly led his boys through a very treacherous route, negotiating a large number of crevasses and a few ice walls. This party constructed a helipad at Point 5615 NL 7145. From this helipad, we were able to 'manpack' a 57 mm RCL (recoil less gun) to Point 5705, to engage well entrenched enemy positions built into the rock face at OP II."

Meanwhile, to further consolidate the deployment, patrolling of the southern glaciers – Langongma, Lyogma, Urdolep and Korisa – was intensified and efforts made to get on to the watershed. The troops could not get on to the watershed in all places, because of the extremely difficult terrain and ice walls. But, the very fact that troops had reached these areas ensured close surveillance of the glacier.

Ski troopers, specially drafted from HAWS were patrolling right up to Indira Col and Turkestan La, to ensure surveillance of the likely approaches to Siachen from the North.

THE FIRST ATTACK

Sanjay Kulkarni, whose platoon was by now well-established on Bilafond La since getting deployed there on 13 April, remembers the first attack which is seared into his mind, even 30 years later.

"Although the Pakistanis had spotted us immediately after we got deployed in mid-April, they did not open fire until 25 April. The fire wasn't effective simply because they were firing from a lower altitude. But we had to be ever vigilant. We couldn't allow them to climb up to the pass (Bilafond La). So there were zero margins for error. Therefore, I had posted one sentry at the very edge of the pass, about 500 metres from where our tents were pitched. The (listening post) sentry would stand at the farthest point possible to look out for any Pakistani troop

The Ski-troopers at Bilafond La. Shokin Chauhan leading them

movement from below. From that position, the sentry could see at least a km into Pakistan territory. It was monotonous and physically very demanding task in the cold and blizzards. But it had to be done.

Bilafond La: The sentry posted at the very edge (see arrow) spotted the first Pakistani attack

"We had put in place a system where every hour, the sentry would come and give a report and I would respond by saying, 'Okay. Or 'Ram Ram' or 'all right'. I used to have a lantern on in the tent so that even in the dark, the soldiers would know that this was the Platoon Commander's post. I had told them, if I don't respond, peep into my tent and see if I am dead or alive. For all you know, I could be dead. But, as it is you sleep less at those altitudes, so I would be mostly awake or semi-awake when they came and gave the report every hour. This system paid rich dividends later," Gen Kulkarni said and went on to describe what happened on 23 June.

"On 22 June, there was shelling on our posts from the Pakistani side. Mostly 120 mm mortar fire. It also snowed heavily that day. In the early hours of 23 June, Lance Naik Chanchal Singh was on duty as the LP Sentry. That morning around 4.45 am, he spotted some movement about one kilometre away. He immediately shouted '*dushman*, *dushman* (enemy). But before Chanchal could run back to the post he was hit by Pakistani firing. The firing was effective. He died on the spot, but had managed to alert us. Because of Chanchal and another soldier, Govind Singh on perimeter sentry duty, we were activated immediately. Once they (the Pakistanis) were spotted, it was a matter of getting our act together. When Hav. Sukhbir came rushing and said, 'Saheb, *dushman*!' I asked him, are you sure you are not hallucinating? He said no, sir, Chanchal has been hit! I immediately rushed out and then it was all out firing from our side. They stood no chance once we had spotted them," Gen Kulkarni recalled. He remembers many Pakistanis being mowed down in that skirmish. "We beat them back and for a full day many bodies lay strewn on the lower slopes," he remembers.

This is how an official report describes the first clash on Siachen:

"*After the first firing incident on 25 April 1984 Pak troops tried to evict us from Bilafond La on 23 June. At approximately 0445 hrs, own listening post located ahead of our own post for early warning, spotted 30-40 enemy troops stealthily moving up the Bilafond glacier. As the leading troops reached 300 to 400 metres ahead of the LP, L/Nk Chanchal Singh and L/Nk Govind Singh of 4 Kumaon opened up with their LMGs on the enemy. The surprise having been lost, Pak troops started firing with all their weapons-HMGs, LMGs and mortars. The fire was very effective. The accurate fire almost made it impossible to carry out any movement between LP and the main post.*

Capt Shokin Chauhan (3rd from right, back row) with
Ski-troopers at Bilafond La, June 1984

*Unmindful of his personal safety, L/NK Chanchal Singh after engaging
with the enemy withdrew. Undaunted and aware of the urgency to
alert the post, he managed to reach the post, and inform the post
commander Capt Kulkarni, and after informing him of the impending
attack, succumbed to his injuries. With the enemy closing onto about
500 metres of the post, our own post opened fire with automatic and
small arms. Caught in the open, the enemy suffered casualties. Despite
losses, Pak troops made two more attempts to capture Bilafond La.*

*"Pak suffered 26 casualties. Pak plans were foiled by the alertness
displayed by the LP and the gallant efforts of the post of Bilafond La.
This bloody nose to Pak in the first major skirmish in the region had a
very salutary effect. Pak troops rolled back from their position at Ali
Brangsa to about 7 km SW of Bilafond La. Our troops occupied the
area Ring Countour 5369 from where they could effectively dominate
the Siachen glacier.*

*"On the same day, Pak troops made an attempt to move forward and
close in on our post at Sia La. The attempt was foiled by bringing
accurate fire on the enemy. Mortar fire on the enemy camp at Kondus
glacier was effective and enemy troops were seen running from their*

tents. Subsequently, the camp was shifted two km south wards along the Kondus."

Pakistan had tried to draw first blood, but was thwarted by the alert Indian troops on Bilafond La. The first ever skirmish in fact alerted the world via the BBC (British Broadcasting Corporation)'s popular radio service. In fact, Gen Kulkarni remembers hearing the news on the morning of 24 June on his small transistor. "I still remember that Hindi news on BBC radio used to come on at 6 am. On 24 June, around 6.20 A M the news bulletin announced that Indian and Pakistani Army troops have clashed at a place called Siachen in the Himalayas. That's how I think the world outside the limited circle of mountaineers, first heard of a place called Siachen," Gen Kulkarni said.

Indeed, no one outside the Northern Command and the highest echelons of the Indian government was told about India's deployment at Siachen. Even the language of the citations for gallantry medals for Gen Kulkarni and his team were kept vague. Sanjay Kulkarni and L/Naik Chanchal Singh were awarded the Shaurya Chakra, one of India's highest gallantry awards. Sanjay remembers the announcement, was made sometime in early August.

But, for Sanjay Kulkarni there was another surprise that he remembers even to this day.

The lonely vigil

"Days after the first clash, Lt Col (later Brig) Pushkar Chand called me on the radio set and said, '*Aise kar. Tu niche utar, ek kaam hai* (come down, there's some work for you).' I refused initially, mainly because going down would have meant climbing up again! But he insisted. I had to go down to the Task Force headquarter. After all he was my Task Force Commander. He was another famous mountaineer who had climbed Everest and Kanchenjunga. As it turned out, after the news of the skirmish on 23 June, Mrs (Indira) Gandhi decided to take a look at the glacier herself. She flew over the area. Of course, she didn't land anywhere. But when she was flying, she apparently saw a flag, our national flag flying on the glacier. At the Bilafond La post, we used to fly the tri-colour. At the base camp, she enquired about this post that had the flag flying proudly. She apparently also asked who was commanding the post. My name was mentioned. She apparently instantly said: 'Send that officer on a fortnight's trip to Europe!' Pushkar Chand told me, 'make your passport and go for this trip, all expenses paid.' That's how I went to Austria, Switzerland, France and Germany with the MoD team. I was included in the delegation as a user member. We went for buying snow clothing, specialised equipment etc. As a Captain, I would not have been on that delegation otherwise! That was Mrs Gandhi for you!"

So, as Gen Kulkarni came down to make his passport and prepared to go to Europe, consolidation of troop deployment had already begun. He never went back for any active deployment on the glacier, until he got posted to Leh in 2013 as Chief of Staff of 14 Corps.

As I prepared to wind up the interview with Sanjay Kulkarni, I had one last query: Did he or others who were involved in the planning and execution of *Operation Meghdoot* in the first few months, ever think Siachen would become so big? His answer: "No, to be honest, no. We knew we were capturing something important, but we had thought it would be like Polar Bear I, Polar Bear II, Ibex I, Ibex II (the long range patrols that used to go up to the glacier between 1980-83). But no, we never thought we would stay there forever. We thought we have captured it. *Ab khatam kahani* (that's the end of story). But Pakistan's violent reaction has forced us to stay there forever."

Much has changed in the intervening three decades. Leh has become a thriving town, the road to the base camp via Khardung La is all weather; the comfort levels on the glacier and the base camp have improved beyond imagination, and the Indian Army has mastered the craft of glacial deployment to an extent that regiments now pro-actively seek postings for their units on Siachen!

Meanwhile, within the first four months of launching *Operation Meghdoot*, Northern Command knew it had to rotate troops because of severe environmental conditions that imposed great physical and mental stress on soldiers.

Gen Chibber wrote: "I had directed that troops deployed on the glacial posts be released periodically in about 3-4 months. 1 Vikas and 2 companies of Ladakh Scouts were earmarked for the second induction."

Before the first turnover began, this is how India's deployment at the end of July 1984 looked like.

Sia La: One Company Minus (half of the usual strength of 100 men) of Ladakh Scouts supported by a section of MMG (Medium Machine Gun), One section of Heavy Machine Gun, 81 mm Mortar, one detachement of SAM-7 missiles and Grad P(multi barrel rocket launcher).

Bilafond La: One company Minus of 4 Kumaon supported by similar weapons as on Sia La.

The early accommodation on the glacier

Gyong La: One company Plus (more than 100 men) of19 Kumaon supported by 3 MMGs, One Section of HMG, 81 mm mortar, Det SAM-7 and Grad P.

Base Camp: 19 Kumaon, short of two companies that were deployed at Gyong La and other locations and supported by one battery of 105 mm guns.

After taking over the responsibility from 19 Kumaon at Gyong La at the end of July, 1 Vikas, made its presence felt. In no time they had established a post at Point 5955 (later named Shiv). The route through Zingrulma was also opened, thus easing maintenance problems of the post at Gyong La to a fair extent. With the occupation of Shiv, the complete area came under India's effective observation. Not resting on their achievements, 1 Vikas continued inflicting casualties on the enemy. For the first time the initiative in Gyong La was with Indian troops.

Meanwhile, at Sia La extraordinary Pakistani activity was seen at camp ND 6001 on the Kondus glacier. In order to pre-empt any enemy aggressive designs, 81 mm and 120 mm mortar and Grad P were lifted to the general area of Point 6630 overlooking the Kondus glacier. On 30 August, Indian troops engaged the Pakistani camp intermittently between 11.30 am and 4 pm.

Northern Command records show that the Pakistani camp was razed to the ground and their mortar position destroyed. "The enemy suffered heavy casualties of over 20 killed/wounded. A group of personnel, many of them in their pyjamas were also seen escaping southwards along the Kondus glacier," the record notes. It goes on to say: "On 23 August at Bilafond La, approximately 30-40 Pakistani personnel were observed moving NE from Ali Brangsa towards our post. Own mortars and Grad P engaged the enemy. The advance elements of 8-10 personnel were killed and more casualties were inflicted when the enemy tried retrieving the bodies."

Perhaps enraged by the continuous reverses it had suffered, Pakistan continued its build up, especially opposite Sia and Gyong La. Logistics infrastructure was considerably improved by the acquisition of Alpine huts and by developing roads and tracks.

90 Till the end of August 1984, Pakistan did not have artillery guns or 120

A Pub tent at Sia La

mm mortars. On 8 September 1984, an intelligence source reported to Northern Command that instructions had been issued by HQ FCNA (Force Commander Northern Areas) to heli-lift one 105 mm Pack Howitzer in support of Operation Ababeel. Subsequently, during mid-October 1984, two more guns were despatched. This movement of guns was later confirmed by Pakistan's firing of ground and air burst shells at Bilafond La and Gyong La. Intelligence also reported that in September 1984, an *ad hoc* commando Company was raised under HQ 80 Infantry Brigade by amalgamating the commando platoons of NLI battalions. This *ad hoc* sub unit was to be deployed in support of Operation Ababeel. In the meantime, Pakistan acquired alpine huts for use in Siachen. Three of those huts arrived in Skardu in September 1984.

DEVELOPMENT OF ADMINISTRATIVE INFRASTRUCTURE

Four months after *Operation Meghdoot* was launched, the situation had somewhat stabilised, and India continued to retain the initiative on the Saltoro ridge. But by this time, it was clear that these positions would have to be held permanently. This meant undertaking huge back up and logistics efforts.

As records of the time show, Northern Command concentrated on improving the administrative infrastructure. The operational track **91** from Sasoma to base camp was improved, and then became possible to move a 3 tonne truck on it. Today, the road is smooth and all-weather.

To enhance logistics, an AN-32 aircraft was inducted to lift additional supplies. "Attention was also paid for improving the material comfort of the troops. Fibre glass shelters, procured off the shelf (ex-trade is the Army term) were constructed by Army engineers at the glacial posts. Recreation facilities including VCRs and TV sets were also installed for improving the morale of the troops and keeping them engaged. Research and development activity to improve living conditions and survival on the glacier were also undertaken. The Snow and Avalanche Study Establishment (SASE), to assist in the collection of data to study environmental conditions in the region was also established."

Nearly three months after *Operation Meghdoot* began the Army Chief, Gen AS Vaidya, visited HQ 3 Infantry Brigade and the area of *Operation Meghdoot*. Till then, he was busy dealing with the fallout of Operation Bluestar and the mutiny in some units following Indira Gandhi's disastrous decision to send the army into the Golden Temple, the holiest shrine of the Sikhs in Amritsar. Later, Gen Vaidya was assassinated by Khalistani extremists in August 1986 in Pune where he had settled down after retirement.

The road to Base Camp today

"Between 18 and 20 August 1984, I accompanied COAS (Chief of Army Staff, Gen Vaidya) and briefed him on the progress of Operation. The visit was particularly useful since we were able to put across in the correct perspective, many pressing problems which required the attention of the MoD. A month later on 19 September 1984, Air Chief Marshal LM Katre, Chief of Air Staff visited the area," Gen Chibber indicated.

India's long engagement with Siachen was now well and truly on its way!

THE THREE MUSKETEERS

Among the ski troopers first sent out on the glacier was Shokin Chauhan, then a strapping young captain, barely five years in the Army. His unit, 6/11 Gorkha was deployed in Uri when he was asked to go and report to the 15 Corps HQ in Srinagar in April 1984, instead of going for a course that would have sent him as ADC to the President. From there, he and another colleague from the same unit, Capt AL Chavan was asked to proceed to the Northern Command HQ (at Udhampur).

They were told the Army Commander was to meet them and 21 other young officers. "We were wondering what this is all about, specially meeting the old man (the Army Commander). No one told us. My CO (Commanding Officer) did not know either. When all of us stood at attention, the first question the Army Commander asked, 'How many of you are married?' Four said they were. Those four were asked to step aside. The rest 19 were told that they are going to Leh and beyond. I being the junior most was tagged along with other soldiers and told to travel by road in the Army convoy to Leh. The Zoji La pass had just opened, so we managed to cross. Capt Chavan and others were flown in to Leh. With me were specially trained ski troopers. Even I had done 15-day ski training in March that year. As we arrived in Leh and started the acclimatisation process, we still didn't know where we were going. Siachen was still unknown," Shokin Chauhan now a senior Major General told me in February 2014.

As Shokin Chauhan and his ski troopers climbed up the glacier gradually, from Camp I to II to Camp III and so on and then finally

93

The make shift dining table

to Bilafond La, they were deployed to patrol the ridge after they were placed under Capt Sanjay Kulkarni. One more party of ski troopers under one Capt Amit Sareen was deployed on Sia La to patrol up to Indira Col. As they reached Bilafond La in their basic high altitude clothing (see photos of the ski-troopes on page 86), and replaced the first batch of Kumaonis, the ski troopers were handed over the special imported snow clothing by the departing troops. There was so much shortage of special imported clothing in those initial months.

Shokin remembers: "We did not have kerosene either, so there was no heating. The only protection from wind and snow was the tent under the parachute (see picture). We ate only tinned food for weeks and ate it out in the open on a makeshift dining table! Since there was no heating, there was no question of even changing clothes. For three months that I stayed there, I couldn't change my underwear! Neither did others. Most of us got chilblains on our feet since the socks would remain wet in the absence of any heating," Chauhan recalls vividly now, even three decades later.

"Those initial days and months were full of firing from the Pakistani side besides primitive facilities. Many soldiers suffered, some died but we were young and came out unscathed. We were also lucky to have in Sanjay Kulkarni a natural leader. He dealt with every crisis smilingly. In Lt Col Pushkar Chand (the task force commander) too we had a leader who trusted and stood by youngsters," Shokin Chauhan tells me. He also remembers individual acts of kindness. "My instructor in IMA, an education officer, realising I had no money, gave me thousand rupees and said, son keep this, you will need it. Then there were helicopter pilots. A guy named Anshuman Kumar Mata, was a daredevil. He would come whenever required and the weather be damned."

In November 1984, after four months of deployment at Bilafond La during which they took on the Pakistanis in the first attack on 23 June, Shokin Chauhan, AL Chavan and the ski troopers came back to their respective units. Sanjay Kulkarni had departed for Europe in August. When Shokin came back to the unit, colleagues asked him, '*kahan gaya tha?* What is bloody Siachen? You must have had a ball.' "That hurt. We had gone into one of the most risky missions blindly and here we were treated so shabbily. They didn't even give us the high altitude allowance at that time saying we have been given the avalanche allowance instead. We should logically have got both!" But things have changed now.

Another incident is etched in Shokin Chauhan's mind even now.

Wing Co Yunus, perhaps just before his last flight

Helicopter pilots used to be the lifeline for those deployed on the glacier, more so then, than now where facilities have improved way beyond imagination. When the time for Shokin Chauhan to go back came, he was to be airlifted and brought back to Leh. But for three days after his lift was planned, the weather didn't permit any flying. So when Sqn Ldr Naqvi finally managed to come to pick up Chauhan he remarked in half-jest: "You are my Jona (jinx in the Game of Housie that is typically played on Sundays and holidays in armed forces gatherings)!"

Two days later, Sqn Ldr Naqvi was to fly back to Hindon, near Delhi and Chauhan was to hitch a ride back, but the arrival of some senior Air Force officer forced a change. Naqvi took off in his Mi-8 for the glacier never to return! His chopper crashed somewhere between Khardung La and the base camp killing everyone in it! Chauhan still has the last photo of Naqvi and the Mi-8.

Shokin Chauhan's Siachen stint ended on that sad note.

His colleague from the same unit, AL Chavan had also come down a few days before him, and Sanjay Kulkarni had of course returned to Leh and gone for his all-expenses paid Europe trip sanctioned by Mrs Indira Gandhi herself! It was not until 29 years later, that all three, now Major Generals, came together in a common area of operation!

In September 2013 when I visited Ladakh and travelled to the Siachen base camp, Maj Gen Sanjay Kulkarni was Chief of Staff in the Leh-based 14 Corps. Maj Gen Shokin Chauhan was commanding the prestigious 8 Mountain Division that is deployed along the Line of Control in Kargil-Dras-Batalik sector, west of NJ 9842. Maj Gen Chavan was commanding the neighbouring 3 Infantry Division that guards India's contested border with China in Ladakh!

The Ibex in the wilds of Siachen

The much needed supplies!

A lonely post

The crucial telephone line

VI

The Conflict Widens

"The scope of Operation Meghdoot has been extended"

If India's military leaders thought that by holding the crucial passes on the Saltoro ridge, they would be able to thwart any Pakistani advances on Siachen, they were sadly mistaken. Stung by being outsmarted and outpaced in the race to the top, the Pakistani Army widened the area of operations, and launched several attacks in the first year after *Operation Meghdoot* was launched.

By 1985, Siachen had acquired political overtones in Pakistan with Benazir Bhutto—daughter of Zulfikar Ali Bhutto, the Prime Minister who was sent to the gallows by Gen Zia—making her come back in the country's political landscape, started taunting Gen Zia ul-Haq for having 'lost' Siachen to India. Within the Pakistani Army too, the loss of the tactical heights at Saltoro was being viewed as a major setback.

Peter R. Levoy in his book *Asymetric Warfare in South Asia: The Causes and Consequences of the Kargil Conflict* wrote: "The Pakistani army sees India's 1984 occupation of Siachen as a major scar, outweighed only by Dhaka's fall in 1971.The event underscored the dilution of the Simla Agreement and became a domestic issue as political parties, led by Benazir Bhutto's People's Party, blamed an incompetent military government under Zia ul-Haq for failing to defend Pakistani-held territory—while Zia downplayed the significance of the loss."

There is no doubt that Pakistan's 10 Corps, which had inkling about the inevitability of India occupying the passes on the Saltoro ridge, was caught on the wrong foot, kept trying to prove that it could wrest back the passes, but failed repeatedly. For India, tactically, it would have been adequate to hold the passes to deny access to the glacier. However, Pakistan's repeated efforts to occupy the ridges, which would have given them no tactical advantage, but only helped in scoring political points, forced India's hand to counter the moves by manning all possible heights themselves.

Therefore by November 1984, Northern Command was putting in place the third turnover of troops on the glacier, since now it looked certain that India would have to bring in more soldiers and expand the area of deployment.

Northern Command records of the time noted: "With the decision to occupy the Siachen region permanently throughout the year, the third induction of troops was planned. Despite extreme winter conditions with temperatures falling below minus 30 degrees Celsius, exchange of fire was almost a daily routine. Logistics problems were further exaggerated because of the increased requirements of kerosene at

Getting to posts like this is a Herculean task

The glacier is snowbound throughout the year

all posts and replenishment of ammunition. The Pakistani build up meanwhile continued unabated especially opposite Sia La and Gyong La."

In November 1984, 2 Vikas located at Tangste under the 114 Infantry Brigade (which looked after the boundary with China in Eastern Ladakh) was inducted to relieve 1 Vikas, which went back to its original location at Kiari under the 70 Infantry Brigade. So one Company of 2 Vikas got deployed at Bilafond La, and two more were deployed at Gyong La by November 1984. Sia La continued to be held by Ladakh Scouts. These troops were to stay at their respective locations till April 1985.

Meanwhile, highly-skilled ski troopers and volunteers for what was initially thought to be a short-term 'High Risk Mission' were also withdrawn since winter had set in and it was getting impossible to sustain them logistically. Northern Command recorded: "During the extreme cold conditions coupled with snow blizzards, we had approximately 10 clear days in a month for flying. The low temperatures reduced efficiency of the troops and weapons to a large extent. Added to this, the wind chill factor made living conditions almost unbearable. **101**

The forbidding Siachen

This resulted in a number of casualties due to extreme cold and chill, further adding to logistics problems of evacuation and relief."

In Pakistan meanwhile, the military was coming under increasing pressure to give a befitting reply to India's occupation of the high passes. Therefore, the build up of troops on the Pakistani side steadily increased. A Northern Command intelligence assessment at that time estimated that Task Force HQ, carved out of 62 Infantry Brigade was established at Khapalu. Elements from the Gilgit-based 323 Infantry Brigade were also pushed ahead for glacier operations. The note said: "The following units were officially part of the Siachen deployment from the Pakistani side by November-December1984: 21 POK Battalion, 1 Northern Light Infantry (NLI) Battalion supported by one company of 9 NLI and one company (Shaheen) of 1 SSG Battalion. An independent mountain battery from the 452 (I) artillery regiment equipped with 105 mm guns, one battery of 88 (independent) mountain battery equipped with 120 mm mortars and an *ad hoc* commando company raised under the 80 Infantry Brigade."

Like Pakistan, India too was building up troops and infrastructure in anticipation of another assault in the summer. No one would have anticipated a major attack in the winter months. But, the attack did come in the last week of February, 1985. An air operations helicopter

102

In memory of the Siachen soldier

sortie to Sia La on 21 February spotted three Pakistani positions near a peak called Saddle which was unoccupied till then. Alerted by the intrusion, Brig Jal Master, who had taken over from Brig. Vijay Channa in November 1984 as the first Commander of the 102 Infantry Brigade (converted from 26 Sector), flew over the area and assessed the intrusion. He immediately ordered a patrol of one officer, one JCO and 20 soldiers to go and occupy Saddle NL 375003, which was strategically located near the Pakistani camp detected that morning. The post at Saddle was now ready for any eventuality, although not fully established. The only question was when would the attack come: at night or early morning?

It did not come until noon the next day!

But, for the next five hours the Pakistanis tried to break through the small Indian force at Saddle, but the just inducted force under Maj MS Dahiya of Ladakh Scouts, repulsed the attack despite not being firmly entrenched. The Pakistanis, beaten back in day time, tried to interdict the track between Sia La and Saddle that night. Alert Indian troops got the better of the attackers, and killed at least five Pakistani soldiers; three fatal casualties were confirmed by Indian intercepts of Pakistani radio chatter. Weather also turned bad at dawn, and in **103**

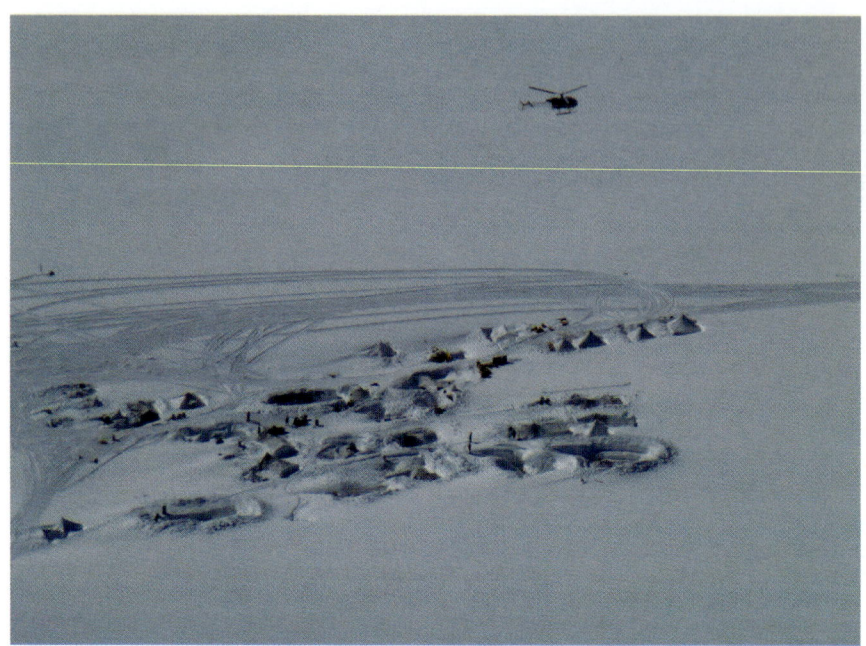

A latter day camp in the middle of nowhere

24 hours only five Cheetah helicopter sorties could be launched to supply ammunition and rations to the patrol on the Saddle. On 23 and 24 February, the Pakistanis launched yet another attack, this time with support from artillery and mortar fire. Yet again, the attack was beaten back. Such desperate attacks were now being launched with increasing frequency.

By the summer of 1985, a year after *Operation Meghdoot* had begun, Northern Command told Army HQ that a larger deployment to thwart frequent Pakistani attempts to wrest control of the passes was now inescapable. Soon, what was initially perceived to be a small military presence of battalion strength at most (about 1000 men), expanded first to brigade level deployment (3,000 soldiers) and now, post-1999 to nearly division strength (6,000 troops). Northern Command, reviewing the situation in the summer of 1985, noted: "By the third week of April 1985 there had been a perceptible hardening in Pakistan's attitude and stance as regards operations on the Siachen glacier. This was evident from the intransigent attitude adopted by Pakistan during various flag meetings culminating in their abortive attempt to evict us from Sia La in February 1985."

104 As Pakistan expanded the conflict, an *ad hoc* Indian response – doctrine

The peaks became important to hold

Soldiers resting in between operations

if you will—evolved around the concept of 'holding every height.' As Pakistan tried valiantly to evict Indians from the peaks and passes, it became imperative to not to lose any post. Instead of a well-reasoned and well-planned operation, the deployment on Siachen was guided by political aims in those early months.

One example of India's decision to occupy as many heights as possible came in June 1985. After thwarting the attacks on Saddle and Ring Contour, and despite occupying those peaks, Indian troops could barely observe Pakistani movement on the Gyong glacier. So, it was decided to occupy a nameless feature at NL 60654. Northern Command records of the time show that Naib Subedar Rinchen of Ladakh Scouts was tasked to go and occupy the feature on 17 June.

"For the next three days the enemy was unaware of our presence in this area which gave us the opportunity to consolidate and expand 'Rinchen' (that is how posts came to be named, mostly after soldiers who ventured into the unknown and established Indian presence. So you have several posts—Ajay, Bhim-Sonam, Amar, to cite just a few—named after daring warriors) into a formidable locality. After establishment of 'Rinchen' and 'Das' (another post named after a soldier), we were able to completely dominate the enemy from Lake Camp to OP II. This strangulation move in conjunction with establishment of 'Das' completely surprised and harassed the enemy. Because of its crucially dominating location, the outpost at 'Rinchen' has inflicted a large number of casualties on the enemy," Northern Command recorded.

Gen. Raghavan later noted in his book: "The summer of 1985 left no doubt in the Indian military mind about the inevitability of maintaining a strong, long-term presence on the Saltoro. That meant additional forces—in fact more than expected—an extraordinary logistics chain and the use of artillery to maintain control. The glacial terrain notwithstanding, the Saltoro needed to be held on the pattern of the Line of Control. That meant no part of the ridge line could be left unguarded. The hue and cry in Pakistan about the Siachen debacle found an echo in India, and the defence of the area got embroiled in the discourse of national honour and self-respect."

In 1985 itself, Gen Chibber was convinced that the Pakistani attacks would continue, since they had logistical advantage over India. "For example, from the road head to Gyong La their (Pakistan's) turnaround

The guns brought a lot of cheer

time is four days; ours is 10 days. To Sia La, they can reach in six days; we take 15 days," he wrote.

Crowding the peaks meant more combat troops, and of course more personnel from support arms. Those who have fought and perfected the art of mountain warfare point out, it takes a full company (about 100 men) from the support arms to equip and supply a platoon (30 men)! In Siachen, where no army had ever been deployed or fought, it was doubly difficult.

Guns had to be hauled up in difficult terrain, men from the artillery, signals and EME (Electrical and Mechanical Engineers) branches had to be trained and acclimatised to stay and survive on the icy heights. As Northern Command came to grips with the enormity of the deployment and the logistics challenge, even a small accretion cheered the troops. Snow mobiles, bought off the shelf from Europe made their debut in mid-1985. "Induction of two snow mobile scooters marked a sea change in the concepts of infantry mobilisation. Both utility snow mobiles are functioning efficiently and further induction of these vehicles is being met by imports," Northern Command reported to Army HQ.

107

Aware of the Indian disadvantage, Gen Chibber had already recommended enhanced deployment and strengthening of air defence, as two important elements that required immediate attention. Additional combat troops were now needed since the Pakistani attacks were relentless. Service arms like the Army Supply Corps, Ordnance and Signals had to have more presence now. Medical attention was becoming an absolute necessity, given the brutal weather conditions.

In a note to Army HQ, Gen Chibber confessed: "Earlier, basically because of problems of logistics and air maintenance, we had taken a decision to adopt 'summer' and 'winter' postures in the area of *Operation Meghdoot*. The Pakistani attempt to dislodge us from the weakened Sia La position in winter, which had to be rapidly reinforced, gave us anxious moments between 21 February and 1 March. With a much shorter turnaround of Pakistani troops from their road head, we could not take the risk of thinning out during the winter. There could be no summer or winter postures, barring pulling back of some posts established in the summer months on the heights which were untenable in winter."

Therefore, he recommended the following enhancements of troop inductions:

Artillery: One Air Defence Battery; one Grad P (multi-barrel rocket launcher); one light regiment; one field regiment of 105 mm guns and one battery of medium calibre guns

Engineers: One field company

Signals: One line section; half radio section and two mobile detachments

Infantry: Two infantry battalions

Air Force: Six Cheetah helicopters; two Mi-8 helicopters; four AN-32 aircraft.

Army Service Corps: Composition platoon; 2 motor transport (3 tonne capacity) platoons.

Army Medical Corps: Advance dressing station; technical support platoon.

108 *EME:* Advance workshop detachment.

The Mi-17s headed to the glacier (top and bottom)

By the summer of 1985, all uncommitted reserves of the 3 Infantry Division were exhausted. More troops and support elements had to be brought in immediately. The increased number of troops was a logistical nightmare. Unlike in most other places in India, where troops are deployed, there is no civilian habitation anywhere close to the Siachen base camp, leave alone the glacier. On the glacier **109**

itself, there are no natural resources. Not even drinking water. Only ice, mud and rock are strewn all over. Every small item, from toothpaste to a tablet of medicine has to be brought in from the outside.

No army in the world has stayed and fought at such altitudes and in sub-zero temperatures. A new doctrine had to be evolved for fighting on the glacier. Officers and soldiers not only had to go beyond their own experience, but had to constantly think on their feet to innovate methods and ensure troops got some basic comforts.

Many uninitiated people have remarked that the Indian Army could have learnt lessons from mountaineers and even early pioneers like Francis Younghusband and the Workman couple in the 19th and 20th century, who climbed the glacier and even passed through it to travel to Yarkand and beyond by surviving in the harsh conditions. But, most forget that mountaineering teams rarely number more than 50 at a time, and the climbers do not have to stay put on the glacier for any prolonged period *and* fight the enemy, as the Indian Army has been doing at altitudes in excess of 18,000 feet for the past three decades!

Climbing towards Khardunga La

Keeping the troops supplied with essentials is a huge challenge in Siachen even now; in 1984 it was a nightmare, with tenuous road links and primitive transport arrangements. Siachen, it must be noted, lies at the very end of the long road that connects Ladakh to the rest of the country. And unlike today, in 1984, the road beyond Khardung La-- in itself a fearful obstacle at 18,340 feet—was rather basic. Only three tonne '*Shaktiman*' trucks could rough it out on the tracks that existed beyond Khardung La. Today, on a good day, it is a 7-hour drive in a light vehicle from Leh to Siachen base camp, a luxury the early troops never had.

The logistics chain is long, arduous and dependent on weather conditions. High mountain passes like Zoji La, Baralacha La and Khardung La are formidable bottlenecks. Even today, Zoji La and Baralacha La are closed for six months because of heavy snow. It is only the determination and innovative spirit of the Army and the workers of the Border Roads Organisation (BRO) that Khardung La is sought to be kept open throughout the year. Even their best efforts sometimes fail, and the pass gets blocked by heavy snow for three-four days at a time, disrupting the continuous flow of supplies that are needed to be ferried across for the Siachen brigade. In 1984, the logistics chain was yet to gear up to meet this new challenge.

BRO workers: Braving all odds

So, as *Operation Meghdoot* completed a year, many changes had taken place in both the political and military leadership. Mrs Indira Gandhi was assassinated on 31 October 1984; India had a young and untested Prime Minister in Rajiv Gandhi. Lt. Gen Hoon moved on to become Director General Military Operations; Brigadier Vijay Channa, the man who headed 26 Sector at the time of the launch of *Operation Meghdoot*, finished his tenure and was transferred to Kamptee near Nagpur to head the Brigade of Guards Regimental Centre.

The changes notwithstanding, India's deployment at Siachen was only set to increase. As Gen Chibber noted in July 1985: "The scope of *Operation Meghdoot* has been extended to the 'physical' domination of the Saltoro watershed, from Sia La in the North to NJ 9842 in the South."

Thus began Indian military's long tryst with Siachen. The Indian Air Force, which played a stellar role right from the start, with insertion of the 4 Kumaon platoon under Capt Sanjay Kulkarni on 13 April 1984, was now called upon to get involved on a much larger scale, performing unbelievable feats that remain unparalleled in aviation history.

Since those early, uncertain days, when neither the Army nor the political leadership knew how the conflict would pan out, Siachen is now firmly embedded in Army plans, just like its presence along the rest of the LoC in Jammu and Kashmir, giving its troops and officers unmatched experience of operating at the highest altitudes possible, an envy of ground forces around the world.

In the initial months of Op Meghdoot, when the glacier wasn't completely mapped nor so many posts established, it was the derring do of Army Aviation and Air Force pilots, which allowed India to take a firm grip on Siachen.

Joseph Samuel, one of the co-founders of Deccan Aviation with the famous Capt CR Gopinath, was a helicopter pilot and instructor with the Army's Air OP Organisation in 1984 when he was posted in Leh.

The Air OP pilots were mainly tasked to carry out reconnaissance

The pioneering helicopter pilots

and observations to assist the artillery units. They formed a vital part of artillery functioning, before the Army Aviation Corps was created in the mid-1980s.

Although Joseph Samuel, now better known in the Army and aviation circles as Sam, was on leave when Capt Sanjay Kulkarni and his platoon went on to take control of Bilafond La on 13 April 1984, and Sam returned to plunge straight into operations in June that year.

He remembers: "We had no idea what Siachen was. We didn't even have proper detailed maps. We were using some maps left over by the Brits from the 1850s! They were beautiful maps, accurate and made with the help of theodolite. I don't how they did all this.

"Our main challenge was since nothing was recorded, there were no benchmarks. There was no precedence of flying there, so we didn't know how to approach, where could we land, what were the landmarks, how much weight we could carry, nothing was known! So we had to formulate our own standards. How much could we go in, that was always the question, since there were no refuelling facilities available? Each helipad had to be organised, mapped, and a name given to them. And what were the helipads like? May be four jerry cans arranged in a square formation so that we could spot them from a distance," Sam recounted over breakfast in Delhi

Samuel Joseph in a Cheetah on Siachen, 1984

in February 2014, nearly three decades after the pioneering work he and his flying mates undertook!

"There were no manuals. So we had to come to our own conclusions about optimum loads, hovering power required etc. We used to start early. We used to take provisions and bring back a lot of casualties. Most of the early casualties were because no one knew how to live at that altitude," Sam recalls.

He still remembers how in the early days, everyone was groping in the dark about locations and deployments. One incident has stayed with him forever. In the winter of 1984, the new Task Force Commander, Kulbir Singh who had replaced Pushkar Chand, one day told Sam to go and confirm some reports about Pakistani troops having built some bunkers and staying put on a peak near Sia La.

"He told me that on the left of the peak at Sia La some intrusion had happened. Why don't you go and have a look? So off we went. Ten minutes of flying couldn't show us anything, so we skirted the spur and started coming back when we located a trail of black spots. *Lagta hai Ibex hai* (Looks like an ibex, an animal found only on Siachen). As we neared the spot we suddenly saw 12 tents. Our first thoughts were: 'Our chaps are very much here. Don't know why we are panicking.' So we went lower and then saw a bunker, just 400 yards from Sia La. We waved at the chaps, 10-12 of them with a machine gun visible. We were just 50-100 feet above them. So convinced that everything was under control we came back to base and I told Col. Kulbir, '*Sir kuch nahin hai*. Our chaps are sitting there, well entrenched.' He said, 'our chaps? Don't be funny. Where? We have no bunker there!' I showed him the spot on the map. He immediately called Sia La to check on the deployment. They said they were not at that spot at all! So I offered to take him up there. As we neared the spot I was a little more careful and kept the chopper much higher. The moment Col Kulbir saw the tents, he exploded, 'Those are Pakis'.

"We instantly came back and there was total panic. The Pakistanis had intruded without anyone noticing! A whole squadron of MiG-23s was moved from Adampur to Leh with the intention to bomb them. The next day, we inserted some 55 additional soldiers at Sia La." A big skirmish followed.

The pilots kept innovating. Sam remembers another incident around Gyong La. "Gyong La was becoming a bit of a bother since it was lightly held. One day, Col Pushkar Chand (the first Task Force Commander) said he had sent a party towards G-3 (Gyong glacier). His troops, the Vikas (regiment) boys with the Ladakhis, were the most suited for the mountains. Pushkar Chand wanted to go and see where his troops were, so we took off.

The early years, pilots landed on unknown mountain tops

Rare sighting of Ibex in the higher reaches

"There is a big bowl. We searched the entire bowl, the climb is steep from 11,000 feet we are suddenly climbing to 17,000. We couldn't find the boys. Suddenly on the ridge I thought I saw some guys. So I told him, *sir wahan to nahin hai*? (Are they there?) Pushkar Chand said they can't be there. I had told them not to go there. So we went nearby and realised that the Vikas boys had indeed climbed what looked like the toughest ridge and had plonked themselves there! Pushkar Chand exploded: 'Oh bloody hell, they have gone there!' He asked me, can we land there? I said let me see. From the sky, the ridge looked only about 50-60 metres long and just about 20 feet wide. And about 200 yards away from the line of sight of Pakistani fire. We managed to go and land there! The tail (of the Chopper) was sticking out of the ridge! Now Pushkar Chand wanted to stay back for an hour with the troops. We went back and then picked him up later. That's how we opened Gyong La 3."

Sam recalls those days very fondly. "Hats off to the guys on the ground though. They braved inclement weather, lack of sufficient food and fought courageously. Those were great days," Sam, who is now a prosperous entrepreneur and social activist based in Bangalore, says. Thirty years later, many may have forgotten Sam and his pilot friends like retired Brig. Baljit Gill, Maj Gen Vinod Tiwari, Col Poovaiah and Col Mike Pereira from the Army Air OP organisation, but in the tightly knit Army fraternity, they continue to be regarded as heroes and pioneers.

The approaches to Khardung La, one of the toughest passes

Army convoy finding their way up to Khardung La

Helicopter with skiis are a great advantage on the glacier

Come sun or storm, helicopters are the lifeline

MASTERING
THE MOUNTAINS

VII

The Air Warriors

'Flying here is certainly not for the faint hearted'

3 June 1990: Two Cheetah helicopters of the Indian Air Force (IAF) are on a regular air maintenance run to the Siachen glacier. As was the routine by that time—six years into *Operation Meghdoot*—the first shuttles were to Amar and Sonam posts, the two highest helipads on the glacier, located at altitudes in excess of 20,000 feet above mean sea level.

Flt Lt. B. Ramesh and Flying Officer Naresh were leading the run and were supposed to land at Sonam. Flt. Lt WVR Rao and Flying Officer Suresh Nair, in the second Cheetah, were scheduled to touch down at Amar, not very far from Sonam.

Rao, how employed with the Tatas in Jamshedpur, remembers that day to be slightly warmer than usual at about 10 degrees Celsius, high for the glacier, but understandable in the summer months. "At those heights, when the temperature goes beyond 5 degrees Celsius, the 'density altitude' at Amar and Sonam is actually close to 23,000 feet, the ultimate limit at which these helicopters can and should fly. But, in those conditions we could carry barely 5 kg load on the Cheetah. The rising temperatures can have such an impact on the load carrying capacity of the helicopters," he remembers.

Rao and Nair landed normally at Amar, but as they revved up to take off, the helicopter engine 'surged' and the machine just sat down on the

Stranded at 21,000 feet

helipad. "Amar is hardly 3,000 metres from a Pakistani post located at a lower altitude. Even as we were struggling to figure out what went wrong, shelling from the Pakistani post started. Remember those were pre-ceasefire days," Rao reminisced.

The two pilots quickly ducked inside the bunker and sent a message to the other helicopter not to come towards Amar, since shelling from the Pakistani post had begun, but Flt Lt Ramesh would have none of it. He made two quick runs to Amar and evacuated Rao and Nair one by one, since it is inadvisable for any one not acclimatised properly to stay at 20,000 feet for more than 15-20 minutes. "Ramesh landed on snow since the helipad was already occupied by our machine. He held the chopper on partial power, lest his helicopter too toppled over and lifted us away even as the ever present danger of Pakistanis targeting the helicopter remained," Rao says, recalling those terrifying minutes.

The pilots were back safely at Base Camp, but the problems for the Air Force were just beginning. The chopper was now stuck at Amar, a juicy target for the Pakistanis. Moreover, how does one repair a helicopter at 21,000 feet? How would the technicians get there? How long would they take to acclimatise? Normally, when Army jawans get deployed at Amar or Sonam posts, they spend at least 10 days at gradually increasing altitudes to get acclimatised. That luxury was

Air Force technicians in front of the stranded helicopter

however not available to the IAF technicians, since the Cheetah was a sitting duck at Amar and it needed to be extracted as soon as possible.

As senior Army and Air Force officers both in Leh and Delhi put their heads together to find a quick solution to this unique problem, troops

The narrow confines of Amar Post

of the Sikh Light Infantry unit deployed at the Amar post constructed a snow wall overnight, a snow column really, to shield the helicopter sitting smugly on the Amar post from any Pakistani firing!

Construction of the snow wall was just the beginning of the innovation employed to retrieve the stranded helicopter from the Amar post. A team of technicians, led by Fl. Lt G. Sreepal was selected and inducted onto the glacier. Because of the urgency to repair the helicopter as soon as possible, the technical team was flown to a post at 15,000 feet for initial acclimatisation. Normally, the first stage acclimatisation for Army soldiers begins at 9,000 feet. After three days of stay there, the technicians walked to a post that is located at 18,000 feet. Finally, they reached Amar on 10 June, a week after the helicopter had soft landed on the post! At the post itself, additional facilities had to be created for the arrival of the Air Force technical crew. Meanwhile, the soldiers on the post had to keep replenishing the 'wall' with fresh ice lest it melted away due to the strong sun, a common feature during summer months!

Now the problem of carrying a replacement engine to Amar still remained.

Rao remembers: "The bosses had to select an aero engine with the least starting temperature. To carry it wasn't easy. The most powerful of the available Cheetahs with the least fuel consumption was earmarked for the airlift of the engine. Now came the question of fitting in the engine in the smallish Cheetah. To overcome the problem of space, the co-pilot's seat was removed, the engine was strapped in and the co-pilot's seat screwed in again. At the Base Camp, strapping the engine to the floor was easy since there were enough helping hands to secure the aero engine. But the same task at Amar became a challenge, since the pilot would have to unscrew the seat himself and would have had to remove his gloves, a dangerous thing to do in those extreme cold conditions. Moreover, flying with cockpit doors open—an extremely hazardous act at 20,000 feet plus altitude—was an additional worry since the cold gets accentuated at that height by the wind chill factor."

Despite the hazards, the most powerful of the available Cheetahs was readied. It was stripped to the bare minimum. "Out went the tail rotor guard, doors, passenger seats and the radio bay panels. The radio transmission set was removed and so was the battery after the

The spare engine

engine was started; we put in only two bottles of oxygen instead of the standard four that were normally carried. But that was not all. In order to save on weight, the helicopter carried fuel sufficient only to fly one way to Amar. It was planned that the refuelling for the return journey would be done at the post itself, even when the rotors would be running and the spare engine would be offloaded," Air Commodore Anil K. Sinha, then a Squadron Leader and Deputy Flight Commander, recalls. Wing Commander Goli, the Commanding Officer and Sinha, decided to take minimum fuel for two helicopters that were to fly into Amar that morning.

As they prepared to fly to Amar, the weather closed in, but Sinha and Goli went up to another helipad at Dolma, some three minutes flying time from Amar and waited. As soon as the clouds cleared, Sinha flew to Amar, delivered the tools , batteries and other essential equipment before Goli landed with the spare engine. "Perhaps seeing hectic activity on the post, the Pakistanis started firing as Wing Co. Goli landed with the spare engine. It was still off-loaded, refuelled even as the engine was still running," Sinha recalls.

Meanwhile at Amar, ground troops were preparing for the engine change. First, they physically shifted the stranded helicopter to the very edge of the table top helipad, so that the incoming helicopter with the **125** spare engine could land and hold till the aero engine was off loaded. On 11 June, the 'half-acclimatised' technical crew had removed the damaged engine from the stranded helicopter.

The technical crew worked through the evening and night of 12 June, taking help from the Sikh Light Infantry troops to change the engine.

Now came the critical part: fly out the repaired helicopter.

It was Friday, the 13th.

Because of the myths associated with the date and day, the CO, the late Wing Commander Goli was not sure if the operation should be carried out that day. But, eventually all of them decided that no matter what happens, they will fly out the stranded chopper that day itself.

In fact, because it was a day of '*Jumma*,' Pakistani troops were perhaps busy with their Friday prayers. Cleverly, the men on the post and the Air Force decided to fly out the helicopter around noon, when they knew the adversary would be busy with the afternoon *namaz*. As Rao says:"Friday, the 13th did not prove to be unlucky for us at all!"

Anil K. Sinha in less 'adverserial' circumstances

Sinha was designated to fly the stranded chopper back. He remembers: "Normally, when you are taking off, you have space around the helicopter. Here there was no such luxury. The helicopter had had a heavy landing after its seizure, and we did not know how deep it was embedded in the soft snow. In my mind, there were many questions. Will the engine start? Will it last the flight? Will I be able to extract it and take it back to the Base Camp safely? As these questions swirled in my mind, I took a deep breath, started and revved the engine and took off. As we landed safely at Base Camp, there were impromptu celebrations!"

Flt Lt WVR Rao and Flt Lt. B. Ramesh quickly followed up with a sortie and flew the technical crew back to the Base Camp.

Even today, 24 years later, the unparalleled feat plays out in the minds of those who accomplished it, as if it happened just yesterday!

Says Sinha, who went on to win a Vir Chakra for gallantry in the 1999 Kargil conflict: "That night we had a wild party at the Base Camp. We were doing back flips and somersaults. We were so happy and proud." Concurs Rao, who left the Air Force in April 2012 and now flies helicopters for the Tatas in Jameshedpur: "We were almost delirious with joy. After all, how many Air Forces in the world can

The Air Warriors on the glacier

boast of such a deed? I remember after that long and most memorable party, my voice was so hoarse that I permanently gave up smoking!"

The events of 13 June 1990 will also go down as one of the best examples of jointmanship between the Indian Army and the Indian Air Force! Both Sinha and Rao say that without the incredibly

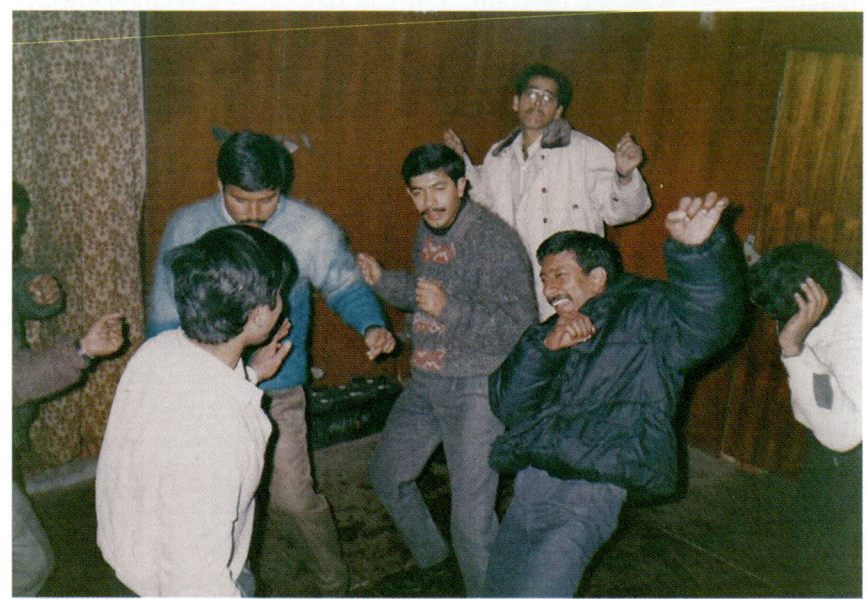

Party scenes at Base Camp on 13 June 1990

committed and selfless Army soldiers on the Amar post, it would have been impossible to even think of changing the engine. "On the first day, when the chopper sat down and we came to the Base Camp, the Sikh Light Infantry troops on the post, at their own initiative removed the rotor blades of the helicopter, and built that snow wall to keep it out of sight of the enemy! All this without any training. But, a more incredible feat was yet to come. On the day we were changing the engine, the portable crane that was airlifted to Amar for hauling the engine up (remember the helicopter engine is located above the passenger seats at a considerable height), broke into pieces because of extreme cold. These brave and extremely fit Sikh Light Infantry troops physically lifted the 182-kg engine at 21,000 feet to help us repair the helicopter," Rao said with justifiable pride.

Sinha added: "The rapport between us and the Army soldiers on the glacier has to be seen to be believed. Without total trust in each other, we can never function as efficiently and effectively as we have done all these years!"

Rao also recalls the simplicity of the soldiers. "Many a time, the troops used to say they had a craving for *aloo parathas*. So, on the days when we were coming from Leh, our wives, on short visits to Leh, used to make them early morning, and in our first flight we used to carry the *aloo parathas* for the troops on Amar and Sonam. The sheer joy on their faces on receiving the *parathas* was priceless!" Almost every helicopter pilot who has operated on the glacier would have a similar a story or two to share. Some remember how eager the soldiers are to receive letters from home.

In fact, a standard practice among the helicopter crew is to carry the mailbag in the very first sortie of the day, since it is the lightest weight they can carry at the beginning of the day when the helicopter fuel tank is topped up full. The coordination, the camaraderie and the brotherhood of soldiers is on full display at Siachen, an emotion that civilians will never be able to fathom or understand!

The engine change and recovery of the helicopter from Amar Post is just one of the many incredible feats achieved by the *Siachen Pioneers*, as the 114 Helicopter Unit is universally known. Established at Leh on 1 April, 1964 (is the Golden Jubilee Year of the unit), it has the unique distinction of being perhaps the only helicopter formation that has been deployed in an operation continuously for three decades!

Its mainstay is the single engine Cheetah (successor of the Chetak helicopter), now manufactured at the Hindustan Aeronautics Ltd (HAL) facility in Bangalore. Originally produced in 1962 in France as Aerospatiale SA 319 Alouette III (known in India as Chetak), its upgraded version, the SA 315 B Lama began licensed production at HAL in 1971. This helicopter came to be known as Cheetah which is the mainstay of 114 HU since 1984! Although it has the ability to operate at the extreme flight envelope limit of 23,000 feet routinely, a single engine helicopter is fraught with risk in normal circumstances. In Ladakh and especially on the Siachen Glacier, the risks multiply manifold.

Remembers retired AVM Manmohan Bahadur: "There are areas in the Glacier where the pilots fly with a prayer on their lips. The crevasses are so deep and wide that they could swallow an entire helicopter in the event of a force landing. The pilots have to brave temperatures as low as minus 60 degrees Celsius at times. Strong winds and poor weather is a constant companion while flying in close proximity of high peaks and rugged mountains. And don't forget the powerful 'down draft' that often pulls down the machine, if the pilots are not careful. In our time, over and above regular flying at the extreme flight envelope, we were also under constant threat of enemy fire. In those days, we always flew low and fast to give minimum reaction time to the adversary. The landings then—as now—on the match box size helipads are precise. The brave jawans on those posts would open the

An advanced light helicopter swallowed by a crevasse in 2013

door, take out the load, put in a casualty or mail, close the door and we would take off in the reciprocal direction. The time taken for this manoeuvre is not more than 20-30 seconds! As we returned to Base Camp, a quick hot cup of tea, another consignment loaded and off we went again. This continued the whole day, weather permitting."

And this routine minus the threat of enemy shelling continues even today. Every day. 365 days a year.

Three decades of flying in such conditions has given the 114 HU an operational experience that is the envy of aviators the world over.

Leh, it is said, is the Mecca of helicopter flying in the world. There is a saying among chopper pilots: If you are an Indian Force helicopter pilot, and you haven't been deployed to fly in Ladakh and particularly in the Siachen glacier, you have not arrived! The lucky few, who get posted to Ladakh, are inarguably among the best helicopter pilots in the world.

Just consider this: In the 1990s, the record for highest mountain rescue in the world was from Mount Everest at 19,500 feet; Indian helicopter pilots land at 20,000 feet four times a day, every day! The Austrian Air Forces' High Altitude Training School for helicopters is located at 9,750 feet! In India, Leh itself is at 11,000 feet!

As aviators who have had the privilege of flying under 114 HU say, 'no amount of money can buy you the experience of landing at Sonam— the world's highest helipad—or the satisfaction of pulling out a sick soldier battling the odds on the Glacier.'

Simply put, the helicopters, both of the IAF and from a later date of the Army Aviation Corps, are a lifeline for Siachen. Without these machines and the magnificent flying men, India would have had great difficulty in defending the high passes on the Saltoro ridge overlooking the Siachen glacier.

But it is not easy.

The shelling may have stopped since November 2003 when India and Pakistan agreed to a ceasefire, but other challenges remain.

The men and machines continue to face the vagaries of extreme cold **131**

A lonely chopper on the glacier

weather and formidable terrain. Like troops on the ground (*see separate chapter on health issues*), pilots too face acute mountain sickness (AMS), High Altitude Pulmonary Oedema (HAPO), High Altitude Cerebral Oedema (HACO), snow blindness, sunburns, hypothermia, chill blains and frost bite. In addition, pilots face constant discomfort and fatigue due to the extreme cold (remember the temperature goes down to minus 60 degrees Celsius in winter), vibrations in the helicopter, risk of hypoxia, lack of concentration and as they some times say 'white out'—a perception and spatial disorientation due to the terrain. When the glacier and its surroundings are totally covered with thick snow, pilots sometimes have no reference points while flying. In other terrains they at least have a cliff, a valley or flat ground as a reference, but on the glacier where there is nothing but snow, just pristine white snow all over, pilots can get totally disoriented since everything around them appears two instead of three dimensional! As a pilot describes it: "The 'white out' can occur on a cloudy day when the skies are grey and the earth and sky appear to merge because there is no contrast of bare rocks, boulders and ridges that stand out so clearly in sunlight. Depth perception is impaired and a pilot must be careful not to get hypnotised because of concentrating too hard."

But if pilots face extreme odds, the machines are not spared either. Prolonged operations in the higher range of its in-built flight envelope in Ladakh, has repeatedly caused structural and engine problems in the Cheetah fleet. Temperature extremes, strong winds, rarefied atmosphere has often damaged the structural frame of the helicopters. Pilots and technical officers in Army Aviation as well as the IAF have noticed frequent rupture of tubular members, cracks on welded joints; rubberised components like gaskets and seals lose their efficiency; the engines face thermal stress and are prone to—like the one that was changed on Amar—surges.

The role of the men on the ground—the technicians—is perhaps more important in Ladakh than anywhere else, simply because there is no margin of error in these difficult conditions. To keep an aircraft flying six hours a day, seven days a week means the technical and ground staff have to be constantly on their toes. The quantum of flying by helicopters under 114 HU is perhaps four times that of any other unit in the IAF. And yet, the technicians cope with the demand admirably. In sub-zero temperatures, the hands don't work. What many of us don't know is that extreme cold can also cause 'cold burns.' One has to be extremely careful in handling metallic objects. If bare skin so much as touches metal, the skin can just get peeled off. So gloves are a must, but then all mechanical work is not possible with gloves!

A typical day at 114 HU begins an hour before sunrise. The technicians get the machines ready, checking for any small defect or shortcoming. No chances are taken. If there is even a minor fault, the helicopter is grounded. Retired Air Marshal KC Cariappa had been part of the heavy lift Mi-8 helicopter team that had supported the 1981 expedition by Col Kumar. He later spent four days flying with 114 HU pilots in 1992. He came away awe-struck at the guts and professionalism of the pilots and the sheer dedication of the Army soldiers.

In 1999, Air Marshal Cariappa described his experiences in an article he wrote for the *Flight Safety Magazine*. "The day would start with a 7.30 am take off from Leh to cross the 18,000 feet Khardung La. The climb out, after takeoff required all attention, as we flew over the boulder-strewn narrow gullies and sometimes steep, nearly vertical slopes. There was no question of 'relaxing' because we were always fairly close to the ground, and any malfunction demanded instant reaction to prevent the chopper from crashing. Once the pass had been crossed, I would breathe a sigh of relief as we could now start the long, shallow descent to Base Camp at the snout of the glacier where the River Nubra had its source. In summer, the Base Camp appears unkempt; it is dirty brown and is an environmentalist's nightmare, 133

A tiny speck in the sky but perhaps the most important machine
at Siachen

because melting snows reveal the detritus of human habitation. But, in winter all is starched, stark whiteness with only rocks that are too steep to permit accumulation of snow, breaking the monotony. On landing at Base Camp we would switch off, get the helicopter refuelled and take on a mere 25 kg of mail or other supplies for a designated picket. After takeoff and en route our destination, the colour of the glacier would change from dirty brown to almost pristine, blinding white. We could see tiny deep blue pools shimmering in the sun, and look down at the awesome, frozen and seemingly bottomless depths or forbidding crevasses from where there can be no rescue. From time to time, we would fly over small columns of troops heading up the glacier to relieve their comrades. They would be 'roped' to each other as a precaution, should someone stumble into a crevasse if an ice bridge were to give way...."

"After about 20 minutes of flying, the first indication that we were near our destination would be when the men there, on hearing our 'chopper' would light up smoke candles to indicate wind direction and its speed. The approach to land had to be perfect the first time, because in this rarefied atmosphere everything is critical: the angle of **134** approach, the speed rate of descent and the weight of the aircraft.

There is no margin for error. On touch down the engine revolutions would be decreased. The troops would scamper up quickly to off-load, and within seconds we would be on our way back to Base Camp. Time is always of the essence here. It is important to get in as many sorties as possible, because who knows what the weather the next day would be like. For the next sorties the load would be somewhat increased, this time to perhaps 50 kg, because we would be that much lighter having consumed some amount of fuel on the outbound and return legs. After four or five such missions, we would switch off to refuel, during which time the technicians would check out the helicopter and prepare it for the next round of sorties. While this was going on we would refresh ourselves with steaming mugs of hot tea and some food. We would then lift off again to fly a few more sorties before 1 pm. Because of topographical reasons, the valley gets extremely turbulent in the mountains. There are violent vertical currents that can toss a light helicopter like a feather in a storm..."

A few words about the helipads: "These are located at heights varying between 14,000 and 21,000 feet. They have been stamped down and hardened by the boots of innumerable troops who then cover the surface with wooden planks to provide a firm surface needed to take the weight of the 'chopper.' The helipads are some 15 square feet and when viewed from air appear to be miniscule, which in fact they are.

Overcoming nature's huge challenge

While coming in to land in the summer months, the helipad merges with the background if the approach angle is too shallow, but once the touchdown is affected, one realises that the chopper is actually sitting on a 'table-top' some 1.5 feet above the surrounding area. Hence, the necessity of a perfect approach because the slightest error could lead to a catastrophic incident..."

Summer operations are always considered more hazardous than those in winter, because of reduced engine power that is available to the pilot. Perhaps the analogy of driving a car whose engine is 'tuned' for driving in the plains and then is taken up into the hills, will illustrate the point being made about the loss of power. Then there are numerous crevasses which criss-cross one's route and from where the chances of rescue are remote should a helicopter crash into one of them (see 'The Chopper in a crevasse' photo). In the winter however, the situation is very different. The engine performs much better, and the helipad sizes seem to be larger, because the amount of snow has increased and had risen to the level of the helipad; even the crevasses disappear...This then is what our intrepid soldiers and airmen are confronted with on the Siachen glacier. No amount of praise is enough and no paeans adequate to tell of their heroic deeds and acts of heroism."

In later years, the Army also acquired the Cheetahs and Army Aviation pilots, along with their IAF colleagues continue to serve at Siachen against all weather odds, sustaining the deployment of Indian Army troops throughout the year.

Mi-17, the heavy duty load carrier

The Cheetah

Flying against all weather odds

Dropping vital supplies in most difficult areas

VIII

Getting the Logistics Right

'Here the hepter, doctor and porter are our real Gods'

As the financial year draws to an end in March, every government department and organisation in India is busy finalising and reconciling accounts.

In Leh, the headquarters of 14 Corps, two Brigadiers in charge of ordnance and supplies have much more important issues than balancing the credit and debit columns.

As winter shows the first signs of receding, and the Border Roads Organisation (BRO) engineers get down to the task of opening the two passes—Zoji La and Baralalcha La—that connect Ladakh to the rest of the country, the two Brigadiers in Leh start monitoring the movement of supplies that have been contracted for the coming year.

Although the Zoji La and Baralalcha La do not become viable for heavy traffic until the middle of April—they are under 8 to 10 feet of snow for over six months in winters—a meticulous timetable is already in place to ensure that a convoy of trucks starts flowing into Ladakh, carrying all kinds of provisions, ranging from tents and snow clothing to ammunition and from fruit juice to high calorie chocolates.

Given that the window for stocking up for the rest of the year is only between April and early November after which the passes close again, and the fact that a full-fledged Army Corps (60,000 troops) is now

The Khargdung La top

deployed in Ladakh, the challenges of maintaining the logistics chain have increased manifold. The planning actually begins 18 months in advance, the two brigadiers tell me explaining the complex operation. The Army has established 'ordnance echelons' at key locations along the long supply chain. Trucks bearing various items begin to move after receiving indications that the passes are open and repaired to take the load. The sequence of travel and loading and unloading is all decided a year in advance.

As the convoys begin their journey from the plains of Punjab, enter Himachal Pradesh or Jammu, depending on their ultimate destination and then traverse the high passes, officers in the Army's ordnance and supply branches get busier. They have to keep tabs on the progress of these convoys coming into Ladakh, either on the Manali-Baralalcha La-Leh road or the Jammu-Banihal-Srinagar-Zoji La-Kargil-Leh route. The long distances and difficult, narrow roads add to the challenge that the truck drivers face. In the summer months, tourists travelling by these roads often encounter these convoys, and many of us would instinctively curse the truck drivers for slowing down, or sometimes even blocking traffic. But, next time any one of you comes across these trucks, give a little thought to the vital tasks they are performing. Without these uncomplaining truckers who take tremendous risks driving in the high altitudes, soldiers deployed in the harsh terrain across Ladakh would not be get their essential supplies in time!

The author at Khardung La, October 2013

For Siachen, the trucks have to cross another hurdle, the formidable Khardung La (at 18,380 feet it is considered the world's highest motorable pass) and then travel another 200-odd km to get to the Siachen base camp or the farthest base in the Turtuk sector. Not every truck has to go up to Siachen base camp though. Over decades, the Army has established various nodes, where depending on the importance of the equipment or provisions, stocking is done. Every three months, stocks are pushed forward either to their final destination, or are kept in transit. An estimated 1,80,000 tonnes of provisions are needed every year in Ladakh.

Soldiers at Siachen Base Camp

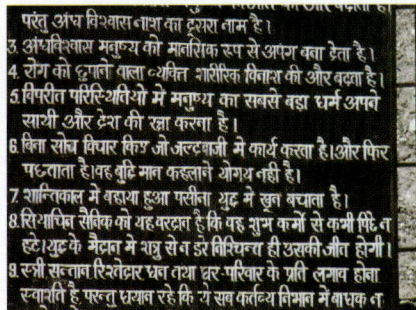

Board at Base Camp cautioning against blind superstition

After years of bureaucratic jostling, special rations are now provided to troops at high altitudes. In Ladakh, two categories of High Altitude Ratios exist. The first category is for those living on altitudes between 9,000 and 12,000 feet. The second for those stationed above 12,000 feet. In Siachen, it must be emphasised, the Base Camp itself is at 12,000 feet! After a detailed study, it was decided that every soldier who gets deployed on Siachen must get 6,000 calories per day diet. So, specially selected food items that include, chocolates, beverages, eggs and dry fruits, are specially flown to the glacier. In fact, soldiers have the option to choose from over a dozen special items to eat, in addition to those available at the Base Camp and lower altitudes.

For every battalion that gets deployed on Siachen, fresh supplies have to be provided. At the very least, 12 units get rotated in a year on Siachen. Then there are personnel from other arms. So, on an average, about 15,000 to 20,000 troops get deployed by turns on the glacier in a year! The highest priority however is to supply Category I and Category II items. They include snow clothing, gloves, three pairs of socks, jacket down, triple-layer snow suits and survival essentials like an ice axe and crampons. None of these are supposed to be reusable.

Soldiers in full winter gear listening to instructions at the Siachen Battle School

The special boots

Gloves and goggles

For the logistician, there is no room for error. When the trucks are unloaded at various points, the stocks have to be divided into 'air portable' or parachute compatible weights. They have to be stored in accordance with the priority of dispatch. Come blizzard or avalanche, the loads in any case have to be carried every day.

Once the provisions are sorted out, stacked and ready for dispatch at various locations, helicopters take over. The larger, sturdier Russian built Mi-17s carry heavier loads. They are not able to land on every small helipad on the glacier. They also have limitations of 'hover' at such altitudes, but are indispensable in dropping, guns, ammunition, tents, snow scooters and spare parts since equipment failure is frequent

Loads ready for dispatch to higher reaches by Mi-17

on the glacier. After all, despite their best intentions, no defence manufacturers would have anticipated the extreme conditions that prevail on the Siachen glacier. The Mi-17s with their ability to carry heavy loads are as indispensible as the lighter Cheetahs. The Mi-17s operate from three places—Leh, Thoise and Base Camp—and have a busy schedule throughout the year.

Then there are the old but reliable AN-32 transport planes which are based in Chandigarh in the plains of Punjab. From the very beginning of *Operation Meghdoot*, these planes have contributed immensely to the supply chain. AN-32s carry heavier loads and drop them by parachute over the glacier. While dropping both by transport aircraft and the Mi-17 helicopters is a pretty sight, for the soldiers on the ground, it is a major task to keep track of the loads and retrieve them. As Lt Gen Ata Hasnain, who commanded his unit 4 Garhwal on the Northern Glacier in 1995-96, reminisces: "On the northern glacier, there are no porters. All the haulage is done by soldiers. The drops used to begin early in the morning. That time (in the mid-nineties), kerosene jerry cans, apart from the other heavy stuff needed for heating used to be dropped by Mi-17s or AN-32s through orange or red coloured parachutes, as near to the posts as possible. At the posts there was an entire arrangement to keep a close eye on the drops. Once the Mi-17s and the transport aircraft had departed, work for

The AN-32 in action on the glacier. Notice the tiny red parachute

The flying machine at the highest possible posts

the ground soldiers would begin. They would fan out to the spots already noted, some on snow scooters, most on foot, roped to each other, locate the parachutes, haul the loads on sledges, tie them up to the snow scooters, or start pulling them to their pre-determined storage points. That is the time the soldiers were most vulnerable to the dangers of crevasses, especially in summer months when they open up in large numbers."

Snow scooters are indispensible on the glacier for the mobility they provide. They were inducted as early as 1984-85, according to the

Load dropped at a remote post

A Cheetah on a 'Pillared' helipad

Retrieving the loads from the valleys sometimes takes days

The snow scooter, indispensible on the glacier

initial notes of the Northern Command. But, the infamous Indian bureaucracy, instead of facilitating easy acquisition, delayed purchases on absolutely flimsy grounds.

As Lt Gen VR Raghavan noted: "The army found that snow scooters can greatly help...and reduce both time and effort...snow scooters are based on a simple technology, are cheap, and easily available in the world market. They do not require complex processes involved in the acquisition of tanks or aircraft or submarines. Snow scooters are meant to operate on snowfields and not glaciers. Consequently, their parts get worn out faster on glaciers. Nonetheless, they are not required in large numbers and the annual purchase of a couple of a dozen would have more than met the needs on the Saltoro. This simple matter was turned into a tortuously complex operation by officials in the Ministry of Defence."

"It first questioned the veracity of the breakdown rates, then the quality of training imparted to users, then the cost-effectiveness of the machines against porters and finally, the need to have them altogether. On one occasion, when a few snow scooters were sanctioned after some years of denial, the troops on the glacier asked that special **147**

George Fernandes (centre) on the glacier.
He visited Siachen a record 34 times!

prayers of thanks be offered to the regimental deity. The story may be apocryphal, but it shows how gallant soldiers are reduced to seeking divine intervention against insensitive official processes."

In fact, it took the personal intervention of George Fernandes, Defence Minister in the National Democratic Alliance (NDA) government (1998-2004) to speed up the process of acquiring snow mobiles. Fernandes, who earned the sobriquet of 'Siachen Minister' because of his frequent – and as soldiers say, morale-boosting – visits to the glacier, administered a shock treatment to civilian bureaucrats, by ordering them to visit and stay in the Siachen area in 1998! An international news agency report in June 1998 said:

"For more than a year, three Indian bureaucrats ignored the request for snowmobiles from soldiers stationed in an icy border wasteland. Now, the angry Defense Minister is reportedly sending the officials to the country's equivalent of Siberia."

"*The Pioneer* newspaper, quoting anonymous defence sources, reported Wednesday that Defense Minister George Fernandes, returning from a visit to the Siachen glacier in April, was displeased to find that the bureaucrats had been sitting on request for 10 snowmobiles. Fernandes ordered that at least 10 snowmobiles be sent to Siachen every year and directed the Defence Ministry officials to spend at least a week on the glacier to familiarize themselves with the needs of troops there.

"*The Times of India* added that such familiarization postings could become standard under the energetic Fernandes, who became Defence Minister when a new government took over two months ago."

Fernandes in fact made almost three dozen trips to Siachen during his tenure as Defence Minister. Describing one of his visits to the glacier, Manoj Joshi, writing for *India Today* in October 1998, said:

"The schedule would be punishing for the 40-year-old, but George Fernandes, Union Defence Minister who celebrated his 69th birthday this June, wouldn't know it.

Take his last trip to Siachen, a place avoided by the healthiest at the best of times. Up at Udhampur at 4.30 a.m., Fernandes was at the airport an hour later for the flight to Leh, which he reached by 7 a.m.

A visit to local officials, the Doordarshan Kendra, a quick lunch, and he was off by road to Khardung La. There, atop the highest motorable

George Fernandes with soldiers on the glacier

149

pass, he held an impromptu press conference with accompanying journalists, even while army officers pleaded with the party to move on because of the danger of hypoxia.

By evening, he reached Partapur, the headquarters of the Siachen brigade. Throughout the journey, he made it a point to stop the convoy to talk to locals and jawans. At Partapur, his first assignment was to inspect the base hospital, which he did, taking notes in a small book.

After dinner, he chatted with friends till 12 midnight, worked on his files till 2 a.m. and was up again at 6.30 a.m. for a helicopter ride to the higher reaches of the glacier.

Special privileges were at a minimum. On the road he was, as always, upfront, next to the driver, minus any special security. Arrangements were not ostentatious and he dispensed with the special table and tucked in with the jawans."

George Fernandes' tours and his special interest in Siachen ensured that acquiring snow mobiles at least has remained a smooth affair thereafter.

In fact, in 2010, the Ministry of Defence claimed: "The Defence Ministry has signed a contract for procurement of 20 snow mobiles with M/s BRP, Finland in December 2010. The complete set was received, inspected and deployed in Siachen by March 2011 in the "record time frame of three months."

Before Fernandes made it a habit to visit the glacier every six months, ministers and Army Chiefs visited Siachen infrequently. Lt Gen PC Katoch who commanded the Siachen brigade between December 1997 and December 1999 tells me: "When I took over the Siachen Brigade (1997), I was told that the periodicity of visits by the Defence Minister and Chief was about once every 2-3 years. While I was still on attachment, Mulayam Singh Yadav came on his

Brig (later Lt Gen) P.C. Katoch

Brig Katoch on the glacier

last visit. He presented four INMARASATs (satellite phones) to the formation and next day national dailies flashed this news with the heading *"Communication Problems in Siachen Resolved"*. Siachen was actually a neglected sector till then." He too credits Fernandes with bringing Siachen into focus.

"On his second visit, in 1998, he (Fernandes) witnessed three bodies that had been recovered from a crevasse in the central glacier after many months, when the crevasse opened up a little more. Skin from the bodies was peeling off and Fernandes was visibly shaken. He was a Defence Minister who visited 'every' post on the glacier where the helicopter landed, understood the difficulties and ensured due priority to this sector including its equipping," Gen Katoch told me in 2013.

In the first two decades of the Siachen deployment, bureaucratic procedures seemed to be the main hurdle. Remembers Gen Katoch: "Every winter, special clothing came much after the winter started setting in (I saw this during the onset of winter in 1997, 1998 and 1999). Of particular concern were lack of socks and gloves. Delhi had the stupid system of an Annual Provisioning Review (APR) that commenced only in the new financial year, that is April. By the time the troops got the stuff, it was late September, at times even October. There was no system of reserves at Army/Command/Corps/Division level, despite knowing the quantum of troops on the glacier and extreme **151** weather conditions. At times, it was painful to know that imports had arrived in Delhi, but clearance from DGQA (Director General Quality Assurance) was being delayed on one pretext or another, while troops suffered cold injuries on the glacier. One protested like hell including visiting VIPs but nothing much happened. Now, I am told the situation is much improved."

The supply chain is now indeed much more efficient and the priority accorded to Siachen, is perhaps one of the highest across the Indian Army.

The trucks, the Mi-17s, the AN-32s all brought goods right at the doorstep of the glacier but in the final analysis, the life saver for troops perched on the Saltoro are the Cheetahs and their magnificent pilots. Light, versatile and flown by pilots of the Indian Air Force and Army Aviation, the Cheetahs have been synonymous with Siachen from the very first deployment. When flight operations begin at day break, a Cheetah, with a full tank, is barely able to carry a 20 litre jerry can on the first trip. So, suppose the Cheetah is going to the highest posts at Amar or Sonam, it would take one jerry can and maybe a mail bag containing letters for soldiers from their families.

On the return leg, having shed the 20-litre jerry can and burnt some fuel, a rucksack of a soldier about to go on leave and therefore needing a lift back to the Base Camp would be brought back. In the second trip, two jerry cans would make their way up and the soldier, whose rucksack had been brought down on the first trip back, would get a lift down to the Base Camp. And so it would go on till noon, the official

A Cheetah in action

cut off time for helicopter flights on the Siachen. So, nearly 20 sorties would take place to evacuate or transport half a dozen soldiers! Such is the difficulty of flying in the rarefied atmosphere on the glacier. In the summer months when temperatures rise, it is doubly difficult to strike a balance between the need to carry as much loads as possible and the safety of the helicopter, since heat makes the already rarefied air at high altitudes thinner, greatly reducing helicopters' power. And yet the pilots take risks, going beyond their normal duties, always game to save a patient, evacuate an injured soldier, or transport an essential spare part in an emergency.

As a young officer, Col Amar Pratap Singh posted on the Glacier told me in October 2013: "Sir, in Siachen, the Hepter (helicopter), doctor and porter, are our real Gods!"

Truer words have never been spoken!

Initially of course, helicopters were a scare resource. Sitting in South Block, in Army HQ, it was difficult for the Staff Officers to understand the criticality of helicopters to sustain the deployment on Siachen. As Gen Raghavan, who also commanded the Siachen sector in the mid-1980s, wrote: "A stage was reached when every helicopter hour was measured. Army and air headquarters were locked in interminable sessions to decide on allocation of sorties to Siachen...a couple of

Between 5 a.m. and 12 noon, choppers try to fly as many sorties as possible   **153**

dozen hours of helicopter allocation was a cause for celebration or despair on the Saltoro. On occasions local commanders were reduced to petitioning senior officers for additional helicopter hours not as an operational necessity, but as a personal favour. It took some years and not a few close calls with military disasters before a full understanding evolved on the indispensability of helicopter support..."

Much has changed since those difficult years. Today, apart from the IAF's 114 Helicopter Unit, the Army has two aviation teams based in Leh, one of them a squadron of indigenously developed and manufactured Advanced Light Helicopters, Dhruv, boosting India's ability to keep uninterrupted supplies to Siachen.

In winter a common sight to avoid skidding

Army ordnance and supply units are vital for sustenance

Heading to the glacier from the Nubra Valley

The advanced light helicopter Dhruv is now a vital part of
Siachen's air effort

IX

The Intrepid Indian Soldier

'Here great courage and fortitude is the norm'

In the winter of 1988, the 5 Kumaon battalion was inducted on Siachen. Gopal Karunakaran, then a young Captain, now Director with the Shiv Nadar Schools, was commanding his company at Sonam, one of the highest posts on the glacier. One day, the Base Camp Commander, Rajan Kulkarni (no relation of Sanjay but commissioned in the same Kumaon regiment like him) called Gopal on the radio set and told him that a telegram had arrived for him from Kerala. Gopal knew it could mean only one thing since Geeta, his wife was pregnant with their first child and was staying back home in Kerala.

"Rajan asked me if the telegram should be sent up to the post. We were in the middle of the winter and there was no guarantee that a chopper would come the next day or the day after. And a climbing patrol would have taken more than a week, if it was scheduled to come. Eager to know the news immediately and not willing to wait, I asked Rajan to open the telegram and read the contents. Now, we the 5 Kumaonis are a very OG (olive green, a propah, sticklers for etiquettes) *paltan* (battalion). Informal and exuberant

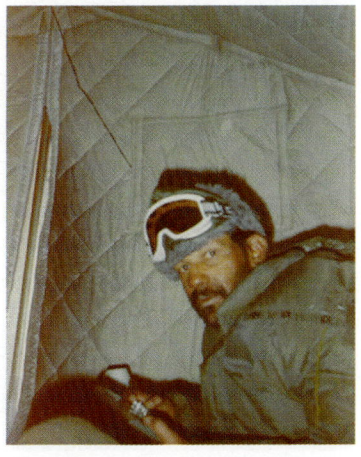

Capt (later Col) Gopal at Sonam

The 5 Kumaonis at the Base Camp

conversations were rare. So when Rajan open opened the telegram and read the contents, he didn't want to say congratulations, a girl has been born etc so he said 'Congratulations, you are a true 5 Kumaoni.' Translated it meant it was a girl! It so happened that in a quarter of a century till then, every officer posted to the unit was blessed with a daughter. Every boy born to them was at a time when they were

Gopal (extreme left) with colleagues at Base Camp

Young Kumaonis before they went up to Siachen

outside the unit! The news came to me four days after my daughter was born," Gopal recalls.

In those days, telegrams were the only means of communication for soldiers on the glacier. That is how Gopal got to know his daughter Priyanka was born in distant Kerala. "Since we were posted on Sonam, people said you should be named Sonam," Gopal told his daughter at our place one evening describing the incident to Priyanka, now studying in Australia.

Over *pao-bhaaji* and *chai* at our place that November evening, Gopal recalled clearly every moment of his stay on the glacier even 25 years later. If Priyanka's birth was the greatest news he could get on Siachen, there was a sad incident Gopal cannot forget even now. Gopal was the unit's Adjutant, a key man in any unit. One day a young lieutenant Sunil (now a serving Brigadier) walked up to Gopal and said, "Sir, young Rajan Singh wants to meet you." Gopal asked him what the matter was.

Sunil said: "Sir, he is super shy and is afraid to meet you but he still wants to tell you something." So Gopal told Sunil to bring Rajan into the tent.

Rajan was a young, 18 year old boy-soldier, straight from the hills **159**

At Sonam

of Kumaon on his first posting after training. As Gopal asked him to speak, young Rajan had an unusual request. "He told me *sahib jab paltan wapas jayegi mujhe MT platoon mein post kijiye* (Sir, when the unit returns from here, please post me to the Motor Transport platoon!)," Gopal remembers.

Apparently, Rajan had rarely seen or travelled in cars or vehicles back home in the hills. But his journey to Siachen had taken him on a plane, a truck and a jeep and he had instantly fallen in love with automobiles! Gopal had no hesitation in agreeing to Rajan's request and promised to post him in the MT platoon on the return journey so that he could enjoy being in the midst of automobiles!

Next day, Gopal and the first lot of his unit started their 20-day walk for Sonam. Rajan was among the first batch of soldiers walking up. Four days later, as they reached the Kumar base at 17,000 feet, Rajan was taken violently ill after developing HAPO (High Altitude Pulmonary Oedema).

"At 2.30 at night, I got a call from the nursing assistant about Rajan's condition. So I went to meet him and sat with him for half an hour. The nursing assistant said the situation was under control since Rajan was being given oxygen. The nursing assistant had already requisitioned a helicopter first thing in the morning. But at 4 am, I was again woken

A helicopter coming for evacuation is always a welcome sight

up. Rajan was sinking and the post was running out of oxygen! The helicopter's arrival was still 90 minutes away.

"By 4.15 a.m. Rajan died, a seemingly fit boy but felled by the unforgiving mountains. That day, we realised the importance of oxygen on the glacier and the vital link that helicopters provide! It was a sad loss so soon after our induction on to the glacier, but we took it on our chins as the accepted dangers of a soldier's life. We shed not a tear, and proceeded to do our duty for the next six months, battling the odds and the enemy, in incredibly difficult conditions," Gopal recalled.

Now, a quarter century later, medical and evacuation facilities on the glacier have improved way beyond imagination with the Army constantly striving to better the situation. Now HAPO bags are available at almost every post which helps soldiers overcome the HAPO syndrome by maintaining atmospheric pressure equivalent to the sea level once they get inside the bag. The soldiers now have the luxury to wait for the helicopter to arrive. Oxygen cylinders, big and small, are available aplenty across the 150-odd posts on the glacier. The number of medics, called nursing assistants, has also increased exponentially. In fact, a whole new 'Siachen Medical Doctrine' has evolved (*see separate chapter*) which has helped bring down medical casualties drastically.

It however does not mean soldiers don't meet accidents or succumb to health issues even now. Since the entire deployment of the troops **161** is in sub-human weather conditions, health issues do crop up, no matter how fit or young the soldiers are. But the response to medical emergencies is faster and mostly available at the posts now.

It wasn't so in the early years. Many a time, unexpected problems cropped up. Lt Gen (retd) Ata Hasnain remembers for instance how toothaches became a major headache! "Before starting the walk to the glacier, every unit went through a very thorough medical check up. Dental health was of great importance. Theoretically, on the glacier, you can, through tele-medicine treat any ailment, even a heart attack. But dental pain can never be treated. And they say a man suffering toothache is almost paralysed. So a dentist and his assistant were permanently posted on the Base Camp, at least when we were there. The dentist used to carry out a large number of fillings. If a tooth was decaying, it would be extracted ruthlessly! Many people have lost their teeth on the Base Camp! All this became mandatory and helpful. Otherwise imagine the cost of evacuating a man by helicopter just because he had a toothache!"

Those who have served on the glacier also recall how a code has evolved over the years on setting priorities for using helicopters. P-I was always for seriously injured soldiers, P-II for less urgent patients, P-III for sending officers up and down and P-IV, the least priority was

The way they live on the glacier

for a body. "A dead soldier was of no urgency since it was always important to save a life than use precious helicopter hours to transport a dead body," Gen Hasnain remembers. But sticking to the order of priority would sometimes lead to unintended consequences.

For example, in the mid-1990s, a Gorkha unit lost a boy soldier due to HAPO on Sonam saddle, which is approachable only by helicopter. On the first day, the body was brought to the helipad so that it could be sent down to the Base Camp. But the pilots were busy ferrying essentials through the day and told the Gorkhas that the body would be taken down at the end of the day. When closing time for flying came, the pilots said they were low on fuel, so they would take the body back the next day. Next day, something else took precedence. And so it went on for two weeks.

Every day the Gorkhas would bring the body to the helipad and every day, unable to load it onto the helicopter, took it back. The daily routine and living with a dead colleague's body for two weeks eventually got to the Gorkha troops. They started hallucinating. And started treating the dead soldier as if he was alive; they kept aside food for him. Ultimately, someone sneaked to the GoC about this post and the body. He was livid. Next day the body was categorised P-I and brought down forthwith!

Gen PC Katoch concurs: "At times, visibility packs off for days

Gen Katoch (extreme right, back row) with troops on the glacier   **163**

together – fogged out at times even for 7–10 days at a stretch. There have been cases where men were living along with the dead body of a comrade in the same habitat because helicopter sorties could not be launched."

Pilots have their own stories about carrying back the dead. Since transporting bodies was P-IV, very often rigor mortis used to set in and the bodies used to be stiff by the time their turn came for getting on board the helicopters. Cheetah helicopters are in any case too small to accommodate the prone bodies, so the soldiers were forced to break limbs to stuff the dead man in a sleeping bag and then send him away.

Brig (retd) RE Williams, who now works with the Jindal group and was also an important part of the initial days of the Army Liaison Cell (ALC), an organisation set up to handle the Army's media affairs at the turn of the century post the 1999 Kargil conflict, has a story to tell too.

He was a young Major in 1987 and was deployed on what is now Bana top with his own battalion, the 8 Jammu and Kashmir Light Infantry (JAK LI). Now the most decorated battalion of the Indian Army, the 8 JAK LI is perhaps the only unit that has actually fought two hand-to-hand battles on the glacier (*see The Tale of Three Battles*). Brig. Williams co-authored a book with filmmaker and author Kunal Verma in 2010, titled: *The Long Road to Siachen: The Question Why*. In the book, Brig Williams describes the pain of sending one's own colleague on his last journey in less than ideal circumstances.

"Evacuating a live casualty was not a very difficult exercise but ferrying a fatal casualty was a very demoralising event...First, even though the method was absolutely inhumane and disrespectful, we were forced to evacuate by actually tying the body to a rope and sliding it to lower altitudes. There was no alternative because when a casualty cannot be evacuated immediately due to operational and other reasons, it becomes very heavy and rigor mortis sets in, making the body extremely stiff. Carrying such casualties in areas where you have place to move is much simpler as it can be carried on a stretcher, but carrying a body in terrain where there is inadequate place to move even two abreast, it is a torturous experience. Ferrying it is bad enough...to see one of your colleagues being evacuated by this method is a psychological setback...to ferry a dead man on a helicopter at altitudes over 20,000 feet is another major exercise. With the body stiff and hard as a rock, the situation becomes more difficult...as a last resort, to accommodate the casualty, some limbs, I hate to mention, have to be forcibly adjusted. Such are the realities of living and dying on the world's highest battlefield."

Rules for flying are also very strict. After 12 noon, helicopter sorties on the glacier normally end, unless there is a dire emergency. Even in an emergency despite the pilots' willingness, the top brass is firm on not breaking the rules leading to a lot of heartburn.

Remembers Gen Katoch: "The hierarchy is steeped in its own rigidity and fails to see logic. The rule, at least in my time on the glacier was that any flying by Army Aviation after noon had to get permission from Army HQ. In one particular case, a jawan got critical with high altitude sickness. Permission from Army HQ was sought through Army Aviation channels which was in limbo because the official concerned was in a meeting. The Army Aviation pilot at Base Camp realising that weather was already turning bad, informed me and took off without permission and evacuated the casualty, saving his life. I commended the pilot, spoke to the GOC and sent up a citation for him. But Army Aviation ceased his flying and pulled him out despite all my protests not to do so."

The synergy between the aviators and ground soldiers is perhaps at

A crevasse, the most feared natural obstacle

165

A deep crevasse

Two Ladakhi porters explaining how they rescue people from crevasses

its best on the glacier. Within Army units, it is exemplary. Another incident Gopal recounts from his tenure on Siachen was about a soldier, who had slipped and fallen towards the enemy side and how he was rescued at Bana top, at 20,000 feet by a brave and courageous officer who went across single handedly at grave risk to his life, to get the jawan back. The soldier spent four hours exposed to temperatures below minus 40 degrees C (later both his arms were amputated). "When I met him in the hospital a month later, he said he knew that his company commander would come to rescue him. It taught me a lesson in trust, faith, camaraderie and leadership which I shall never forget for the rest of my life," Gopal said with justifiable pride.

Soldiers, by the very nature of their profession, develop enviable camaraderie and devotion to duty. On the glacier it simply gets accentuated.

Lt. Gen (retd) Rostum K. Nanavatty, who commanded the Siachen Brigade between October 1988 and November 1990 and later also became the Northern Army Commander, reminisces: "My lingering memory of *Operation Meghdoot* is that of the Indian soldier who, irrespective of his background or regiment (I had 18 major units turnover during my command), unerringly performed their duties to the country in the face of insurmountable odds. He demonstrated doggedness, tenacity, spirit of sacrifice and commitment that was only matched by the Pakistani soldier on the other side of the Saltoro. The latter, it must be said, astonished us on more than one occasion with his innovativeness and derring-do. It compelled me to coin the maxim 'Welcome to Siachen: here great courage and fortitude is the norm.'"

Gen Nanavatty's maxim, finds a pride of place even today, 25 years later, on the glacier.

Those who have served and continue to serve on Siachen, form an elite band of brothers, difficult to emulate anywhere else. When wearing a uniform, a small sky blue/white ribbon on top of the left pocket finds pride of place on the uniform worn by a Siachen veteran! Everyone, soldiers, JCOs, young officers, aviators and senior commanders, have their favourite anecdote, stories of triumph and tragedy to share.

Lt Col Sagar Patwardhan, who was deployed on the glacier with his unit, 6 Jat in 1993-94, had a couple of unforgettable experiences on Siachen. The first time when he went for a reconnaissance, the accompanying soldier developed a stomach ulcer and couldn't carry his rucksack after reaching half way up. "At such times, you have to step up and carry the colleague's bag no matter how much the discomfort of taking the extra load. We also lost our way in total 'white out' conditions. The 'link' patrol took us up to the designated point, but the other patrol coming to guide us further was yet to arrive. So we stumbled through and somehow found a small post. Now that post didn't have enough place in the tent for us but we all 'adjusted' and slept."

Next morning, Sagar, answering nature's call, got out of the tent and went some distance down the slope, away from the tent and promptly 'sunk' up to his waist in fresh snow! "As I tried to extricate myself, one loosely tied boot got stuck inside the hole! Desperate to get back into the tent, I put my foot back into the boot, by now full of snow! Since wind had picked up speed and I was some 10 metres away from the tent, there was no point shouting for help. No one would have heard me. Using all my strength, I somehow freed my stuck leg, stumbled back into the tent and shouted for help! Everyone pitched in. I first got into the sleeping bag and desperately tried to warm myself! Saving the foot which had got exposed to snow was now the first priority. As others tried to turn snow into warm water on the stove, I started rubbing the foot after having taken off the wet socks. It took us three hours to get me back to normal! I thought to myself, if this has happened to me on my first reconnaissance patrol, how will I survive the 90 days I am supposed to be here?"

But survive he did!

After spending his mandatory three months on the glacier, Sagar was back at the Base Camp and was promptly made in charge of the Siachen Battle School that imparts basic training and etiquette about survival on the glacier. Three months into his tenure, a post called Bhim with 8-10 soldiers got buried in an avalanche. Helicopter sorties showed no sign of life there. The worst was feared but the bodies needed to be retrieved, so Brig. Tej Pathak, who later retired as a Lieutenant General and was the Siachen Brigade Commander then, sent for Sagar and asked him to take a 25-member team up to Bhim to try and locate the post.

"Orders are orders! Normally, if you have done two tours on the glacier, you are not sent back but here I was, trudging up again on an 11-day trek to Bhim on what was nicknamed 'Patrol Sagar.' As we neared the post, a snow storm hit. We were cut off for three consecutive days. On the fourth day, we located all the bodies. Now came the tough task of taking them all down with the help of choppers. By the time we finished the task, it was another three days. After I came back, the commander sent a congratulatory message and later recommended me for a citation. Nothing came of that recommendation, but the satisfaction of having done my bit has kept me going even after so many years," Sagar tells me.

Devotion to duty under such extreme conditions is what sustains India's deployment on the glacier.

Gen Nanavatty also remembers one such tragic incident.

"I vividly recall a JCO in-charge at an advance support base who, even as avalanches were crashing down about him, simply refused to abandon his post and calmly signed off – forever – saying '*Sahib, main yahan se nahi nikal paunga: sab ko meri Ram Ram bol dena*' (Sir, I won't be able to make it back from here. Convey my greetings to everyone)."

He also off hand very fondly remembers an Artillery Observation Post officer at 6,400 m, who conscious of the fact that the enemy

Making their own way

Keeping a watch

was monitoring radio traffic, refused to divulge that he was grievously wounded and continued with his mission until a lull in the battle.

A soldier narrates his experience to the author on the Base Camp

Soldiers interacting with the author

In October 2013, when I revisited the Base Camp, 2 Bihar and 7 Kumaon battalions were manning the central and the northern glaciers. As I sat down to interact with the soldiers, all of them were eager to share their stories. Havildar Rajiv Kumar of 2 Bihar talked about the extreme cold. But what he was most amused was how cooking food was the most difficult part of staying on the glacier. "*Wahan chawal pakane ki liye pressure cooker ki 21 sittiyan lagani padti hai sahib* (we needed 21 whistles of the pressure cooker to cook rice up there!)," the simple soldier recalled. Another colleague of his, a cook said although high-calorie and high-protein diet is provided for everyone, hardly anyone ate. "*Uppar to bhuk hi nahin lagti hai sahib* (there's no appetite up there, Sir)," he confesses. So he would often make a variety of dishes ranging from maggi *kheer* to a milk shake!

Capt Deepak Chauhan of 7 Kumaon can't forget his stay at Amar either. "When I was going up to Amar, everyone was telling us, even the unit before us that it is the toughest post but I thought to myself, what is so tough? I have done the commando course, I shouldn't find it difficult. At Amar, there is a 1,000-feet wall to be climbed before reaching the top. Once we reached the 'wall base' the first 200 feet is a 60 degree incline, the next 400 feet is a 70-degree slope, but the last 400 feet are the toughest. As the people who are already on top throw **171**

Soldiers making their way up from Base Camp

a rope down, the final 400-feet stretch seems unending. It is at an 80-85 degree incline and you have to haul yourself up by the rope. In all it takes about two-and-a-half hours to climb the 1000-feet wall," the young captain, who stayed there for 100 days, tells me.

As a Company Commander at Amar, for Chauhan, like many others before him, the main challenge was to keep motivation levels high. "So, I used to get them to rearrange the tent, change guard duty every 5-6 hours and order different dishes to be made. So our boys even made *jalebis* (an Indian sweet dish) at the post," Chauhan revealed. Many who have served on the glacier several years ago, cannot forget the innovation by the cooks. Gen Katoch, who was the Siachen brigade commander between 1997 and 1999 tells me: "Once staying on the central glacier, I was given excellent *Dahi*, which I was told is set inside the HAPO bag – some innovation! Similarly, the best sizzler I have ever had in my life was at Base Camp cooked by an artillery unit."

Most soldiers complain of insomnia at those altitudes. Doctors attribute sleeplessness to lack of oxygen and extreme cold. As a jawan said, all that he managed to do was to sleep fitfully for three to four hours at a stretch. But unlike earlier times, soldiers now manage to take a 'dry bath' and change their undergarments every fortnight or **172** so. Now, every post has a common heated tent where soldiers can go, dip their towels in medicated hot water and sponge themselves. This is a big change from the early days.

Despite improvements in basic facilities, standard drills of wearing proper snow clothing without exception are still a must. Old timers and the current lot, both are unanimous in saying that units which rigidly followed the teachings of pre-induction training, did not and do not have a single weather casualty during their entire tenure on the glacier. Pre-induction training, at Base Camp is comprehensive, and it is generally found that only those suffered weather injuries who either did not follow the acclimatization schedule, or take standard precautions (nothing can happen to me attitude). Usually, nine pairs of imported heavy woollen socks are issued to each individual for the glacier tenure. But those who don't use them suffer, as Gen Katoch recalls. "Once, a Kumaon unit deployed on Northern glacier started having multiple cases of chilblains and frostbites. I went up to the Sonam post and asked the men to individually show me their nine pairs of imported heavy woollen socks. Some of them had brought only four-five pairs up .They sheepishly admitted that the remaining pairs had been kept behind to take them home and present the socks to the *budhao*, the old man, usually an ex-fauji himself!"

Practising the 'four-pointer' climb (using all four limbs)   **173**

Crossing the crevasse safely is a coordinated operation

Gen Katoch also admits to being foolish himself. "Once staying on a company post on the central glacier, I was to visit a forward post early morning. The first part of the journey was by snow scooter and the time was an hour plus before sunrise. Like a fool and displaying stupid bravado, I was wearing my stitched up balaclava in the icy winds. I could hardly feel my ears. I visited the post and by noon had come down to Base Camp by helicopter. By evening, both my ears were black with frostbite. For a month I could not sleep on my side as the treatment is only application of medicine!"

Following SOPs (standard operating procedures) is the only trick that works.

Col (retd) Danvir Singh concurs. He remembers when his battalion, 9 Sikh Light Infantry, was told that it would be going to the glacier, started training and preparing the soldiers both physically and mentally.

"We started psychologically training a year in advance. Lots of photographs and video films were shown to the troops. We got officers and men who had previously been deployed on Siachen to come and speak to our boys. All their fears were addressed. Fear of crevasses, **174** fear of frost bites. It was drilled into their minds that only training,

Driving a snow scooter across a crevasse

training and training will keep them alive. When I went to the glacier as an advance liaison officer, I saw at first hand and narrated the experience to the boys. So by the time we were inducted, most of our troops were well aware of what they were getting into."

Danvir said any battalion which can imbibe training requirements fully, survives and performs the best. "I was personally afraid of falling into a crevasse and sure enough I did while walking to Indira Col. But since all four of us were properly roped up and were following the SOPs, I came out safely," he told me in Delhi one afternoon.

The range of experiences that soldiers undergo is mind boggling. Capt Bharat, a young officer of 2 Bihar, narrating his experience in walking up to a post called Pehalwan, reputedly the closest post to a Pakistani post on the central glacier, recalled how the 20-member patrol party has to walk according to everybody's convenience. "People realise that individually no one can survive the glacier. It is team work that matters."

"One incident I cannot forget is that during my stay there was an accident on the Pakistani post just about 350 metres away from our post. Their tent caught fire and was reduced to ashes in a matter of **175**

Col Danvir Singh Chauhan

minutes. Since we were so close, we shouted across to check if we could help. They declined. Of course, help fetched up for them but I must say, unlike in our case where helicopters fly to every post almost daily, in their case, I saw helicopters coming to their post only twice during my 110 day stay at Pehelwan. When you compare their facilities with ours, one feels proud of our system and our Army," the young, barely in his mid-twenties, Captain tells me at the Base Camp.

But no matter how many attempts are made to increase comfort levels, there are some posts where lack of space creates its own problems. Gen Hasnain recalls: "At the the Bana listening post, located on the peak of the Bana saddle, the bunker used to be wide enough to have an ice bed as wide as a 3-tier berth in Indian railways. So an officer and a soldier who form the total strength of that post, slept with their legs over one another. The officer would get the first turn to put his legs over the jawan's. After a while the jawan would tell the officer, '*sahab bahut ho gaya, ab jyada weight ho raha hai. Ab thodi der ke liye mein paon upar rakhta hoon* (Sir, it is unbearable. Now my legs will rest on yours for a while)!"

Many such tales remain to be shared but one thing is clear, that over the past three decades the bond between the Saltoro and the Soldier has deepened. The inhospitable terrain of Siachen brings the best out of the Indian military. All that the soldier asks for is that the nation keeps faith in him. And give him the respect and dignity he deserves.

MY SIACHEN DIARY
Brig. Abhijit Bapat

In July 2007, me and a cameraperson colleague from NDTV, Manoj Thakur had travelled to Siachen Base Camp to make a film on Siachen. Later that year, the first civilian trek on Siachen in many years was being permitted by the Army. We spent four days on the Base Camp, living with the 5/9 Gorkha Rifles unit, then commanded by Col. Abhijit Bapat and his merry men. We ate meals with them, looked at their routine, spoke with the soldiers and officers alike, trying to absorb what it takes to be on Siachen. The film can be viewed here: A 20 minute film obviously cannot capture the range of experiences and emotions that the soldiers go through on Siachen. I therefore requested Abhijit, now a Brigadier again posted in Ladakh, to pen down his most memorable experience. Read what he chose to focus on!

> *"Yeh Labz – E – Mohabbat, Bas Itna Sa Fasana Hai,*
> *Simte Toh Dil – E – Aashiq, Nahi Toh Zamana Hai,"*

This couplet comes to mind, as one slowly makes one's way on the Siachen glacier, panting and gasping for breath. The icy and subzero weather conditions along with the huge mass of pure 'white' for as long as one can see, beckons the MAN in every individual. It brings out certain emotions and a sense of sacrifice which cannot be described in words. For every man who serves there, breathes the pristine and pure Himalayan air, it is an episode to remember for a lifetime.

It is an extremely humbling experience as one gets to see the immense power of Nature, and, the manner in which it is able to overwhelm whatever the puny 'human mind and body' is able to put across. It is also the ultimate test for both – man and machine, in their quest for survival.

My story is about a soldier and his sacrifice and courage under

Abhijit Bapat with the then Army Chief Gen J.J. Singh

extreme stress and duress, that, one feels during a tour of duty on the Siachen glacier.

It highlights the true glory and the bedrock of an Indian Soldier's fighting efficiency – regimentation. It is a word from which a soldier fighting for his country derives true inspiration and strength, the will to make the requisite sacrifices, and, the courage of conviction to do the *Harder Right than the Easier Wrong*. The Siachen glacier projects a radiant aura, and, also has a certain glamour associated with it. But all that would lose sheen, had it not been for the courage and indomitable spirit of our valiant soldiers who man it, protect it and make the supreme sacrifice in order to defend it.

The Saga of Havildar Man Bahadur

Man Bahadur was recruited in the Army in 1993 and was an able and sincere soldier. This hardy mountain boy belonged to a remote area bordering Sikkim and West Bengal. The natural hardships had toughened him physically and mentally. He was extremely meticulous and hardworking, and soon gained the confidence and respect of his subordinates, peers and seniors alike. His abilities made him stand out, and he was always at the helm of most of the responsibilities meted out to a person of his age and service bracket. As is generally the case, his mother found him a suitable bride after he had completed five years of service. Soon, Man Bahadur was blessed with twins. Having lost his father at an early age, Man Bahadur was very close to his family, especially to his mother. He slowly rose up the ranks, and was rewarded for his professionalism when he was made a Havildar in 2006.

Man Bahadur's unit was inducted onto the icy Himalayan heights of Eastern Ladakh in September 2006. With his customary enthusiasm, Man Bahadur quickly learnt the method of operating in the hostile climate and terrain of the Karakoram Ranges. He was the guiding beacon for his subordinates and a source of inspiration for his peers. He volunteered to serve in a location that is probably the highest conflict location on this globe – Bana Post. The tenure was for a period of four months including time taken for induction and de-induction. Meticulous preparations are made by every individual, as it was an onerous responsibility. Daily sustenance is done through previously stocked rations. Otherwise individually, a very systematic plan has to be made, as all personal requirements for the entire period have to be catered for. These include personal clothing, reading and writing material, hygiene and sanitation arrangements, and the mandatory medical, as well as, insurance formalities.

The complete load has to be packed and balanced in such a manner, that the trek on the glacier until the final destination, is smooth and without a hitch. Depending upon the weather and climatic conditions, such treks can take anything up to 10 to 12 days or more.

The Tragedy

A day prior to the date of induction, the unit received a telegram. It was meant for Havildar Man Bahadur. It stated that a serious epidemic had struck his village. It had claimed the life of his beloved Mother. His wife and twins were also seriously ill, with both the children in particular, being critical. The entire unit and its hierarchy were shocked with the sudden tragic turn of events. He was advised and permitted to proceed on leave by all his superiors.

Abhijit Bapat (centre) with Gen J.J. Singh and
Defence Minister A.K. Antony

Havildar Man Bahadur did not utter a word on hearing the news. There was not a flicker of emotion on his face!! Nobody realized that he was made of sterner stuff!! In the evening, his superiors asked him to fill up his leave dates so that he could proceed on leave the next day. But, Havildar Man Bahadur refused to do so. Everybody was surprised and also worried. Havildar Man Bahadur was then taken to his superior officers, as it was felt that he probably wanted to share something personal with them. Or, probably he wanted some financial assistance which he was too embarrassed to talk about openly.

The 'Real' Man Bahadur

On being asked as to why he had refused to proceed on leave, the reply that was given by Havildar Man Bahadur stunned everybody present there – senior and junior alike. He said, "Sahib, my mother is already dead and gone ten days back. The telegram has taken so long to reach. It will take me a minimum of seven days to reach home from here after I start tomorrow. By the time I am able to reach home, even the rituals which are to be done 13 days after the demise, will be over. As far as my wife and children are concerned

Sahib, God gave them to me. I am sure that he will keep them safe for me. Today, the unit has entrusted me with a responsibility. How can I let my seniors and juniors down? Life and death are two sides of the same coin. I too could fall in a crevasse during my tour of duty and die. So are we going to stop doing what we are supposed to do? Sahib, I would like to be inducted as has been planned. There will be no effect on my performance, I wish to assure you. My only request is that I be permitted to go on my full authorized leave on completion of my tenure on the Siachen glacier."

Everybody present in the room was stunned and too shocked to speak. In today's materialistic world, where anybody and everybody, looks for quick success and an easy life, here was a rare human being. The sincerity and devotion to duty displayed by Havildar Man Bahadur on that day was something that would be cherished by the unit. Havildar Man Bahadur completed his tour of duty in the most gallant and sincere manner. He was also decorated for his outstanding achievements.

As I said earlier, the Siachen glacier witnesses such tales of sacrifice and courage, almost on a daily basis. Some do get reported and publicized, but most of them remain under wraps. This was one such tale which has not got the deserved publicity. You could not have found a better person than I, to narrate this story, as I was blessed to have commanded soldiers like Havildar Man Bahadur on the highest, coldest and I dare say, the toughest battlefield on this planet. It has been an exhilarating and humbling experience serving on the Siachen glacier, as well as narrating this tale.

It changed my outlook to life in general, and, increased my respect for the profession of soldiering. Sometimes, as I look back at the years gone by, and I wonder to myself – Do I really know the men I command today, or have already had the privilege to command. I close with a couplet from a well-known poet:

Hamne Mohabbat karna Nahi Sikha,
Aapne Mohabbat ke Alawa kuch Nahi Seekha,
Zindagi jeene ke Sirf Do hi Pahalu hai Ghalib
Ek Aapne nahi Seekha, Ek Hamne Nahi Seekha

THE LEGEND OF OP BABA

During the making of the film on the life of soldiers before they head to the glacier, Manoj and I were looking for, what Manoj called an 'opening shot,' a scene which would show the human side of tough soldiers. In the first 24 hours, we could find nothing unusual. The soldiers were of course training at the Siachen Base Camp in the day, playing basketball in the evening, writing letters and generally

The OP Baba shrine

Myth? Reality? No one knows

carrying out daily chores even as helicopters came and went, either emptying a load or lifting essentials for the higher posts. That night just before hitting bed, Manoj in fact sounded worried: "Sir, *ek killer sequence abhi mila nahi hein!*" My reply was: "*Tum dhund hi loge, Manoj.*"

Call it luck, or call it OP Baba's benevolence, next day, a column of the Gorkha unit we were staying with, was descending from the Northern glacier after the three month mandatory stay. As the soldiers trudged down in single file, their white snow clothing now almost black, faces tanned and framed by unkempt beards, Manoj started shooting their return. Silhouetted against the imposing mountains, the single file of soldiers looked absolutely tiny. That is when Abhijit Bapat, then commanding the unit—now a Brigadier— told me about a ritual his soldiers were about to complete. "They will now head to the temple there," he said pointing to the complex at some distance "and report to OP Baba before coming and giving me the debrief," Abhijit said. I was intrigued. Which other army does this, I wondered, as Manoj and I headed to what looked like a temple, as we neared the area.

An officer praying to OP Baba

And temple it indeed was.

Temple of OP Baba.

Capt Tarun Tiwari (who must be much senior by now) led his soldiers inside the temple, bowed in front of a bust, shouted "OP Baba ki jai," and stood in silence for a minute. So did all the returning soldiers. They were all thanking OP Baba for their safe return from the glacier.

So who is OP Baba?

A board at the temple complex reads: "The true origin of the legend of OP Baba shrine remains obscured in the mist and frozen mass of the Siachen glacier. The shrine itself originated in the Malaun Post Bila complex in the northern glacier in the late 1980s. As legend goes, a soldier named Om Prakash was instrumental in single-handedly beating back an enemy attack on Malaun post, while soldiers of the post had been temporarily called to the rear headquarters. Who the soldier Om Prakash was, and what became of him is the mystery of the legend.

A soldier's silent prayer

"It is the firm belief of the troops that the soldier Saint Om Prakash, fondly revered as OP Baba, is their Guardian Deity who protects them not only from the depredations of nature on the glacier, but also from the enemy by forewarning them of impending dangers by appearing in their dreams. A formal military report is given to OP Baba by the troops prior to and on accomplishment of every mission on the glaciers. So strong is the faith in OP Baba that all troops pledge to give up consumption of alcohol and tobacco during their stay on the glacier."

The faith in the shrine of OP Baba is almost fanatical for soldiers posted at the Base Camp of the Siachen glacier. Built near the snout of the glacier in 1996, elaborate ceremonies are performed as soon as a soldier finishes his posting of 90 days on the glacier, something allotted by rotation. Living under sub-zero conditions on a mass of ice can be fatal, or cause loss of limbs or eye-sight or even sanity even amongst the most hardened even when all precautions are taken and right training imparted. Coming back from the glacier intact is a cause for celebration.

In the shrine complex, there are statues of deities surrounding OP Baba's bust. There is a simple red flag with *Jai OP Baba* written on it. Muslims, Buddhist, Hindus, Sikhs, soldiers of all faiths come and pray here. No one thinks twice.

Many other myths abound. Stories are passed on from one unit to the other. Posted at forbidding heights, soldiers need to keep faith in someone and something. OP Baba fulfils that need. Many believe that disobeying OP Baba brings death. In October 2013 when visiting the Base Camp, a soldier narrated the story of a Doctor who had fallen into a crevasse and could not be rescued. Two months later, his parents came visiting the Base Camp and wanted the army to search for him. A local porter volunteered to look for the doctor's body. As he went inside the crevasse, the porter located the doctor's body. But, as he tried to pull the doctor out, other bodies in the crevasse also suddenly came alive and whispered in the porter's ear: "we also want to come out." The terrified porter abandoned his mission then and there and ran for his life!

Apparently, those who disobey OP Baba, suffer. Sometimes a simple act like kick starting the snow scooter, or a generator becomes difficult for a variety of reasons, but soldiers believe if they pray to OP Baba, these problems are instantly overcome!

The army never questions the simple faith of these simple soldiers.

The guns blazing away in 1990.
Thankfully, they are now silent

A gun position

Terrifying chasm!

Keeping weapons in working condition is a major task

X

The Tale of Three Battles

'I don't care what sacrifices we have to make'

Three years after the Indian Army seized Bilafond La and Sia La and then consolidated its presence on the Gyong La, a platoon of Pakistan's Special Services Group (SSG), the commando force, through a fine feat of mountaineering managed to occupy the southern shoulder of

Bana Top as seen from Bila Saddle

Bilafond La Pass, also known as the 'left shoulder. At 21, 184 feet, the huge massif dominates the entire Bilafond La, area. An observation post on top of this feature gives a clear view right up to 20 km on either side. The Pakistanis had occupied the peak without the Indians at Bilafond La or on the Amar and Sonam posts, getting wind of the operation and named it Quaid Post, after the founder of Pakistan, Mohammad Ali Jinnah.

On 18 April 1987—almost three years to the day when *Operation Meghdoot* began—a medium machine gun on the Quaid post opened fire on the Sonam post, about 1500 metres below and killed two Indian soldiers of 5 Bihar regiment then posted there. The Indians were caught by surprise. Now helicopters ferrying supplies to Sonam and the neighbouring Amar post, started coming under frequent fire from the Quaid post. Indian presence at Sonam and Amar looked increasingly untenable.

Quaid post had to be eliminated. The question was: How?

The sheer 85 degrees incline for over 500 metres was impossible to climb silently and without detection, when the Pakistanis were sitting on top of the peak; helicopter gunship operations could not be

Snow, snow everywhere

contemplated in that rarefied atmosphere and on a narrow peak. What was the alternative? A frontal, almost suicidal attack seemed the only answer. Brig. CS Nugyal, then commanding the 102 brigade, conferred with his battalion commanders and formulated a plan. A supremely fit soldier, Brig (later Maj Gen) Naugyal was a Sikh regimental officer, known for his impeccable integrity, courage and professionalism. As the second commander of 102 Brigade, Brig. Naugyal had major tasks in hand: consolidate Indian positions and eliminate any possibility of Pakistanis getting the upper hand anywhere on the Saltoro.

April is still winter on the glacier as we know from the first ascent in 1984. It was also turnover time. The 5 Bihar battalion was being replaced by 8 JAK LI (Jammu & Kashmir Light Infantry). Aware of the Quaid post, Brig. Naugyal and Col AP Rai, CO of 8 JAK LI, decided to send a recce party and get ready in anticipation of the clearance from the highest levels. Second Lieutenant Rajiv Pandey, on his first posting, was chosen to lead the nine-man reconnaissance team to Sonam. It was flown in from the Kumar base. The effort to fly the nine member team was herculean. One Cheetah trip could at best carry one soldier with his personal weapon at a time. Even the kitbag of the soldier had to be carried in the next trip, so severe are the restrictions on carrying weights to the 20,000 plus post. Helicopter pilots recall that it took some 35 sorties to fully transport the 9-man team! It took almost three weeks to build up resources.

Finally, On 29 May 1987, a 10 man patrol under the extraordinarily brave, resourceful and gutsy 2/Lt Rajiv Pande left for the post. Facing this dynamic young officer was a 90 degree climb on slippery ice walls that were 1500 feet in height, which had to be negotiated to reach *Quaid* Post. On top of that, the weather was abysmal and visibility more so. This young man's bravery has never really been given its military due. It was his tenacity, cold courage, high morale in sub-zero conditions, where every step was an ordeal, especially when it came to fixing ropes against a vertical ice wall under intense shelling, surviving for over 48 hours without water and food, that really laid the foundations of the success that eventually followed. Unfortunately, nearing *Quaid*, they were detected by the SSG commandos and eight Indian soldiers, including Lt Pande and his JCO were killed. The officer was posthumously awarded a Vir Chakra.

Though the death of 2/Lt Rajiv and his men was tragic, the CO was now even more determined to succeed. What rankled the officers and **191**

The peaks rising above the glacier

men of the battalion, was that the bodies of the dead lay for three weeks in front of them; unrecoverable because of the shelling and Pakistani visual domination.

Launching an attack on a well-fortified post which has the advantage of height was not going to be easy. It needed reconnaissance, preparation and more importantly, volunteers who were willing to go into battle knowing fully well they may not return. Evicting the enemy would almost certainly involve hand-to-hand fighting and even use of artillery which meant escalation on the glacier. So Northern Command had to keep Army HQ informed too. Army HQ and the then Army Chief, Gen K. Sundarji took the matter to the Cabinet under Prime Minister Rajiv Gandhi. Some accounts of the time suggest that he had to do a lot of convincing at the political level to get his way. Although the rumblings in Sri Lanka were getting louder, fortunately India had not yet got embroiled in the island nation's war.

After the patrol had observed the area, the battalion started gearing up for the eventual assault. But there was a problem: Every soldier wanted to be part of the operation! Writes Brig. Rajiv Williams: "When volunteers were asked to raise this force, there was not a single

192

person who remained silent; everyone wanted to participate and take revenge. The objective had to be captured, and the Pakistanis had to be put in their place. Since the men were distributed at various posts in groups of 10 to 15, with a mix of personnel from supporting services, it was not possible, since it was not possible to get personnel from just one company...After a quick, deliberate selection process, keeping the factor of immediate availability, a force of 50 men was selected with Major Virender Singh as 'Task Force' commander and Capt Anil Sharma as his 2IC (Second in Command)."

By end of May 1987, the Task Force had moved to the administrative base about a km from the target, the 'left shoulder' at Bilafond La. It had taken the Cheetahs over 200 sorties to ferry troops and their equipment to Amar and Sonam posts. Both the posts were reinforced and readied for the eventual assault. Just ahead of the Sonam post, Capt Ram Prakash located a ledge that could accommodate a medium machine gun and a rocket launcher to be used in the final assault. Capt. Balraj Sharma with his seven man team occupied Amar and like near Sonam, this team also built an observation post. The Pakistanis on the Quaid post could see the Indian movement, and gradually realised they were being isolated. The Quaid post was left with just one route to replenish supplies.

Now primed for attack, the Task Force Commander, Major Varinder Singh launched Operation Rajiv (in memory of 2nd/Lt Rajiv Pandey) on 23 June to capture the *Quaid* Post. A total of 62 people participated in the final operation. The team included two officers, three JCO's and 57 jawans. Among the JCOs was Bana Singh.

Born on 6 January 1949 in a Punjabi Sikh family, at Kadyal, a border village located in RS Pura, the famous *basmati* rice-growing belt outside Jammu, Bana had enrolled in the Indian Army on 6 January 1969 into 8 JAK LI. He was considered a keen, enterprising and intelligent soldier by his officers, handling diverse responsibilities. He had also been trained in mountain warfare by the High Altitude Warfare School in Gulmarg and Sonamarg and was eminently combat fit; in other words he was, at a young age, an all round combat soldier whom his officers and peers respected.

The platoon sent on 23 June under Major Varinder Singh, Bana's aggressive and bold company commander, had to unfortunately come back half way, losing two soldiers in the bargain. A month before this **193** attack, Lt Pande had managed to fix ropes on the sheer ice wall that would lead to the Quaid post, but due to heavy snow fall, the ropes were untraceable. The ropes had to be fixed all over again.

The second platoon led by Subedar Sansar Singh with 10 jawans, made an attempt on 25 June. This time, there was no problem with the ropes, but due to a communication gap with the controlling headquarters, the mission had to be aborted. Col Rai, determined to succeed at all costs, had conveyed his determination to his command: "I don't care what sacrifices we have to make, but *Quaid* will be captured!"

So, Naib Subedar Bana Singh, hand-picked by his CO for the challenging assignment, led the last attack, along with Riflemen Chunni Lal, Laxman Das, Om Raj and Kashmir Chand. It was exactly at eleven minutes after noon on 26 June 1987, when the final phase of "Operation Rajiv" was launched in heavily snowing conditions and gathering darkness. A strange thing had happened the night before. Recalls Bana Singh: "one day before the assault, I was feeling depressed. So I started praying. I heard the voice of Guru Gobind Singh, who said said: 'I was only testing you.' Then my depression disappeared. It is the first (and last) time that I had such an experience."

When Bana Singh and his men started to move towards Quaid, the heavy, persistent snowfall and the poor ambient light conditions, made the soldiers wonder if it was day or night. On top of that, the Pakistanis knew something was going on, because of the artillery shelling that the Indians had started from the gun areas in the base camp, which forced them to put their heads down and remain confined to the bunker.

As Bana and his team started the torturous and silent climb on the 85 degree incline, all their limbs were aching; they were longing for rest, some rest but aware that this was their last chance, they kept climbing one foot at a time, resting every 10 minutes to give some respite to the aching arm and legs, catching their breath. The snow was falling steadily. They seemed to be heading to certain death, especially if the Pakistanis on top of that feature were to be alerted. Mountaineer Harish Kapadia, who had spoken to some of the participants of Op Rajiv, describes the 500 m climb in his book *Siachen: The Battle of Roses*: "To reach the post they (Bana and Co.) had to use a mountaineering technique called *jummaring up*. You ascend a slope by using a clip named *jummar*. A *jummar*, when attached to a rope, slides only upwards while you stand on slings attached to it. As it goes up and is released from pressure,

Some of the bravehearts who took part in
Op Rajiv, Bana Singh (bottom left)

the lever in the *jummar* locks and does not allow it slide down. You have to push yourself up with a heavy load on your back—it is hard work that even a fit mountaineer finds strenuous. Progress is slow and precarious, as great balance is required to stand on the attached slings. The soldiers put hot water bottles in their jacket so that after a few feet of climbing on the rope, they could warm their hands enough to hold the cold *jummar* clips. Even 50 metres of *jummaring* when everything else is quiet, is a challenge—here they had to *jummar* up 500 m where the enemy could fire upon them."

195

Ardous climb

Foolhardy? Perhaps, but only the Indian soldier could have carried on in such adverse circumstances.

Bana Singh remembers there was a single, deep bunker on the top, as they crested the peak. The Pakistanis must have become complacent because of the foul weather, and the heavy snowfall, and their success in warding off the previous two efforts by the Indians to capture the post. Manning the post was Naib Subedar Atta Mohammad from the Shaheen Company of Pakistan's elite commando force, the Special Services Group (SSG).

Three days of attacks by the Indians had not yielded any result, but as Bana and his men silently climbed the top of the Quaid post, he opened the entrance door of the bunker, threw his grenades inside and closed the door. Bana and his men set up their light machine gun on a single shot. In that extreme climate, the automatic weapon could fire only single shot. As the surprised Pakistanis rushed out of the bunker, a short but intense close quarter battle took place, killing six Pakistanis, two or three in hand to hand combat.

Naib Subedar Atta Mohammad and his men too fought bravely, but
196 were overpowered. Apparently, a couple of injured Pakistani soldiers

fell off, or jumped off the cliff, and survived to tell the tale. Brig Williams writes: "His (Naib Subedar Atta Mohhammad's) part of the story would never have been known had it not been for these men. They vividly described their last days on the Quaid post. "Naib Subedar Atta Mohammad was everywhere. When we saw the enemy (Indian soldiers) climb the towards our post, despite bleeding profusely after being hit by an enemy burst, our Naib Subedar kept going around and assuring us that reinforcements would soon arrive. The reinforcements never came, but we stood our ground and delayed the capture for three days till our ammunition finished..."

For his bravery, Naib Subedar Atta Mohammad was posthumously awarded one of the highest Pakistani gallantry awards.

Bana recalls that following the protocol and ethos of the Indian Army in treating the dead, the bodies of the six SSG personnel were brought back by the Indians, and later handed over to Pakistan during a flag meeting at Kargil.

On the morning of 27 June 1987, the Brigade Commander, Brig CS Nugyal who had been intimately involved with the planning and execution of the operation, arrived by helicopter at the battalion's launch base. Fiercely hugging Bana and his soldiers, he announced that hereafter, the **21153** feet (6749 metres post so brazenly taken away from Pakistan by Naib Subedar Bana Singh and his men, would be called *Bana Top* in his honour; a decision that a grateful nation and a very proud Army indeed, have accepted for posterity.

Naib Subedar Bana Singh was awarded the Param Vir Chakra, the highest wartime gallantry medal in India, for conspicuous bravery and leadership under most adverse conditions. "Operation Rajiv" overall, resulted in the award of one MVC (for Subedar Sansar Singh), seven Vir Chakras and one Sena Medal, besides the PVC. The CO and the Commander were awarded UYSMs. 8 JAK LI and 102 Infantry Brigade had reason to be proud; very proud indeed, for their stupendous skill at arms in the toughest high altitude terrain the world has ever known so far.

Sub (later Hon. Capt) Bana Singh

As Gen Raghavan wrote: "The operation required an amazing degree of commitment from the troops and outstanding leadership from the officers. The battalion and brigade commanders were on the Saltoro themselves, directing, controlling and fine tuning the whole operation. There is no parallel in military history of an attack of this kind conducted at over 21,000 feet."

But losing the 'left shoulder' now named Bana top to the Indians, did not stop Pakistan's (mis) adventure. In September 1987, the SSG launched yet another attack on Bilafond La. Literature and news reports of the time suggest that this attack was planned by Pervez Musharraf, then a brigadier in the SSG.

Codenamed Operation Qiadat, the attack was aimed at capturing two posts named Ashok and U cut, north of Bilafond La. In September 1987, Ashok was manned by just eight soldiers led by Naib Subedar Lekh Raj. In the third week of September, Pakistan intensified artillery and mortar attack on all posts around the Bilafond La area, and particularly on Ashok and U Cut. Those who were there, remember

War Memorial built by 8 JAK LI at Siachen Base Camp

the entire area becoming black with shells exploding in soft snow. 8 JAK LI was about to complete its tenure and 3/4 Gorkha Rifles was about to take over responsibility of the Northern glacier.

On 23 September 1987, the Pakistani attack on Ashok post commenced. That time, no one knew who participated from the Pakistani side. Later, it came to light that soldiers of the 1 and 3 Battalions of the SSG and the 2 Northern Light Infantry were involved, in what turned out to be a suicidal mission.

Brig. Williams, then a Major posted at the neighbouring post of Sonam, and the seniormost officer at Bilafond La at that time describes the battle: "At precisely 5.55 am, the brave, young and courageous men of Pakistan's elite SSG obeyed orders of their commander, and at the break of dawn were seen trudging along the narrow ridge leading to Ashok. The deployability along the ridge was no more than two men abreast, and therefore we could observe scores of rows following one behind the other. The attack had commenced...Ashok Post was held by a only a weak section of 8 men of 8 JAK LI and later strengthened by reinforcements from 3/4 Gorkha Rifles...

"Having waited for the attack till close to 3 am, we had barely slept on the night of 22-23 September, when I received a radio communication from the JCO positioned at Ashok, saying that the Pakistanis were coming on to the post in large numbers. Initially, I thought the report was not correct , because who in their right mind would venture an uphill assault in the early hours of the morning. However, the report was correct and the enemy was climbing that steep ridgeline and could be observed distinctly—a delightful opportunity for target practice for our troops. The Pakistanis were appropriately welcomed by Lekhraj along with seven other men. The (Pakistani) numbers swelled, but Lekhraj kept assuring us that nothing would happen to the post as long as he was alive...It was not more than 15 minutes after he spoke with me over the radio set when a TOW missile fired from the enemy fire base hit the bunker directly and killed the JCO instantaneously along with two other men."

Over the next two days, as India reinforced the Ashok post and used artillery extensively, the battle raged on. India's counter-punch was codenamed Operation VajraShakti. As Suresh Nair, who was a young artillery officer then posted on Siachen with 314 Field Regiment, recalls in an interview to me: "The 314 Field Regiment was a very

On razor's edge

young unit having been raised only in 1984. Immediately on raising we were sent to the glacier, and believe me we could not have got a better training ground.

In this Operation, artillery proved to be the major battle winning factor, due to speed, accuracy and quantum of fire brought down on the enemy. The arty fire was expertly handled, and was brought down at the right time and place exerting decisive influence in the battle."

Suresh Nair continues: "On 23 September when the attack began early morning, and as the section located on the Ashok post kept fighting gallantly, we in the artillery started firing our medium, light and field guns on the enemy positions. By 1130 am the enemy had to withdraw and take cover behind the Tola hill and the HMG ridge. The arty duel carried on with deadly salvos of air burst and ground burst ammunition. Mainly air burst ammunition was used with great effect. The adversary once again started shelling, Ashok and U Cut on the night of 24 September and seen approaching Ashok in a platoon strength with some civilian porters. The platoon was followed by a whole batallion in four columns. Our artillery fire was readjusted on these advancing columns and they were stalled.

200 "During this battle we employed three 130 MM guns, three 105 MM

LFGs and three 120 MM Mortars. Artillery in the three nights fired over 3,000 rounds of ammunition, which must be a record for firing from the small number of guns. One 130 MM gun burst on the last night due to the intensity of firing, as also the large number of rounds fired. An intercepted radio communication revealed a Pakistani company commander telling his superiors that that no movement was possible due to the very heavy and accurate artillery shelling."

Nair remembers one more episode very clearly even after all these years: "I must mention one very memorable incident with regard to battle field leadership which I had witnessed. Our Commander then was Brig Nugyal. He had come to visit the forward positions. He came in and enquired about us. After some time, a helicopter came in and he flew out. Later, the CO asked me about the Commander and whether he had mentioned that he had been injured. It came as a complete shock, for Brig Nugyal did not utter a word about his own injury when he was visiting us. He had apparently been injured in shelling. During his visit he never mentioned to me or the men that he was in pain and required any medical aid!"

Brig Williams concludes: "As per Pakistani reports and signal intercepts, the enemy suffered a loss of approximately 300." Raj Chengappa, then writing for *India Today*, reported in October 1987: For days the Indian Army pickets stationed at Bilafond La, almost 20,000 feet high and overlooking the frozen wastes of the Siachen glacier, were expecting the Pakistani troops below to attack. Through their binoculars they had watched with consternation as the Pakistanis brought in more men and arms than ever before. The Indian commanders even informally sent word to their counterparts, warning them not to launch an offensive.

But the Pakistani soldiers paid no heed, and around noon on September 23 started shelling the Indian pickets with mortar shells. Said a senior Indian officer just back from the fighting: "They came to us from all fronts, firing mortar shells. shooting long-range missiles, hoping to inflict heavy casualties. But we were ready for them." The Indians were well prepared and pounded the ridges below with medium range gun-fire and mortars inflicting heavy casualties.

The battle raged well into the night, and the Pakistani raiders were beaten back, but continued their attacks for the next two nights. On September 25 after the Pakistanis finally withdrew, the Indians claimed that they had killed at least 150 of them, injuring an equal number. 201

While Defence Ministry sources said that only around 20 Indians were killed, others put the toll at roughly 50. It was easily the biggest offensive by Pakistan since India first established its pickets at strategic points near Siachen in 1984. Said a senior Indian Army officer: "It seemed a do or die attack by Pakistan, and for them it ended in a die and not a do."

While Indian Defence Ministry officials announced the successful repulsion of the attack, Pakistan disputed it immediately. Rana Naeem Mahmood, Pakistan's minister of state for defence, said: "Reports of the encounter as disseminated by the Indian side are highly exaggerated and the casualties reported on the Pakistan side are preposterous."

The key question is why did Pakistan choose to launch its biggest offensive to date at this particular moment? One answer is that was timed when India was busy dealing with Sri Lanka, and serious trouble brewing on her northern border in Tibet. Also, President General Zia-ul-Haq was under pressure from the Opposition to establish Pakistan's claim over the region.

Although both countries have vowed not to use force, and to sort out any dispute in the Siachen region amicably, this has been continuously flouted. Indicative of this breakdown is that despite there being a hot line between the directors of operations on both sides, there was no communication. Pakistan, in fact, tried another abortive attack on Indian posts in the first week of October. This too was repulsed.

The Indian Army is confident of defending their posts in the region and a senior officer said: "We are on top of them now and I mean that literally. We are in full control of the region. If Pakistan wants to dispute it, they would have to do so with casualties and they would have to pay for it dearly." But that is hardly going to deter Pakistan from trying again."

If the battles in 1987 and another one in 1989 in the southern glacier remained out of the public domain at large, it was because all of them were fought in remote, inaccessible areas where even the military reached with great difficulty.

The loss of Saltoro heights in 1984, and the subsequent defeats in 1987 and 1989 continued to rankle the Pakistani military brass. Pervez Musharraf, who as a brigadier had planned and executed the September 1987 attack that resulted in the loss of over 300 Pakistani soldiers in the suicidal battle for Quaid post (now renamed by the Indians as Bana top), had by October 1998 become the Chief of the Pakistani Army. He conceived the Kargil intrusions in 1999 along the LoC starting from Zoji La to the very edge of Siachen, up to Point 5770.

By May 1999, the Indian Army had realized the extent of Pakistani 'creep', and the 8th Mountain Division had been rushed into the sector to evict the intruders and reclaim Indian territory. Over the next two months, fierce battles all along the LoC followed. Kargil War, as the localised conflict came to be known, is generally seen as the first 'televised conflict' in the sub-continent's history since the media, including me, reported from the area for over two months, bringing the stories of incredible valour and sacrifice of the brave Indian soldiers to the Indian people.

But none of us managed to get to the extreme eastern fringe of the conflict beyond Partapur (the HQ of 102 'Siachen' Brigade) and Turtuk. Most of us concentrated at the easily-accessible Kargil-Drass sectors and reported from there. The Batalik-Yaldor-Chorbatla – Chalunka-Turtuk sector remained totally under reported. I myself remember managing to go up to Batalik in the first few days of landing in Kargil but being turned back.

Soldiers of 27 Rajput after capturing Pt. 5770

But away from the media glare, and dare I say, even from the gaze of the higher military authorities too, a major victory was achieved by 27 Rajput in May-June 1999. For unexplained reasons, the incredible action by 27 Rajput that summer in wresting back a key peak in the Turtuk-southern glacier area – thus saving the Shyok River Valley which was won by the heroic exploits of Major (later Col Rinchin) in 1971 (see chapter III, *Getting Ready*) – is not seen as a major battle victory during Kargil. It was an important breakthrough, because had the western approaches to the Shyok Valley been exposed, the Thoise airfield and the entire Nubra Valley would have been threatened, rendering, in one stroke the holding of Siachen glacier and the Saltoro ridge untenable.

Pakistani maps captured subsequently, showed a straight line drawn from NJ 9842 to the Karakoram Pass and even DBO, showing Pakistan's continuing interest in Siachen. But, in the initial stages of the Kargil war, no one, least of all, Indian military planners took Pakistani advance in the Turtuk sector seriously. It was only when Pakistani artillery fire in the area intensified, and the sorties by Pakistan's Lama Helicopters increased, that Pakistani intentions became clearer.

By the middle of May 1999, once the extent of Pakistani intrusions was realized, the Siachen Brigade Commander, Brig. (later Lt. Gen) Prakash Katoch told Col K. H Singh, then commanding the 27 Rajput and deployed under 102 brigade to check out the spread of Pakistani presence in the area.

Singh, who in February 2014, became the first north-easterner to attain the rank of Lieutenant General in the Indian Army's combatant stream, sent out a reconnaissance patrol, only to discover that the Pakistanis had indeed occupied Point 5770. By 2 June, Singh received concrete evidence of the Pakistani presence on the peak when his unit patrol was fired upon. Fortunately, there were no casualties.

Singh, a jovial but firm and inspirational leader had to motivate his soldiers, mostly drawn from the desert state of Rajasthan and neighbouring Haryana, to climb altitudes they had never seen in their life, leave alone climbed such heights. Not only climb, but fight and capture the peak.

Singh of course had one advantage: there was no media to scrutinize the operation and he could prepare taking adequate time. Evicting the

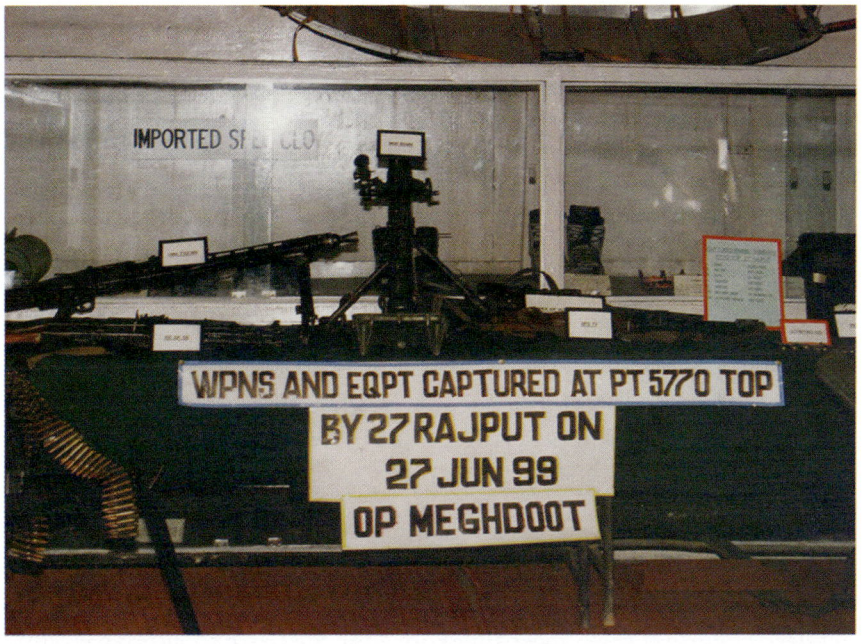

The captured booty (top and bottom)

Pakistanis from the vantage point of Pt 5770 was easier planned than achieved though. For it meant launching an almost vertical attack, climbing the 1800 feet 90 degree incline to the top of pt 5770 which itself was located close to 19,000 feet. Conventional wisdom said, there would be heavy casualties in what looked like a suicidal attempt. But, neither Singh nor Brig Katoch was even thinking about that.

"We were totally focused on the job. Any action in the mountain requires thorough preparation and accurate reconnaissance. We had done the recces earlier. Now, we were focusing on getting the boys ready both mentally and physically. They were well acclimatised and raring to go. But I wanted to plan the operation meticulously so we took our time," Singh told me in February 2014 as I took him back 15 years in time.

Singh selected Major Navdeep Singh Cheema to lead the company for the attack. Cheema's company was supported by a team from HAWS led by Capt Shyamal Sinha and four soldiers from the local Ladakh Scouts. Their first task was to fix ropes for the team to climb the 1800 feet vertical cliff. This was done on two successive nights on 17-18 June, silently and successfully.

Thereafter, soldiers took a week, to get prepared. In the intervening night of 23-24 June, the company started climbing, but 200 feet short of the top the weather deteriorated, with a blizzard blowing across the region and day break just an hour away. Singh, in constant communication with the assault team from a vantage position, decided to call off the attack.

The next day another attempt was launched—in day light. Again, climbing up silently wasn't easy, but as two columns under Cheema and Sinha made their way up, a lot of time was consumed. It was already getting close to sunset and Singh did not want to risk fighting in darkness. Fifty feet from the objective, the team was called back!

The two columns who attempted the first two attacks were by now exhausted. A fresh team was selected, but the officers leading them remained the same. At 3 am on 27 June, the third attempt to capture Pt 5770 began. It was a Tuesday, considered auspicious by the God-fearing Rajput troops. Moreover, it was 27 day of the month, the battalion's number in the Rajput Regiment! Soldiers are nothing if not believers. They believed it was going to be their day. And so it was.

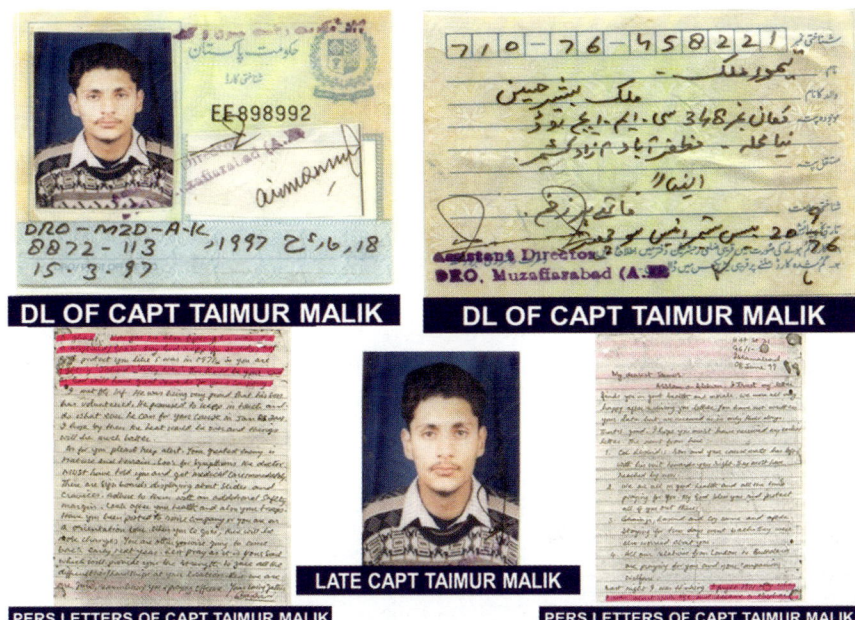

DL OF CAPT TAIMUR MALIK

DL OF CAPT TAIMUR MALIK

LATE CAPT TAIMUR MALIK

PERS LETTERS OF CAPT TAIMUR MALIK

PERS LETTERS OF CAPT TAIMUR MALIK

Capt Taimur Malik's letters

Around 2 pm, nearly 11 hours after they started climbing, the first assault team was poised just below the big rock on which a Pakistan soldier was sitting, perhaps writing a letter. As Singh gave the green signal to rush the objective, the sentry was silenced and the bunkers were attacked. The Pakistanis were utterly surprised, and could offer just token resistance. Capt Taimur Malik and 10 soldiers of the 3 Northern Light Infantry were killed. Miraculously, the Rajputs did not suffer a single casualty!

The Indian Army had achieved its first success against Pakistani intruders, but Turtuk was far away from where the media was, and the top brass too was busy concentrating on evicting intruders from Tiger Hill, Tololing and the areas around the Kargil-Drass sector, for anyone to notice this tremendous success without artillery or air support! The battles of Tololing and Tiger Hill became a matter of folklore in later weeks, as media was at hand when those successes were achieved at heavy cost.

All these thoughts were far from KH Singh's mind. After capturing the peak, his men buried the fallen Pakistani soldiers with full military drill, and then proceeded to consolidate their position in the area, even as war raged elsewhere along the LoC.

207

Army exhumes body to fulfill grandfather's wish

• Following a special request to Chief of Army Staff, Army hands over bodies of 5 Pak soldiers killed in Kargil

GAURAV C. SAWANT
NEW DELHI, AUGUST 28

ON A special request by Pakistan, the Army exhumed the bodies of five Pakistani soldiers killed during the Kargil war and handed them over late evening yesterday.

The bodies were handed over to the Pakistani soldiers at a border post in the Kargil sector itself. The soldiers killed during the shelling by Indian artillery guns ahead of Kargil posts on the southern Siachen sector had been buried according to full Islamic rites by Indian soldiers, sources said.

Top level sources in Army Headquarters said that the grand-parents of one of the buried soldiers, Captain Taimur Malik, are non-resident Pakistanis living in England. They approached the Indian Defence Attache in London and pleaded their case. He in turn got in touch with Chief of Army Staff General Ved Prakash Malik in New Delhi.

Pakistan's request also came in the Director General Military Operations (DGMO) level talks that take place every week. Sources told *The Indian Express* that Malik's grandfather in a moving letter wrote that he was certified blind and his wife was suffering from angina. The couple have been living in England for the past 49 years.

The septuagenarian Malik also wrote that Captain Malik's mother was suffering from skin cancer and doctors had given her little time to live.

[...] area of Peak 5770, his mother wants [...] buried at the ancestral grave and wants to pray by the grave side for her remaining years," the letter read. The family wrote that their hearts were not for the issue, the pain and pain suffered by Indian soldiers and their families during the Kargil crisis.

Moved by the letter, the Army decided to exhume the body of Captain Malik and four other soldiers with him. "We want to return all the bodies and also the prisoners of war. To honour their request the bodies were handed over yesterday," a top officer in Army Headquarters told *The Indian Express* today.

"Apparently this Captain's family is also very well connected politically and their was tremendous pressure on the Pakistan army to retrieve his body. And because they knew the general area where the officer had gone missing, they approached on" said another officer.

Army officers here said that initially they were not too keen to exhume bodies, "but the Pakistani side was pleading," and therefore to honour their request it was done. The bodies were exhumed two days ago and then brought down to Kargil.

"Here at Post 43, where all the corpses take place the five bodies were handed over with full military honours yesterday evening. The Pakistani Army has thanked us for this gesture and have gone home that once the prisoners of War (POW) wrangle is sorted out, the eight soldiers in Indian custody could be repatriated. We told them we hoped for the best outcome and were more than keen to return them. But the ball lies in their court," he added.

A humane gesture

Col (now Lt Gen) K H Singh with Tipsy

There is a postscript to the story. Exactly two months after the capture of Pt 5770, KH Singh and his troops were exhuming the bodies of the killed Pakistanis and sending them back to Pakistan through Post 43 in Kargil!

As it happened, the young Pakistani captain killed in action belonged to a well-connected family. His grandparents, based in London, got in touch with the Indian Defence Attache, requesting the Indian officer to try and send his body back to Pakistan as a special gesture. Phone lines burnt at the highest levels, and it was decided to exhume Capt Malik's body to be sent back to Pakistan (*See the report by Gaurav Sawant for the Indian Express of that time*). But KH Singh, ever the officer and gentleman, insisted that all Pakistani soldiers who laid down their lives in the battle for Pt 5770, and not just Capt Taimur must get the privilege of being sent home. And so it was. A true soldiers' code: respect the enemy and respect the dead!

Col K H Singh with his victorious troops

Years later, KH would command the 25 Infantry Division that guards a large portion of the LoC south of Pir Panjal in the Jammu division, and is now poised to command a Corps, exactly 15 years after he took on the Pakistanis in Siachen! One of the abiding memories he has from the Turtuk stint was the company of a local dog he named Tipsy. "She was my constant companion and a valuable asset. At least on a couple of occasions, Tipsy alerted us on suspicious movements and continued to stay with us."

THE CITATION
Nb Sub Bana Singh, 8 JAK LI (JC-155825)

Naib Subedar Bana Singh volunteered to be a member of a task force constituted in June 1987 to clear an intrusion by an adversary in the Siachen glacier area at an altitude of 21,000 feet. The post was virtually an impregnable glacier fortress with ice walls, 1500 feet high, on both sides. Naib Subedar Bana Singh led his men through an extremely difficult and hazardous route. He inspired them by his indomitable courage and leadership. The brave Naib Subedar and his men crawled and closed in on the adversary. Moving from trench to trench, lobbing hand grenades, and charging with the bayonet, he cleared the post of all intruders. Naib Subedar Bana Singh displayed the most conspicuous gallantry and leadership under the most adverse conditions.

209

A DOCTOR REMEMBERS

I was inducted on the Northern glacier in July 1987 for a four month tenure. Reaching Kumar (15000 ft), where the Battalion HQ of 8 JAK LI was located, one heard stories of the heroic capture of Bana top (22000 ft) by the brave soldiers of this battalion about a month ago. The battle was codenamed OP RAJIV, after 2/Lt Rajiv Pandey, VrC of 8 JAKLI and the son of an AMC officer, who was martyred while establishing a rope base under the nose of the enemy. In the officers shelter at Kumar, was pasted the birthday card sent by Rajiv's sister which sadly reached a day after his martyrdom. One must admit that as a young 25 years old doctor, the experience of reading this card after knowing the circumstances, left one teary eyed.

The Medical officer whom I was relieving, narrated the bravery exhibited by 8 JAKLI in which the entire battalion volunteered for Op Rajiv. He told me that while he handled a lot of gunshot wound injuries, the casualties due to severe frostbite far outnumbered the actual battle casualties. This was because the men had been fighting endlessly at Minus 30 degrees celsius at 21000 ft for three nights.

After acclimatization, I was moved to the 18,500 ft at Bila base. This was selected as the location of the Regimental Aid Post (RAP) of the RMO because it had a helipad (for casualty evacuation), and also was the confluence of two routes of evacuation, the first one being OP75 to Bila top and the second from Ashok/ U Cut to Bila saddle to me. The deployment on these posts was essential to defend the Saltoro ridge. The Company Commander of the area was located at Bila saddle for strategic reasons, as he could monitor the Forward Defended Localities (FDL) at Ashok and U Cut. It was here that one learnt the strategic significance of the Saltoro. The one who controls this ridge, controls the northern glacier.

As September came, a festive mood engulfed the jawans of 8 JAKLI. And why not? The Army Chief, Gen K Sundarji, had visited us and conveyed his appreciation of the battalion's grit and determination in capturing the Bana top. Moreover, 3/4 GR was being inducted to replace them by late September. 8 JAKLI had done its bit and was in the process of handing over charge of the northern glacier to 3/4GR.

Things however changed dramatically around 20 September. On that night, I received my first two war casualties. OP75 a post ahead of BILA TOP was hit by an artillery shell fired from an enemy held HMG RIDGE. Two soldiers were brought at around 10 PM with severe splinter injuries all over. However, as the RAP had a *bukhari*, I could start an IV line and render the necessary medical aid. At first light the next day, the brave AIR OP pilots landed their helicopters at my post and evacuated these casualties to the Advanced Dressing Station (ADS) at base camp. At that point of time, our helicopters did not have night flying capabilities. We witnessed heavy shelling over the next few days, with one shell landing barely 50 m ahead of our RAP hut.

On the night of 22 September, my Sepoy/ Nursing Asstt Ram Sewak Ojha located at bila saddle called me on the telephone to convey that the senior JCO of 8 JAK LI had been grievously injured in enemy shelling. He urgently required an IV drip, and it was impossible to do the same in the snow bunker of his RAP, where the temperature had dipped to –40 degrees C. Therefore, despite the intense shelling, he was moving to a tent which had a *bukhari* so he could maintain the lifeline till morning, when he could be sent to me for further management and evacuation. I could only marvel at the bravery of this 21 year old AMC nursing assistant, who was prepared to put his life at risk to maintain the IV lifeline of the Infantry JCO. On 23 Sep at around 0300 hrs, he informed me that the JCO was recovering and he would be sending him to me soon for further management. I was overwhelmed by the professional skill of this young paramedical worker. My joy was shortlived. Around an hour later, the Company Commander rang me up to tell me that a shell had fallen on the tent in which the casualty was being treated and Ojha was seriously injured and bleeding profusely. I requested him to tie a tight shell dressing across the wound and evacuate him to me immediately by snow scooter, or a sledge for further management. Both the casualties were managed at my location and evacuated at first light. Despite acute pain, the eyes of Ojha lit up when I told him that it was only because of him that the injured senior JCO will live. RS Ojha was awarded the Sena Medal (Gallantry) for his exemplary courage and professional skill, in saving the life of the JCO.

Since the Nursing Astt at Bila saddle had been evacuated, and the fact that the battle was to be focused in this area, I was moved up to this location. It was a chilling one Km walk to this post with shells flying all around. The men at Bila saddle (both of 8 JAK LI and 3/4 GR) were overjoyed to see me. I actually realized that the mere presence of an RMO in the battlefield contributes significantly to boosting morale, thus helping the war effort. A new RAP was dug. It was essentially a large bunker in the snow covered by a CGI sheet. Unlike Bila base, I did not have the luxury of a fibre glass hut with a *bukhari* inside to serve as the RAP. Intense shelling and the fact that Ojha had been evacuated a day earlier, ensured that everybody operated only from the bunkers. There was no scope of cooking, and all were to survive on biscuits, chocolates or *Chikki* till the battle was over. It is at these heights that you realize the importance of cooked food. The men as such did not like biscuits and chocolates. In any case where was the time to eat?

The night of 23 September saw a fierce attempt by the Pakistanis to capture our post. Sheer guts, raw courage and determination ensured that the enemy was beaten back. The toll on both sides was heavy. I received innumerable casualties from Ashok and U Cut. All had serious gunshot wounds. The main problem remained maintaining an IV lifeline. While we physically thawed the IV fluids by putting them in warm water, but the moment we started a lifeline the IV line would freeze. Finally, assisted by some men of 3/4 GR we used burning stoves under the IV lines to keep them going. Warmth to these men was provided by extra sleeping bags and pain killers were administered copiously. There was no other option, but to tie a tight shell dressing as a tourniquet to control bleeding in a large number of cases. Additional casualties were treated in another bunker. We had by now become experts in timing our movement while going from one bunker to another, as taught to me by the JCOs. The moment a shell landed or burst we would come out and sprint to the next bunker, thus taking advantage of the time between two bursts. Thereafter, the snow scooter did shuttle service between my RAP and the helipad to take these brave injured soldiers to the ADS once the choppers arrived at first light.

Though we beat back the enemy on that night, but it had taken its toll on us. The loss of friends, dehydration (as it was difficult to thaw ice for water since the entire area was coloured black due to the soot of the enemy shells) and non availability of cooked food did bother us. We were also running short of manpower to fight out the attack that was slated for the night of 24th. Reinforcements were picked up by chopper from the inducting troops of 3/4 GR from Camp I and Camp II which were at significantly lower heights, and dropped on the battlefield. It is a tribute to the acclimatization schedule developed by the Indian Armed Forces Medical Services, that once the acclimatization schedule was followed, we had negligible cases of HAPO. However, this was battle and it did not give any time for acclimatization. Since these men picked up by the choppers, were not acclimatized, almost all of them were complaining of a splitting headache and some were vomiting. They were exhibiting signs of Acute Mountain Sickness. Two developed HAPO. However, seeing the current situation, I could only afford to evacuate the HAPO cases. The rest had to fight regardless of their current medical condition due to the call of duty. I gave them a pep talk, a tablet of an analgesic and a tablet of Lasix, in an attempt to ward off HAPO. This was all that was available in my drug list to take care of AMS and hopefully prevent HAPO at that time.

Another case demonstrating the spirit of camaraderie, brotherhood, determination and selflessness by the infantry soldier merits narration. At around 1700 hrs on the 24th, a group of nine soldiers of 8 JAK LI trooped into my RAP to have a chat with them. They had come from Ashok and U Cut and were to go back for the night defence again. Each of these brave men had not eaten for 48 hours and were feeling numb in their feet (wet socks and the inability to remove shoes due to battle conditions) due to severe frostbite. They were fully aware that if they survived the battle, they would be losing a substantial part of their toes to frostbite. They asked me if I thought that they were medically fit for war. I did not have the heart to lie to them, and told them that they are fit cases for casualty evacuation, but then who will fight the war? The senior among them pointing to a young 20 year old boy among themselves said "We have not come to be evacuated. The post has to be defended as it is the question of *IZZAT* of the *Paltan*. But Sir, this boy is the nephew of Nb/Sub Lekhraj who died yesterday. Their family cannot afford to lose another boy in this battle. He is the only male member left in their joint family. Please evacuate him only". The boy was evacuated by me as a case of severe frostbite. Out of the balance eight brave hearts, four lost their lives on that fateful night defending Ashok and the rest sustained significant injuries. Till date I feel humbled by the selflessness exhibited by these men. It also brought out the role played by the RMO in not only treating casualties, but also building morale and thus contributing to victory in battle. For this the men must have complete faith in the RMO and the latter should be honest with them.

A stroke of luck occurred on the 24th evening. By accident, we latched on to the enemy radio frequency and thus were capable of monitoring their move and taking appropriate action. This greatly helped our artillery battery commander who could bring down focused fire on the enemy based on their location. At around 4 am on 25 September an officer casualty of 3/4 GR who was brought to me and told me that the enemy had reached the top, and the Gorkhas were doing hand to hand fighting with their "khukries". In a tactical masterpiece, the Air Defence Artillery gun located at Bila base was tasked to fire in a ground role by engaging the top of the ridge where the enemy was advancing. It was the first time in the history of air defence that this gun was used in a ground role. This, and the bravado of the Gorkhas broke the back of the enemy. Daylight forced them to call off the battle. The Indian Army had successfully defended Saltoro ridge in the battle codenamed OP VAJRASHAKTI. On Republic Day 1989, I was awarded the Yuddh seva medal, the first AMC officer to be awarded this honour. My nursing assistant Ram Sewak Ojha deservedly got the Sena medal (Gallantry) for his act of valour.

This battle demonstrated the closeness with which the Armed Forces Medical Services integrate with the fighting arms in war. We live with them, rejoice in their moment of glory, and grieve with them as a part of them, besides providing medical care to them. It brings out that an AMC officer is a Soldier doctor, and not the other way around, in the true spirit of the Corps motto viz *"Sarve Santu Niramaya"*.

The medical support of the glacier is provided right up to the FDL with the medical officer being deployed at each company (Coy) location (as against the traditional deployment of a medical officer only up to Battalion HQ level). The MOs and nursing assistants totally integrate themselves with the infantry subunits they are with, and this keeps up the morale of the soldiers, thus minimising psychological problems and enhancing operational efficiency in such harsh conditions. Operations in the glaciated environment of Siachen have opened a new chapter in the history of modern warfare. Never before has man battled with nature and fought in such extreme conditions. Siachen has turned a new leaf in medical tactical doctrine. Conventional thinking and textbook philosophy do not apply in this unusual environment. Innovations and improvisations entailing a high degree of mental mobility are a must for the successful conduct of operations in such an environment. The Indian Armed Forces Medical Services have done a tremendous job in providing health care and succour to our soldiers on the glacier. The medical chain has always functioned as a well oiled machine, thus not only saving a large number of brave lives, but earning the appreciation of Commanders at all levels. Siachen has indeed brought out the best in our men, clearly proving the immortal words, "When the going gets tough, the tough get going".

In the summer crevasses open up in large numbers

The glacier in all its majesty

XI

Medicine Men: Siachen Saviours

'Nothing that is learnt in Medical School applies here'

The Siachen glacier presents an unique set of environmental challenges for the human body. These include low oxygen, partial pressure due to reduced barometric pressure at high altitudes (HA), extreme cold, high levels of ultraviolet radiation and low levels of humidity. Survival on the glacier involves battling not just these gruelling environmental conditions, but also combating long periods of isolation, making do with tinned and preserved foods, battling to obtain clean drinking water, living in cramped inhospitable temporary shelters without electricity, and the absence of a host of things considered essential and taken for granted by civilised society. Add to this the constant threat of enemy action, which requires man and machine to be fighting fit and alert 24 × 7.

Siachen therefore becomes the toughest call of duty for Indian soldiers. As an Army doctor says: "The human body makes adjustments in its functioning to enable individuals to live and work at these extreme altitudes. These adjustments constitute the phenomenon of altitude acclimatisation. Acclimatisation, which largely involves increase in the rate and depth of breathing, and increase in haemoglobin levels in the blood, however, does not allow the human body to function on Siachen as it does at sea level. At an altitude of 5,000m for example, the levels of oxygen in the blood of a healthy soldier would be similar to that of a patient with a severe lung disorder at sea level. While such patients are admitted to ICUs, confined to beds and treated with

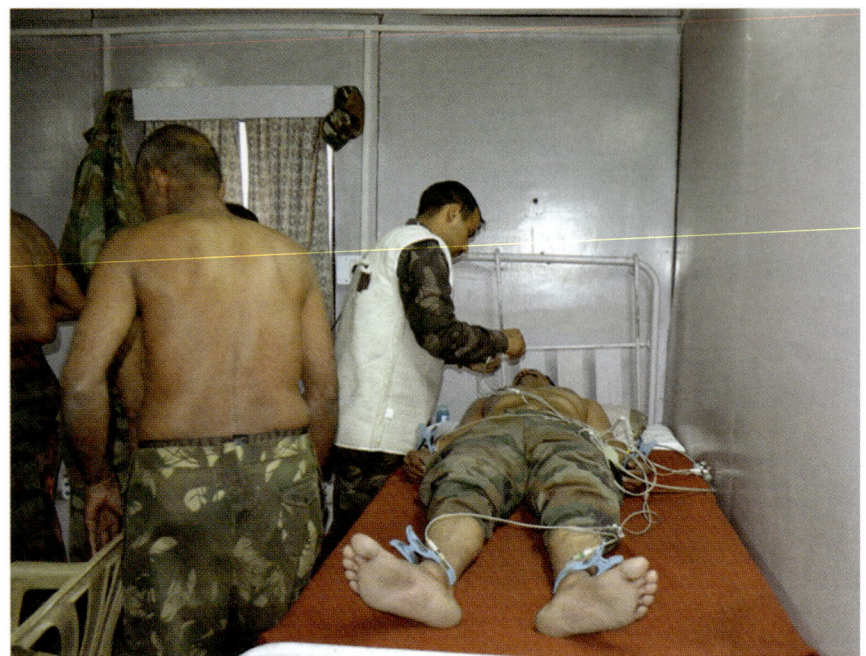

ECG being recorded on study subjects at the Base Camp

continuous oxygen therapy, and soldiers at 5,000 m with similar levels of oxygen in their blood perform intense physical activity and fight the enemy!"

Studies have shown that medical problems can occur within a few days of reaching high altitudes, or at times even after months of stay on Siachen. Acute Mountain Sickness is one of the commonest acute high altitude illnesses encountered by almost 20 to 30 per cent soldiers on arrival at high altitudes. Tough doctors say this condition is largely benign and self-limiting if recognised and treated in time, but it is extremely distressing and often demoralising for soldiers. This is quite understandable since a healthy, physically fit soldier suddenly finds himself experiencing headache, nausea and loss of appetite for no apparent reason which spooks him, often causing him to wonder what other terrible things lie ahead.

Prolonged stay at these high altitudes presents a completely different set of medical challenges. The human body is not designed to reside and function at such altitudes, and successful altitude acclimatisation does not occur at such heights. With added effects like impaired **218** absorption of food from the intestine, dulling of taste sensation and severe loss of appetite, combined with low oxygen levels, impaired nutrition, raised haemoglobin levels, lack of mobility and dehydration makes the soldier susceptible to a host medical ailments. These could range from raised blood pressure, increased susceptibility to infections and weight loss, to life threatening events like blood clots in the lungs, brain, intestines, spleen and heart. Many soldiers also report sleep disturbances, impaired memory and loss of libido. Whether these conditions are reversible on returning to sea level and what, if any, are the long term consequences of having served at such extreme altitudes, still remains to be scientifically studied.

This is where medicine men step in.

Over the years, the Army Medical Corps (AMC) has instituted an excellent system whereby health lectures begin at the sea level, and continue through every transit camp on the way up to high altitude posts. The soldier is made aware of the likely response of his body to the peculiar set of challenges that high altitudes throws at the human body. This knowledge empowers him to recognise features of high altitude illness right at the beginning, and seek medical attention promptly to ensure quick recovery.

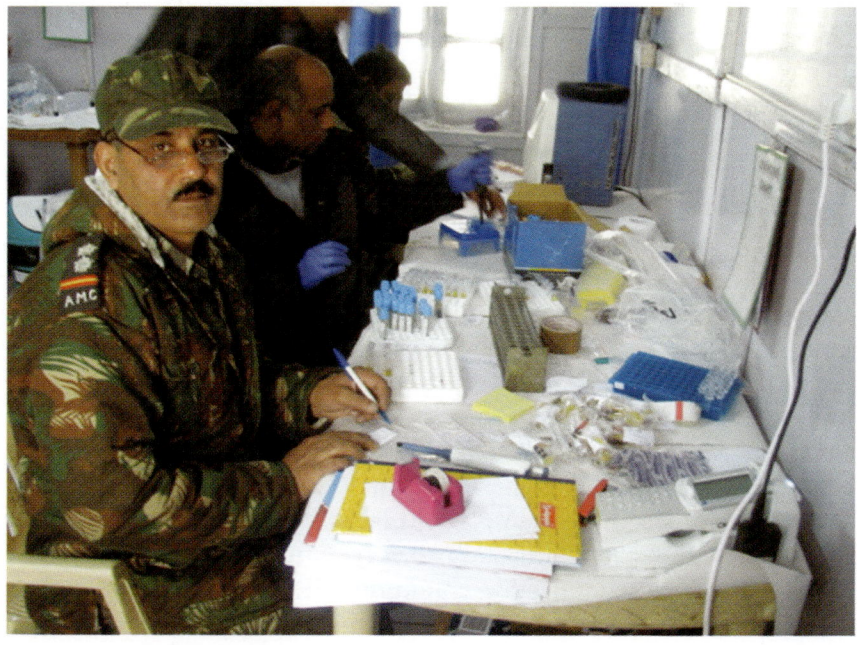

A 'field' laboratory set up at TsangTse

According to a number of doctors in the AMC, a more serious health concern during the first week at high altitudes is pulmonary edema or fluid accumulation in the lungs, and cerebral edema or fluid accumulation in the brain. These two conditions can be fatal if not recognised and treated promptly.

It is a tribute to the efforts of AMC doctors and nursing assistants – who also brave high altitude hardships with other soldiers – that high altitude pulmonary edema (HAPE), which once afflicted on an average 15 out of 100 soldiers who served on Siachen, now affects less one soldier per 100 soldiers stationed there today.

Such an impressive reduction in morbidity due to high altitude illness, is largely due to the focussed approach of the AMC teams who have spent months on the Siachen glacier, shoulder to shoulder with their fighting counterparts.

The first-hand experience of having served on Siachen has motivated these brave doctors in uniform to research the physiological effects of high altitudes, and suggest methods to improve survival and physical performance at such heights. Today, in fact, deaths due to pulmonary edema and cerebral edema are a rarity on the glacier.

Doctors on Siachen are indeed a rare breed of professionals. No medical school in the world prepares doctors to serve in conditions that prevail on Siachen. Isolated on Siachen, with a body of troops that rely on you to save their life in any eventuality, with the most elementary medical equipment which can malfunction in the exacting environmental conditions, the young medical officer faces the test of his life. Where intravenous fluids freeze, and the normally simple act of hearing patients' heart and breath sounds with a stethoscope means asking him to disrobe in sub-zero temperatures, the doctor faces an arduous task.

Nothing that he learnt in medical school would apply in such circumstances. No blood tests, X rays, ECGs or fancy investigations are possible. Often, the toughest decision to take is whether to evacuate the solider to Base Camp, or to hold on and treat him on the glacier itself. Evacuation by air, although an easy option, is often at the mercy of the weather gods and terrain conditions. Helicopters do not land on every post, and carrying a medical casualty across the crevasse ridden glacier on foot is a daunting and often impossible task, when some time one needs to climb near vertical ice walls, and when every step in the rarefied atmosphere makes the lungs scream out for oxygen.

As a senior doctor, who has spent time on the glacier remembers: "Improvisations and presence of mind makes the difference between life and death. As a young medical officer, I recall the day we suffered three casualties due to enemy shelling. As we watched our OP (observation post) come under artillery fire, there was little we could do but hope for the best. A call on the radio set confirmed our worst fears. Three soldiers were wounded with multiple splinter injuries. The wait for the shelling to stop was agonizing. I was desperate to know how much was the blood loss. As night fell and we were permitted to move, we asked a neighbouring post to begin evacuating the wounded down towards us, and we set off towards them trying to meet the wounded halfway, so that they could be treated as quickly as possible. We met an hour later, on the vast desolate openness of the glacier. Under muffled torch lights, a quick examination of the wounded revealed that they needed pain relief on priority. It was perhaps the most difficult injection that I have ever administered to a patient. At 17,000 feet, and sub-zero temperature, the vast emptiness of the glacier, the sky as our roof and the threat of fresh enemy fire, that was the place where I treated the injured! We brought the casualties to the company base using skid

The HAPO bag: A life saver

boards, as ice sleighs and parachute strings as harnesses, sliding them over the glacier, taking turns every few minutes to ensure we did not tire ourselves. The night was spent in our tent using kerosene stoves to provide warmth. We sang songs to keep our wounded friends awake, joking how they would have pretty nurses looking after them in a few hours' time. Silently we prayed for clear weather the next morning to permit an early evacuation."

So have things changed over the last three decades?

Yes, they have. The vast experience gained by the Army Medical Corps in the field of High Altitude Medicine and Physiology has translated into improved practices on the ground. Acclimatisation schedules for troops inducted at high altitudes have been refined, modified, experimented with and implemented meticulously. The results are plainly evident from the mortality and morbidity data of the last three decades. Though the glacier still claims lives, many of these deaths are accidental. The focus of the high altitude medical researchers has thus shifted from prevention of high altitude illnesses, to areas such as improvement of physical and mental performance of the soldier at those heights. Strategies for rapid induction of troops in those areas, and molecular and genetic studies to identify soldiers

Talking to the AMC soldiers at the Leh's Army Hospital

who may be genetically susceptible to high altitude illnesses are in place now. Therefore, such individuals are screened at the sea level and not deployed at high altitudes. The DRDO (Defence Research and Development Organisation) has partnered the AMC in these ventures, providing both human and material resources to ensure optimal benefits to the soldiers on the ground.

A STUDY OF VENOUS THROMBOSIS AT HIGH ALTITUDES

The field of high altitude medicine is, however, still young. Even today, new effects of high altitudes, on the human body are being discovered. In the last 30 years, sporadic instances of clotting of blood in the veins of previously healthy young soldiers at high altitudes have been reported internationally. With the large presence of our army at high and extreme high altitudes (EHA is above 18,000 ft), such cases have been occurring with regularity.

A specialist doctor tells me: "As a haematologist (specialist in disorders of the blood) I have personally treated a number of soldiers afflicted by this malady, both in the eastern and northern theatre. The consequences of blood clots in the veins of a living human can be disastrous.

"I particularly remember the case of a young officer, of the Dogra Regiment, that occurred in 2005. This officer was stationed at an altitude above 18,000 ft on the glacier when, within days of arrival, he developed clots in the veins of his brain, both legs and one arm. Bad weather on the glacier prevented his evacuation for a number of days. He was brought comatose to Army Hospital (R&R), Delhi, where I first saw him. I had never seen such extensive clots in anybody before! The delay in evacuation must have been responsible for allowing the clots to grow. It took us, a team of doctors, weeks to bring this officer back, as he battled for his life. Repeated surgeries and weeks of clot busting drug therapy later, this officer all of 30 years of age, survived, but in the bargain both his legs and the left arm had to be amputated. It was such a tragedy, especially for one so young. But like a true soldier and hero, he has overcome his loss to lead a near normal life today, but his case highlights the health risks that may strike the unsuspecting combatant as he ascends to extreme altitudes and the cold of the glacier, wilfully, to defend his motherland. (*See box*)

Doctors say clotting of blood in the veins is a very rare event at the sea-level, and almost always occurs with the setting in of other co-

The HAPO bag saves precious lives

morbidities such as cancers, polycythaemia (excessive red blood cell formation) or dehydration and prolonged inactivity. Thus, the occurrence of clots in the veins of the legs, lungs, brain and other organs in healthy people at high altitudes is indeed surprising. Early research in India and abroad could not identify much that was wrong with the clotting system of the body at extreme heights. It was therefore natural that this was blamed on known factors such as inactivity due to bad weather, dehydration due to the excessively dry atmosphere and thickening of the blood caused by an increase in RBC counts. An increased RBC number is a mechanism of the body to combat the low oxygen at high altitudes.

Intrigued by the phenomenon, in 2009 a team of doctors were finally tasked with studying venous thrombosis (clotting of the blood in veins) at high altitudes. The commanders were worried about the number of soldiers getting afflicted by this ailment and the effects it had on their life, as also on the morale of their colleagues.

Says the leader of this team: "I grabbed the opportunity with vengeance, being determined to do something to prevent this disease and/or reduce its impact on the lives of our brave soldiers on the glacier. We found that health data from 1987 onwards showed that a large number of soldiers were referred to various Armed Forces Hospitals from high altitude areas because of blood clotting. The largest number of these, it came as little surprise, were from the extreme altitudes of the Siachen glacier.

"I, along with some colleagues, therefore set about designing and conducting a study. In the beginning, the one thing we were very sure of was, that the study must be done in actual ground conditions. We would never be able to simulate the multiple effects of altitude ascent and stay, in any laboratory. Therefore we designed a 'prospective longitudinal cohort' study to elucidate the mechanisms of blood clotting at high altitudes, and the risk factors that predispose a healthy soldier to develop a clot at high altitudes. The idea, so to say, was to unravel the plot behind the clot!"

The study entailed repeat examinations and tests on hundreds of soldiers at every stage, starting from the plains to extreme altitudes and back over a duration of more than two years. No such study had been done anywhere in the world till then. The logistics challenge itself was mind boggling.

The very first problem was to build a team of doctors and scientists who would not only have the requisite expertise but, perhaps more importantly, the passion and endurance to go through with the project involving as it would multiple visits, each spanning weeks, to various locations in the plains and at high altitudes.

With the full backing of the Armed Forces Medical Service (AFMS) the team leader was given total freedom to choose a large number of specialists from the many hospitals that the AFMS runs across the country. There was one condition: Each specialist needed to have spent at least one tenure at high altitudes, not necessarily on Siachen. Eventually, a team that included specialists in blood diseases, pathologists, physiologists, medical specialists, radiologists as well as scientists from the DRDO, was put together. It had doctors from Army Hospital (R&R), Delhi, AFMC, Pune, Command Hospital, Chandimandir, 153 General Hospital, Leh, the High Altitude Medical Research Centre, Leh, a number of field hospitals of the Army in Ladakh and the DRDO's Defence Institute of Physiology and Allied Sciences (DIPAS) in Delhi.

The study was, however, easier designed than done. The next problem **225**

Study team members with soldiers freshly descended from the glacier

area was to find the right subjects, i.e. a multi-ethnic group of otherwise healthy soldiers scheduled for induction to high altitudes and the glacier. The need for a multi-ethnic group was prompted by stray reports of ethnic pre-disposition to ailments at high altitudes.

Says the team leader: "We found the 'ideal' subject group in a battalion of infantry soldiers in the Grenadiers Regiment. This battalion is composed of Jats, Rajputs, Gujars and Hindustani Muslims hailing from the states of Rajasthan, Haryana, UP, MP and Bihar."

The study hinged around analysis of blood samples by various tests of coagulation and proteomic and genomic studies. Blood had to be drawn repeatedly from the same soldiers first at their plains location, Jammu, and then as they proceeded through various stages of their stay at high altitudes.

"Since we conduct a large number of tests every time on every soldier, a fairly large sample of blood (40-50ml) had to be drawn at every contact. As we know, in India blood donation, or removal of any blood from the body generates unimaginable fears of ills ranging from loss of strength and stamina to decrease in libido!! Thus, a structured educational initiative had to be undertaken which involved lectures as well as individual counselling. The initiative was successful, and today our subjects not only voluntarily allow us to repeatedly (3-6 months apart) draw blood, but have also become a force multiplier spreading the word that removal of small amounts of blood from the body does no harm to health at all! The first time we had drawn blood samples, in spite of our education initiative, the hospital fruit vendor would run out of his daily stock of pomegranate (*Anar* – traditionally considered to be a health food) well before the day was over, selling *Anar* juice to our subjects," the team leader remembers.

Blood testing posed some more problems. A number of the tests require sophisticated equipment which was too unwieldy to be taken to field areas, or be used in any conditions other than the exactingly controlled conditions of a high tech laboratory. The laboratories are based in Delhi at the Army Hospital (R&R) and DIPAS. So thousands of samples collected from Jammu, or the two high altitude locations (Tsang Tse and Base Camp in Ladakh) had to be carried to Delhi by road and by air. There was an additional problem: the samples need to be stored at minus 40°C. For short periods, minus 20°C temperature is tolerated. To overcome that problem, a portable deep freezer named "Bevena", capable of maintaining temperatures at –20°C was designed to carry the samples.

However, since it had no battery back-up, it needed to be plugged into a power supply every 3-4 hours for temperatures to be maintained.

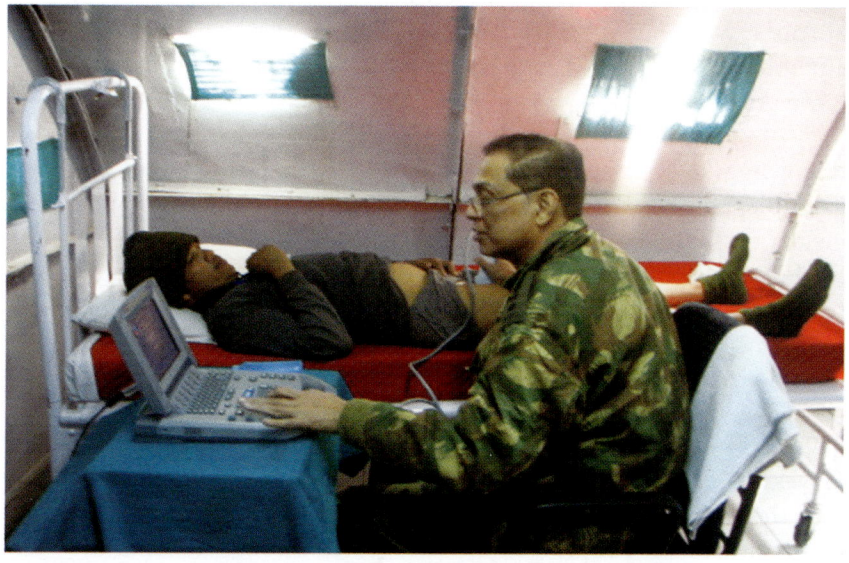

Doppler examination of the legs being performed at the ADS in TsangTse **227**

The biggest test for this device was the time when the samples had to be taken by road from Jammu to Delhi in the peak summer months of June and July 2012.

Remembers the team leader: "Our passionate pathologist friend, not ready to trust his precious cargo to anyone else, travelled in a mini-truck carrying the deep freezer twice from Jammu to Delhi, plugging the device into the power supply at toll posts and once even at a police station in a small town. His hard work paid rich dividends and the samples reached Delhi safely!"

But the sword cuts two ways. Where the cold of high altitudes helped store blood samples with ease, the low pressures at high altitudes disabled two portable semi-automated blood analyzers the team carried to do simple blood tests, such as measurement of haemoglobin and blood cell counts! The machines which analyze small samples of blood through a micro-tube, would not develop sufficient vacuum to suck in the blood samples. The equipment manufacturers' engineers were dumbfounded when asked to suggest a way around this problem, not having encountered such a problem before.

Once again it was the pathologist who came to the team's rescue. That, in a way, is characteristic of working at high altitudes. Most equipment is meant for temperatures and pressure conditions found at sea-levels, usually in controlled environments of a laboratory or hospital. Whether it will work in a field setting at high altitudes is anybody's guess, till it is actually used in such a setting. Constant innovation becomes a way of life in the challenging environment.

Recording a routine ECG in a pre-fabricated fibreglass hut, for example, can be a problem. A fully dressed individual is comfortable inside these huts. But, recording an ECG requires removing the clothing, and suddenly one has a shivering subject whose ECG trace resembles a jagged sawtooth rather than the organized 'P' 'QRS' and 'T' waves caused by electrical impulses of the heart, that a doctor is looking for.

"We warmed the huts and buildings with all manner of *bukharis*, stoves and kerosene heaters. We allowed people to crowd inside so that the heating devices and body heat in closed spaces warmed the temperatures till people actually felt warm enough to take off their clothes for the ECG! Quite a feat at subzero temperatures and rather unconventional, considering the strict concern for individual privacy that we doctors practice at all times. But, the soldier is not squeamish about partial nudity amongst colleagues, and as I said before 'innovation is the name of the game.' Of course, the smoke from all the heating devices was causing discomfort which none minded. Warmth was paramount," the team leader tells me.

Every trip to Ladakh entailed carrying more than a thousand kilograms of equipment. For this and for transporting blood samples from Leh to Delhi the staff of Indian Airlines was most helpful and accommodating. Repeated exposure of the research team members to the high altitude environment brought up issues of acclimatization too. Working on tight schedules, the team had to make do with a minimum safe period for acclimatization at Leh before ascending higher. A few doctors did suffer AMS (acute mountain sickness) in the first few visits, but as is typical of high altitudes, their illness decreased in severity with subsequent visits.

Recalls the team leader: " As per our study protocol, we have studied soldiers in four different phases. The first phase involved baseline studies when the soldiers were healthy in the plains at Jammu. The second phase entailed studies at high altitudes after a month or so of acclimatization at Tsang Tse and at the Base Camp. Shortly (within days, often, the very next day) after this phase, the soldiers ascended

Speaking to the team of doctors at Leh's Army Hospital

the glaciers. All going to posts in excess of 17,000 ft and many to posts as high as 20 to 22,000ft. We again examined the soldiers as they came down after spending between 90 and120 days at extreme altitudes. This third phase of our study helped us to determine the effects of stay at extreme altitudes on the clotting system of the body and other physiological parameters. In the fourth phase, in Tsang Tse again, we examined the soldiers approximately six months after descent from the glacier, to elucidate the residual effects of stay at EHA. The final, fifth phase of the study is yet to come when we shall examine them after descent to near sea-level. We hope to study the residual effects, and the time taken for the body to return to normal after a gruelling two years at HA and EHA."

The main aim of the study is to find markers to identify an "at risk" group, if any, who are pre-disposed to clotting of blood at HA or EHA. The study will also define how long the clotting tendency induced by HA lasts. At the moment no data exists.

Interestingly, the doctors during their regular interaction with the soldiers, found a number of other health related issues cropping up. A few common complaints they had after returning from the glacier were loss of weight, excessive sleepiness, a tendency to be forgetful and for some, a loss of libido too. Weight loss appears to be a universal problem with decrease in fat as well as muscle mass. Most soldiers report altered sleep patterns on the glacier, with a general decrease

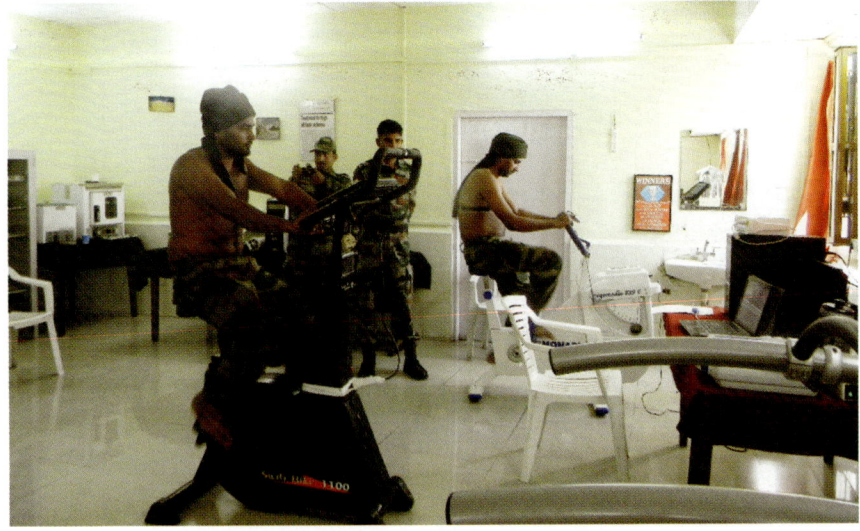

Soldiers undergoing a crucial test

in the number of hours they slept daily. What is remarkable about the sleep deficit, however, is that at extreme altitudes the decreased sleep appears not to translate into excessive daytime sleepiness!! It was only after they descended, that the soldiers started feeling excessively sleepy, and this continued for some days at Base Camp as if catching up on lost sleep.

Forgetfulness was the most common malady that affects almost all those who have descended from EHA. Doctors say: "This appears to involve immediate tasks at hand. For example, one commonly forgets where one has put down an object say a torch, a few moments ago. Most of these phenomena are anecdotally known to reverse with time at low altitudes or at the sea-level, but their exact time course and permanent residue if any is yet to be studied."

The study is far from complete, but its range and scope was wide, and through its conclusions the team of doctors are hoping to unravel a few of the mysteries about venous thrombosis at high altitudes, and offer succour in some form to the heroic soldiers. As the team leader told me: "The amazing spirit of the battalion that has volunteered to a man, to become the subject of our study is just another example of the selfless nature of the common soldier who leaves the comforts of home and hearth with not a complaint, indeed with a cheerful smile, to defend his land and his people at any cost to his own self."

MEMORIES OF A REGIMENTAL MEDICAL OFFICER ON THE SIACHEN GLACIER

My ascent to the "Chandan" post on the central glacier complex began in early March 1995. After the customary prayer ceremony at the Base Camp in early morning, we slowly started climbing the 30° incline up the valley floor, till a spur put us out of sight of those watching and waving to us from below.

A week earlier, on reporting to the ADS (Advance Dressing Station) at Base Camp I was greeted by Capt Srinivas, three years my senior in college. A generous and cheerful man he guided me through the nuances of early diagnosis of high altitude ailments especially the dreaded HAPO and frost bite. "Remember, being at high altitudes

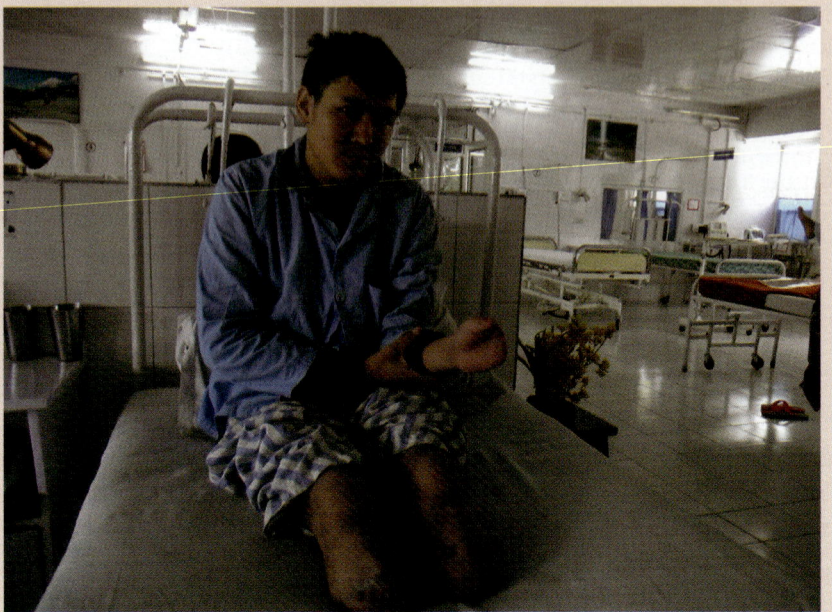

Nima Norbu lost three limbs after being stuck in a crevasse for 25 hours

does not mean that the patient shall suffer only high altitude ailments. Always consider all likely disorders before you diagnose a HA ailment *and* do not panic if you have a patient of HAPO or HACO. Just send them down to me! If evacuation to Base Camp is not an option for any reason, a little bit of descent and oxygen will do a world of good to them and in fact to anybody with any ailment on the glacier," was his first basic advice which stood me in good stead many a time in the next five months or so that I spent on the glacier.

While training in the Siachen Battle School, I met my classmate from school. So SBS training and my stay in Base Camp turned into an enjoyable experience. We worked hard through the days and partied harder at nights! The number of friends I made in that one month is more than I made in the next 19 years of service.

We started climbing under a bright sun, and the sky remained clear till we reached the first staging camp within three hours of starting the ascent. But, then to my utter surprise, in a matter of minutes, the azure blue skies were covered in clouds. It snowed for the next 10 days. So I stayed at 14,000 ft for the duration of the bad weather and felt lucky to have got so much time to acclimatize.

The next ascent would be a cake walk I thought, and eagerly set off. But the snow was waist deep and we were wading through it rather than walking. My breath was coming in short bursts. I had to stop and rest every 4-5 steps and my throat felt parched and my legs heavy. Soon it was clear to me that this would be far from a cakewalk. Having commenced the ascent at 9 am, we finally arrived at the half-link point at 1 pm, a four hour walk for a two km stretch!

I was ascending with a group of highland native soldiers who had been at those altitudes for 2-3 months by then, and were fleet footed at those and higher altitudes as the deer in the Rajaji national park!

The obvious impatience displayed by some of them at my slow climb embarrassed me, and after a half hour stop for rest and lunch half way to the next post, I decided to move faster. But my intentions were scuttled almost as soon as we started. For, within a few hundred yards of where we had rested, we had to walk on a path along the mountainside which came to a stretch where it undulated 4-5 feet some 7-8 times over the next 50 meters or so. Here due to the heavy snowfall in the last 10 days, and it being the hottest hour of the day, snow fell in the form of small avalanches at regular intervals. Therefore, our group leader, a young Naik, decided that we must run across this stretch with him in the lead, keeping an eye out for an avalanche. He was good. He got us across, stopping twice to avoid small avalanches. That turned out to be the last straw for me. As soon as the others stopped to take a breather, I sat down heavily in the snow and thereafter refused to budge. I told my fellow soldiers that they should carry on as I would sleep the night there and join them the next day!!

I do not know if they were bemused or angry. What I do know is that at that moment, I was being totally honest, for I had a headache of gargantuan proportions; the mother of all headaches. The sort I have never had before and after, and pray to never get again in my life or would never wish upon anybody. They spent the next hour feeding me Frooti, tea and biscuits and gently convincing me to come along. Then, all but one carried on.

As I sat there with my silent companion wondering when the headache would recede, and if I would be able to sleep at all at night, along came an angel. He sat down by my side and gave me sweet (over sweet) tea and spoke to me at length of this and that, of the ongoing cricket series, political happenings in Delhi, everything and anything, but the situation at hand. Another hour must have passed when feeling better now (for the headache had receded somewhat) I agreed to walk along with him, and stopping every few steps we made it to the next camp just as the sun set.

The warmth of the camp, the litres of tea, bowls of '*Thukpa*' and a few Brufen tablets had me feeling healthy again within a few hours and I spent the next day playing 'Sweep' with the soldiers even as we all laughed at how I had been the day before. Was it dehydration and fatigue or was it AMS (Acute Mountain Sickness)?

I still do not know. But, at that time it did not matter. All that mattered was that I had learnt that such things could happen to people as they ascend in trying conditions, and I had also learnt how to treat them. I was learning medicine from experience and the experienced and not books!

Illness on the Glacier

A soldier leads a busy life on the glacier. A day's routine work involves link duties (carrying rations and other material from a halfway point at which the lower staging camp people leave them, and doing the same for soldiers at higher camps), helipad maintenance, telephone line maintenance and camp maintenance, all of which involve a fair amount of labour. Work usually proceeds at a slow pace, for at extreme altitudes on the glacier, mild to moderate amount of labour such a shovelling snow or walking up a gentle incline carrying a weight makes one breathless. Yet, or maybe because of it, most of our soldiers are healthy at high and extreme altitudes.

The "routine" ailments of everyday life in a peace station are rarely seen here. Few if any soldiers develop viral infections, gastro-enteritis, fevers, common cold and the host of illnesses and injuries that are the bread and butter of a Regimental Medical Officer (RMO)'s practice in the plains. The reasons are probably two-fold. First, that except for some infections carried by ascending soldiers, there are few pathogens (disease causing viruses and bacteria) in the sparsely populated extreme cold environment here. The second

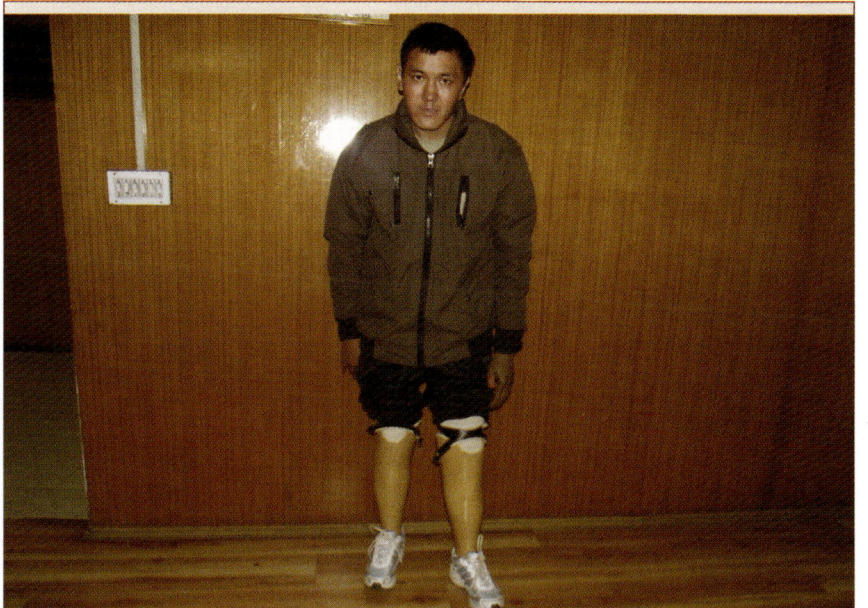

Nima Norbu after his recovery

reason would of course be that every CO ensures that only the fittest of soldiers are allowed to ascend to the glacier.

What does a doctor do then? The day's routine would begin for me with a leisurely breakfast in bed at around 8 AM. After this, while the soldiers completed their morning chores, the company commander and I would practice skiing under the tutelage of a long haired youngster. Ski classes done, we would catch up with the soldiers who having completed the days' tasks would be taking a break enjoying tea and "*pakoda*". The balance of the day would be spent playing games of cards, chess or noughts and crosses, telling tales (rather tall ones at times!) to regale the company and talking of home and family. We lived as a family. Usually, all the soldiers assembled in and around one hut during the day, and as they chatted and joked I assigned to myself the role of a listener, except when alone with the company commander. Another good pastime was to ring up all the satellite and staging posts, and chat to anyone who picked up the phone. While this kept me busy, it also allowed me to catch on early when somebody was feeling unwell. I think my most important role there was to listen to the soldiers to reassure them when they came to me for advice, and keep a stock of jokes and puns ready to make them laugh once in a while.

For a doctor, the critical period is when a new group of soldiers are "inducted" on the glacier. Most altitude related ailments are reported in the first week, as the body tries to compensate for the decreased air pressure and consequent fall in pressure of oxygen. As compensation is completed in a week or two, the risk of altitude related ailments rapidly decreases. Thus, it came as little surprise when a new battalion started being inducting to my post, and a number of them developed AMS en-route, or on arrival at the post. Thankfully, this ailment is self-limiting and the patient recovers with rest and/or simple medication, over a day or two. I do not recall the need for supplemental oxygen or Acetazolamide (a drug used specifically for treating moderate to severe AMS) having arisen in any individual. We preferred to save oxygen, which was available in limited amounts, for cases of HAPO and HACO, two potentially fatal and dreaded conditions amongst fresh inductees to such altitudes.

Once, two boys of the newly inducting battalion developed HAPO on arrival at the Zulu post. This post was notorious for the occurrence of HAPO, probably because it involved a climb of almost 4,000ft in a day. So a soldier started from approx 15,000ft early in the morning, was at almost 19,000ft by evening! The last part of the ascent is up a steep ice wall, all of 100 feet, on which the camp is located. The two who had developed HAPO were diagnosed by evening on the day after arrival at the post. Both were treated through the night and helicopter evacuation asked for. To everybody's dismay, however, the morning arrived densely clouded with heavy snow fall. The battalion being replaced were highland natives, and as mentioned earlier, very competent at these altitudes.

Oxygen reserves being low, it was decided to evacuate the boys to the lower staging post where both would definitely improve. One of the patients was badly off and unable to walk, while the other could walk. The bedridden soldier was put on a stretcher which was lifted by two of the highlander soldiers, as they began the descent down the ice wall on which the camp was located. Barely had they reached the base and begun to walk, to the horror of all straining to watch them in poor visibility conditions (due to the falling snow), the stretcher bearers along with the stretcher disappeared from sight, as if swallowed by the ground. They had walked into a crevasse, one of the many that dotted the valley floor. We lost both the stretcher bearers and the patient.

"Telemedicine is the invention of the army," a senior once proclaimed.

I agree.

Much before I had heard him speak, or heard of telemedicine at all I had practiced it, as every young doctor in the army does. It was usual for us to ring up our senior in the Base Camp, or specialists in the field hospital for advice on a puzzling case every once in a while. But during a new induction I had a "telemedicine" experience of a different kind. A new group of soldiers had arrived at Zulu the previous evening, when I got a call at 4 am from the officer there. One of the soldiers was unable to sleep, was very breathless and had a severe cough. It sounded like HAPO and I asked to talk to the patient. The moment the patient came on line it sounded like I was standing next to a gurgling stream of water. His lungs were full of water, so full that every inspiration and expiration produced loud bubbling sounds. I could not have got better diagnostic evidence if I had taken an X-ray. That was the only time I asked for a patient to be put in a HAPO bag along with doses of drugs and oxygen. Thankfully, two hours later he was better, and with sunrise he was air evacuated. In the Base Camp, the doctor diagnosed him as a case of severe HAPO.

Weather was and is the biggest enemy.

The casualties due to weather were far many more than due to illness, which outstripped casualties due to enemy action, not that enemy fire did not cause damage. We lost our artillery observation post officer, a bright youngster full of enthusiasm and zeal, fresh out of OTA. He died in artillery fire by the enemy, taking splinters through his chest and head. His radio operator too had a splinter through the chest and over the liver. But neither his lungs nor liver were damaged, the splinters had deflected off bone and lay harmlessly in the surrounding muscle. He survived. We (our battalion) also lost three boys in artillery firing on an adjacent post in a separate incident. In the same time duration, we lost three people in a crevasse accident (mentioned earlier) and a post on the northern glacier that sat atop a mountain was blown away in a night of gale force winds. Neither the five soldiers living there, nor any vestige of their camp could ever be traced. News of loss of life and limb in avalanches and blizzards would filter in every once in a while. The smallest mistake in judgement could be harshly punished. In the summer months, avalanches and new crevasses opening were a constant threat. A crevasse covered by many feet of snow in the winters, would have a progressively thinning layer of ice over its mouth in the summers, waiting to swallow an unsuspecting soldier who walked over it every day, and would be surprised to have the ground crumble under his feet on a given day.

Dogs are very useful creatures even at these altitudes. Other than company, they also offer invaluable service. We had a little pup, a local mastiff, carried up by one of the ascending soldiers. Named "Stupid" because of his habit of storing leftover pieces of meat in our sleeping bags, it started accompanying "link" patrols as it grew up. And on more occasion than one, it saved our lives. For it would dig in its feet and refuse to move, barking in protest the moment it approached a hidden crevasse! Soon we learnt to respect his judgement and avoided many a hidden crevasse that might otherwise have claimed life or limb.

I moved after three months from "Chandan" to "Darshak" a post a little higher in elevation and much more in the eye of enemy action. Here we lived in a fibreglass hut inside an ice cave, for this was where enemy artillery fire had claimed the lives of three as they slept in their huts "protected" by a ridge of ice. This had prompted the soldiers to dig a cave into the ice and move into it. No artillery fire can penetrate more than one foot of ice they say.

The post sat on a ridge approximately 1,800 ft above the valley floor. We climbed the steep mountainside to the post, using ropes secured by pitons to the ice covered mountainside. Every so often, one of us would survive a slip on the ice-wall. It would be a sobering thought for all of us when we considered what would have happened if the person had gone all the way down. Certain death! But nature can be a merciful teacher too. A young Naik, part of the battalion training team in the Siachen Battle School, got too sure of himself one day and undid his securing rope at the top of the ice wall. Such was his fate that within a few steps he slipped and went all the way down to the valley in an area observed by the enemy. The enemy helped us

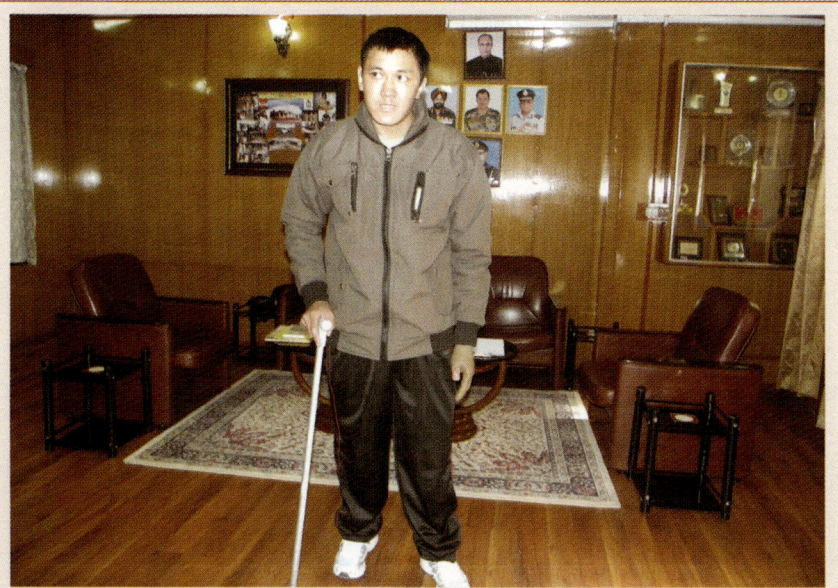

No one can make out Nima has three artificial limbs

search for him. We contacted them on radio, told them of what had happened and informed them that we would be searching for our man. There was no response on the radio, but that day they did not fire on us, as 10 of our boys spread out searching for the "fallen" soldier amongst the crevasses in the ice wall and on the valley floor. Where we expected the worst, late in the evening, as the sun set along with our hopes, one of our search parties heard groaning sounds coming from a crevasse at the bottom of the mountainside. The relief was palpable. He was pulled out of the crevasse, and from his examination I could find nothing but maybe a few fractured ribs! We bundled him off down to Base Camp. Next day we heard that "our man" was hale and hearty with not a wound, except maybe a wounded ego!

Were we scared? Did we think of death and danger often? No.

I did not, and I know the others with me did not either. Such thoughts eat away at your spirit. I think we all learnt to consciously put such thoughts aside. When the enemy got our people we seethed, till we got some of theirs in turn. When nature took our people, we held their memories to our hearts and learnt to respect caution over bravado. The boys carried on and worked with greater zeal

239

and caution, their spirits never flagging, making sure to maintain a cheerful face, taking greater care of each other. The spirit of our soldier is indeed insurmountable.

WINNING AGANST ALL ODDS

Capt Rajesh Mehta, of the 10 Dogra Regiment would never have thought that posting to Siachen would alter his life so drastically. When he ascended to 18,000 feet after proper acclimatisation, he led his men to the northern glacier in early 2005. Before going to the glacier, he was active in a counter-insurgency area, and also did a commando course, earning the coveted instructor grading. In February 2005, days after settling down at his post, Capt Rajesh developed clots in the veins of his brain, hands and legs. Doctors advised immediate evacuation, but a severe snow storm for 10 days however prevented any helicopter flying. His condition deteriorated. When flying resumed, he was first airlifted to Partapur, then flown to Chandigarh, before being admitted to the Research and Referral (R&R) hospital in Delhi.

The clotting was so severe that doctors had no option but to amputate his right leg from his hip, and the left leg from the knee, and the left arm from his elbow. Any lesser person and any other organisation would have given up. But, army doctors with their skills and care and Capt Rajesh with his indomitable spirit, helped on by his equally courageous wife, proved everyone wrong.

The army provided singular support to Rajesh by way of intensive medical care, and suitable employment in the army to rehabilitate him. Four years of treatment enabled Rajesh to recover. Artificial limbs were provided once his medical condition stabilised. Nearly nine years after he was evacuated from the glacier in a near-dead situation, Rajesh was promoted to the rank of Lieutenant Colonel, and is now posted in Pune.

As another retired officer describes: "Despite the physical and mental challenges he faced, Rajesh Mehta has continued doing his work devotedly and always with a helpful attitude to find solutions to the problems of soldiers. In such adverse physical conditions many would give up hope, but not this young man, a trained

Rajesh Mehta before he lost his limbs

commando and an inspirational leader of troops who lives up to the motto "*Mushkil waqt commando sakth* (*When the going gets tough the commando gets going*)."

As Rajesh says: "I am especially grateful to my wife, her courage, fortitude and support during our ups and downs. My young son

Lt Col Rajesh Mehta with his artificial limbs

241

too is a spirited and wonderful company for me. I feel great pride in being part of such a wonderful organisation, the Indian Army' and its humane approach to employment management, and thank them for taking care of me and my family in every way."

"I wish to share with you what helps me cope with my disabilities of triple amputation and CVA (Cerebral Vascular Accident)? As per medical prescriptions, I was bound to be on lifelong medication. During the post amputation period, when my entire time was spent on a hospital bed with hardly any scope of exercise except being picked up on a wheelchair and taken around. Fortunately for me, it was my doctor who suggested that I could follow the *Yoga/Pranayama* being telecast live on TV in the early mornings. Initially it was difficult for me to pick up the technique of *Anuloma pranayama*) that is breathing through alternate nostrils.

But after a period of one month, my body got used to deep slow inhaling and absorbing oxygen in abundance. I continued with medication till mid 2009 and also kept doing *Pranayamas*. I had to tolerate the strong side effects of the medications. But, in January 2010, my neuro-physician after detailed assessment of my progress felt I could taper down my medication.

And by the end of 2010, not only was I rid of my medication, but could also do 50 sit-ups on the bed. I continued with the same routine, and as on date I am able to do 200 sit-ups every day followed by an hour of *Pranayama*. Finally, I would advise all friends to allot some time every day to breathing exercises or *Pranayama*, and continue a medicine free healthy life."

The story of Nima Norbu, a porter from Warshi village, very close to the Siachen Base Camp is equally inspiring. A pleasant young man started carrying loads up the glacier like all his friends and family from the area when he was barely 20.

In December 2012, he was accompanying a platoon of soldiers and a group of fellow porters when he slipped into a crevasse all of a sudden. The crevasse was barely two feet in diameter, but was deep enough to swallow him. Initial efforts to pull him out failed and as night fell, rescue attempts had to be abandoned. Early next morning the search for Norbu began again. Through the day, soldiers and porters looked for him. Incredibly, as day light started fading again, Norbu was located nearly 25 hours after he fell in. Brought out unconscious, he was immediately flown to Partapur hospital and the next day to Chandigarh, and then to Delhi's RR hospital. Prolonged exposure to cold forced the doctors to amputate—much like Rajesh—three limbs.

From then on, life looked futile, but the army's fantastic support system came into play again. Voluntary personal donations, funds from the army welfare fund and world class medical attention allowed Norbu to rebuild his life. When I spoke to him in his village, at first glance, Norbu looked absolutely normal. Three artificial limbs now allow him to move about on his own. Family and friends have rallied around him. With a corpus of about Rs 11 lakh has given Norbu, a base to begin life anew.

"I cannot be my old self again, but such generous help from the Army has given me renewed hope. I am going to educate my child so that he does not have to become a porter," Norbu tells me.

What about his fellow porters? Do they fear going to the glacier?

Norbu says: "We never fear the mountains or glaciers. They are our natural abodes. My friends continue to go up. And they will continue to help the Army. After all, the Army is here to protect us Ladakhis," he tells me proudly.

This then is the story of Rajesh and Norbu, two different personalities, victims of two different circumstances, but both displaying an indomitable spirit.

A doctor at Norther Glacier

Dr. Sagarika Patiyal, Commandant of Leh's Army Hospital in Oct 2013

A medical post at Khardung La

A civilian being given oxygen at Khardung La

Doctors at Leh Army Hospital with the author

An instructor at the Siachen Battle School explaining the precautions
to be taken while deployed on the glacier

XII

A Civilian Perspective

'Our group was like a bunch of excited school children'

As I mentioned earlier, civilian treks to Siachen were restarted by the Army in 2007. In 2008, a young colleague from NDTV, Ketki Angre, then working out of Bombay (Mumbai if you like), volunteered to go on a three week trip. Here is her account:

Staying in Mumbai at mean sea level, the attraction of experiencing life at 15,000-feet has a certain ring to it, an allure, a thrill, a 'once-

The 2008 civilian trek participants receiving final instructions

The O P Baba temple complex

in-a-lifetime' opportunity written all over it. There was no way I was going to miss this chance.

The Army was conducting its second ever civilian trek to the Siachen glacier in 2008 to let 'civilians' like me, see firsthand, what it was like to be manning the highest battle ground in the world.

Our group was like a bunch of excited school children that has been taken out for a picnic, eager to live the adventure of a glacier so often spoken of, yet not open to all. We went through basic training that included walking in 'Scarpa' shoes that I can only describe as adding two kilos of weight to each foot, using an ice axe to climb a wall of ice, walking on horizontally placed ladders to cross a valley or deep crevasse, among other things.

We were introduced to the legend of O P Baba, who is the guardian angel of the soldiers on the glacier – no expedition to the glacier can start without seeking O P Baba's blessings. We bowed our heads in reverence, said a silent prayer and set off.

But nothing could have prepared us for what was to come. As you walk on the moraine, the only thing you become increasingly aware

'We have to go up there'

of, is not the beauty that surrounds you, or the clear blue sky and sun that shines on you. It is, instead, the heavy panting of your own breath, that is your constant companion, your lungs struggling to take in every little bit of oxygen there is at a height of 10,000-feet.

All around you, the mighty Himalayas rise in magnificence, at times mocking your small being, at times egging you on to continue. And then you notice the porters, (usually local mountain folk who carry provisions for the group) carrying more than twice the weight you have on your back, and literally walking with a spring in their step, as if they were out on a stroll. It is devastating for your morale, I can tell you, but it is also a good reminder of just what we were dealing with.

As I also had to film the trek for a documentary that I would put together later for my organisation, I hit on my next challenge. How do I keep the camera steady? I hadn't carried a tripod, as it would only increase the weight we were carrying, and shooting was only possible when we took breaks, or stopped for other groups to catch up and re-organise. Panting as I was, keeping the camera steady for getting some decent shots was turning out to be more difficult than what I had thought. At the end of the first day of our week-long trek, we reached Camp 1. It was no small achievement, I thought, covering some 10 odd kilometres. Except that what we took a whole day, while our jawans are used to doing in a couple of hours. We nursed our bruised egos with hot *chai* and dry fruits that the jawans had kept ready for us. **249**

At Camp 2, we got snowed out, and bad weather meant we could not move for two days. We realigned our plans and instead of Kumar Post at 16,000 ft, the highest we would reach was Camp 3 at 15,000 ft. That night at Camp 3, in minus 25 degrees Celsius, we were frozen to the bone. I know that unlike me, some were silently pleased that we would be starting our descent the next morning. There was relief that there would be only two more nights when we would struggle to crawl into the sleeping bags, and wake up with a start when the air you've exhaled has condensed, and the icy cold droplets trickle from the sleeping bag onto your face. In addition, to keep the camera batteries from draining out, and the camera from malfunctioning in the cold, I had to stuff both the camera and the spare batteries in the sleeping bag. I did have a battery charger, but it fused out the first day I tried to charge the cells. (There was a bulb in just one tent, a true luxury extended only for ladies, and it wasn't built to take too much wattage). It was like having a camera on life support! I had to make the batteries last till the whole trek was over, without the possibility of recharging them.

In our heads, the trek was no small achievement. We had braved the biting cold, the tough terrain, struggled to breathe, walked on slippery ice, and triumphed in our own little ways, knowing fully well that what we experienced was just the tip of the iceberg, as they say.

A long walk on the glacier in the summer months

All roped up!

More soldiers have been lost to extreme weather, than to enemy fire. At some of the highest forward posts, the night temperatures can go as low as minus 60 degrees celsius. You see the same faces around you for weeks, where even having a conversation means precious energy wasted, energy that you would rather conserve, acutely aware that it is after all a battle field. Though choppers fly to many forward posts, the weather is as fickle as it comes, sunny one moment and cloudy the next. Even everyday routine like brushing and washing up is a tedious job. And then there is the serious worry of frostbites and snow blindness. High altitude pulmonary edema and high altitude cerebral edema can strike unannounced and when it comes, evacuation is only possible if the weather doesn't play spoilsport. Or worse, feeling helpless, watching your colleague struggle to breathe, when the inclement weather has forced a rescue chopper to return. Even worse, seeing his limp body lie there waiting for the weather to clear out so that he can get back to his family, albeit, in a body bag.

For us, this trek was an adventure. Something we could narrate to our friends and families when we went back home. But for the jawans, who are on the forward posts day in and day out, in the most punishing of winters, in the most trying circumstances, simply surviving is an everyday battle.

251

Taking a break

Mayank Singh, a widely-travelled journalist and enthusiastic history buff works with *The Sunday India* magazine. He too was on the same civilian trek with Ketki Angre. Here is his account.

HEIGHTS OF VALOUR

Siachen is different in every sense, as once you reach there, your closest friends are hard ice and the Karakoram and Saltoro mountain ranges.

My meeting with Major Gopal reinforced this view in every sense.

Posted at 22,000-feet for three months, the mandatory maximum duration of stay at such heights, Major Gopal and his colleagues had been hit by the so-called *"Siachen Factor"*.

In 2008, down below, the entire Army was agog with the Pay Commission controversy, but Major Gopal and his fellow soldiers were blissfully unaware of the issue, which had seen an unprecedented stand taken by the military in protesting discrimination against the men and women in uniform.

As I broached the subject, all he and others could think of, were their homes, sitting before television sets, newspapers in hand, some warm soup and a normal domestic life.

Major Gopal was on his way down from the Bana post.

We first reached Base Camp, at 12,000-feet. Our instructor, Lance Naik Mohammad Latief Khan, told us to avoid being adventurous, and to stay calm, but at this height, where one felt so close to the Almighty, I just wanted to walk across the mesmerising terrain.

But, within the first hour, we thanked Khan, breathless as we were, since it took us four days to acclimatise, and it was then, that we saw the porters and link commanders. The first were people who carried our heavy luggage, scampering about like mountain goats; the second, soldiers who knew their way between camps blindfolded, as heavy snow obliterates all landmarks. Our true friends were the porters and safety ropes, the dividing line between life and death.

Hence, if the Almighty was even within reach, he had already sent his seconds-in-command – the porters and link commanders -- and their hopes lay in "OP Baba".

Every step is a struggle to inhale oxygen uncomfortably. The path to various glacial posts and camps is a test of both nerve and spirit. The crevices were like mouths open to engulf into their limitless nadir, and the ladders placed over them were precarious. The sound of gushing

Big challenge: Crossing a crevasse

253

water added to the fear factor. Temperatures inside, we were told, reach as low as minus 200 degrees Celsius.

We saw the bodies of two retrieved soldiers in an intact state, and were told that they had fallen into the crevice 14 years ago. This frightening scenario notwithstanding, what seemed beautiful was the tender blue reflection of pure ice.

Nights were even more beautiful, with the stars at their clearest.

Experiencing life in Siachen, makes one realise the importance of a lungful of breath, as at this height, oxygen is rarefied.

A harsh terrain, uncertain and inclement weather and a rarefied atmosphere are principal causes of casualties on the Siachen glacier.

The situation has, however, improved. Earlier soldiers succumbed commonly to wind chilling frostbite and hypothermia, well beyond human endurance. The lack of oxygen due to the very low atmospheric pressure exposes troops to "altitude sickness", which includes dizziness, headaches, vomiting, insomnia, dehydration, heart palpitations, pulmonary embolism and pulmonary oedema.

Many are also affected by the "Siachen Syndrome", or psychological problems linked to physical stresses arising out of extreme altitude warfare.

The bitter cold aggravates even minor ailments or hurts old ones on a body. Touching metal can result in your skin peeling off.

A team mate, Moses Kunzang, was aware that pouring hot water over a part stuck with metal releases the skin.

Answering nature's call while sitting on a plank of wood perched over two kerosene drums, tests your balancing skills.

To save one from snowfall and high winds, a metal pole was erected wrapped with a parachute cloth.

In answering the call of nature, Moses lost his balance, but grabbed the pole to save himself from falling on moraine. So, half the water meant for washing self, poured slowly between palm and metal pole. Amit

Accommodation for the civilians

Kumar, another team mate, started panting, lost his nerve, and then had that empty feeling.

Luckily, Captain (Dr.) Manish Mishra, who was with us, correctly assessed that Amit had had an anxiety attack, but could be evacuated safely and immediately by helicopter from Camp I. But, situations can take a turn for the worse, and nobody can do anything – not even a doctor.

Avalanches are common due the extremely steep gradients of adjacent mountains. The glacier is also lacerated by treacherous crevasses. The ambient surface temperature drops below minus 40°C during the long and fluctuating Himalayan winter. High altitudes combined with low temperatures and glaciation, frequently results in blizzards with wind speeds in excess of 150 knots.

Coming face-to-face with a life threatening situation did not take long. At Camp II, some troops moving down from 20,000-feet and we moving upwards met, and suddenly the weather changed. It started snowing and visibility dropped to 10 meters. A soldier, Sepoy Amarjeet Singh, started having loose motions. A doctor gave him some pills, but there was no relief. His condition deteriorated. In such conditions, **255** helicopters cannot fly and nobody is allowed to move, as soft snow covers all marks, which keeps one away from crevices at every step.

For the next two days, we faced incessant snowfall. Luckily, Amarjeet experienced relief by the next morning. In all this, our food stock was reduced gradually. After two days, with the weather clearing, our first target was to restock Camp II.

Proceeding to Camp III, we reached there by the evening after a seven-hour-long walk. Camp III is much narrower compared to Camps I and II. The height was 15,000-feet and the wind was picking up speed. By night, a sense of uneasiness prevailed even inside our double layered and specially ordered tented accommodation from Austria. Temperatures plummeted to minus 25 Celsius at night, and by morning, small granules of ice had formed at the spot from where I was breathing out.

But our motivation was that next day, we were going to Connaught Place or Camp IV, which is also known as the Kumar Post, and acts as the Base Camp for the higher and largely isolated reaches.

The heights and difficult conditions isolate the men, but while we were there just for a fortnight, our morale was high.

But, just think of those lodged inside the six by six feet cabins for months. The blizzard gave us time to interact. We played *Antaakshari* all the while, and the phone line to Bana post was linked to soldiers up there hearing us sing.

"Please come up here for a day so that we too can enjoy," they said.

Their emotions were best summed up by Corporal Pramod: "We heard 20 days ago that you were coming. Since then, we have been waiting to see someone not in olive."

We were to reach Camp IV next, but had to return, because of foul weather.

On our way back, we discussed what life after Siachen would be like.

Wing Commander Shobit Prakash said he would send pictures to his colleagues: They must realise what our soldiers' face.

Yana Bey, the lady from the Indian Mountaineering Federation, said "compared to other treks, this one was much too overwhelming. I feel lost in this huge and harsh reality."

Her pictures from Siachen will be in her drawing room, a constant inspiration.

As for me, Siachen was heaven, because it took me closer to the infinite. But, for the soldiers living in those tents, it is close to realising what hell is all about.

Indian and Pakistani troops face each other at altitudes in excess of 6000 meters above sea level. They are literally fighting on the roof of the world in extreme weather.

These extremities have been faced by our soldiers with individual courage, ingenuity and innovation in matters of survival.

The dispute over the Siachen glacier cannot be analysed in abstract. Its strategic importance needs to be assessed from a wider focus, inclusive of the state of Jammu and Kashmir.

Each step for the civilians can be painful

Summiting Sia Kangri in the Siachen glacier complex when the weather is clear, one can see Tibet, Xinjiang in China, Afghanistan and the Central Asian Republics.

Most fascinating during the walk on ice, was the thought that China was on my right and the Pakistani camps on my left, besides the knowledge that the whole area consisted of a network of strategic highways.

At stake in the Siachen dispute, is control of the northern reaches of Kashmir, not to speak of national prestige.

Siachen soldiers giving a guard of honour at the Base Camp

A camp in the higher reaches

A photographer's delight

A well organised camp: Big change from early days

XIII

Why India Cannot
Give Up Siachen

'Don't forget, Kargil happened because of Siachen'

In April 2012, Pakistan's then Army Chief Ashfaq Pervez Kayani suddenly called for demilitarisation of the Siachen glacier for the "development of Pakistan and environmental reasons." "India and Pakistan must live in peaceful coexistence as defence without development is neither viable nor acceptable," he declared. He saw all issues dividing India and Pakistan as capable of resolution and Siachen and Sir Creek, as convenient starting points, low hanging fruits to be plucked as strong confidence building measures.

This was completely out of character and a departure from Pakistan's position on the Siachen glacier.

So what prompted the change of heart?

Actually, it was the tragic death of 130 troops of the 6 Northern Light Infantry in a massive avalanche at Gayari on 7 April that year which triggered Gen Kayani's new thought process. After visiting the site of the accident, Gen Kayani spoke at Skardu about the need to demilitarise Siachen. He said Pakistan was not manning those treacherous heights out of choice. "The world knows why we are in Siachen," reiterating the Pakistani position that it was India which started the dispute in 1984.

But, even while announcing the desire to make peace with India on 'Siachen and Sir Creek', Gen Kayani was economical with the truth.

The ground reality is that Pakistani troops are nowhere near the Siachen glacier. Its deployment is on the western slopes of the Saltoro ridge, far away from the glacier and at much lower altitudes.

Indian positions on the other hand are on absolutely dominating heights on the main passes of the Saltoro ridge, Sia La and Bilafond La. As far as the Indian Army is concerned, it sees no need to withdraw from the commanding heights it controls given Pakistan's perfidy in the past, especially in Kargil when it tried to cut-off Siachen in the summer of 1999.

Three months after Gen Kayani made the offer to demilitarise Siachen, I was in Kargil, west of Siachen and at a much lower altitude along the Line of Control (LoC) with Pakistan. Every year on 26 July, the Indian Army celebrates its victory here. Having reported on the area for 45 days during the 1999 conflict, I try and visit Kargil every year to participate in the function that pays tribute to the 500 plus soldiers who died fighting the Pakistani intruders and eventually evicting them.

But in 2012, I had one more task at hand. I wanted to formally interview for NDTV, the channel I work for, Lt Gen KT Parnaik, a highly respected General and then India's Northern Army Commander.

The Northern Command, Indian Army's operationally most active command, has the unique task of guarding India's vast land borders with both China and Pakistan. Its responsibility stretches from the forbidding heights of Karakoram down to the plains of Jammu. Moreover, it has been involved in counter-insurgency operations against the infiltrating terrorists from Pakistan in the state of Jammu & Kashmir continuously for over a quarter century now. Of particular interest to me in 2012 however, was Northern Command's reaction to Gen Kayani's rather unexpected call to try and 'resolve' Siachen.

As we sat down to record the interview, I worked through the usual questions about the threat posed by terrorists, the fragile peace in the Kashmir Valley and the deployment along the LoC. But, I was actually itching to seek his answer on the Siachen issue. Finally I asked him:

What is it that the Indian Army is concerned about with respect to

Siachen? His answer, later circulated widely, put paid to any hopes Pakistan may have had in India agreeing to demilitarise the Siachen glacier area.

Gen Parnaik said:

You see, to understand Siachen, I think one needs to be geographically oriented to the region. And let me simply put it, because I'm telling you without a map, that the Siachen glacier is bounded on the west by the Saltoro Range, which is a very high range and to the east by the Karakoram Range and the Nubra River. So, per se the Siachen glacier is a sort of an iced river, which flows in between them. The Saltoro Range, actually provides domination of the entire area...There is a strategic implication of the Saltoro Range, and the implication is you have the Pakistanis sitting in the northern areas, which we keep saying is illegally occupied, it's Pakistan occupied Kashmir. Now out of the other areas that they have occupied, they have illegally ceded the Shaksgam Valley to the Chinese. Shaksgam Valley lies to the north of the glacier. And if Saltoro Range was held by the (Pakistanis), it practically enables them to bridge the Aksai Chin and northern areas gap, which is with China, and also exercise complete control over the Karakoram Pass. Therefore, strategically, it is an important area. And we feel, by holding these areas, we would effectively deny approaches to Kargil and Leh. Now, in security parlance, for the country it is of strategic importance. That is one reason. The second reason is that we have had a number of rounds of talks on this. A large number of solutions have been offered. One of the biggest issues that has not been resolved yet is that we insist that for anything to happen in Siachen, the Pakistanis must first accept the actual line of ground position, and delineate the line along the positions that are being held by the troops today, both theirs and ours, as is, where is. They do not seem to be amenable to this sort of a thing. They continue to say that we should go back to 1971 and 1953, when this whole area was not demarcated, so you should vacate it. Don't forget, Kargil happened because of Siachen... If you peruse their own records, which are now public, one of the major objectives of what they did in Kargil was to force us to vacate the Siachen glacier. Now, if that is their intent and that is their credibility, it is up to you to judge whether we should be really vacating the glacier or not.

As a follow up, my next question was: Does the government understand these strategic implications?

Gen Parnaik said emphatically: *See, the offer that was made by the Pakistan Army Chief, probably in the wake of the tragedy that took place in Gayari. If they find it difficult (to remain there), they are most welcome to withdraw to safe places. And let me assure you, the Indian Army has no evil designs to set across for those areas and capture those territories. This aspect is also well known to our leaders. So that is where it rests."*

In one short, swift answer, Gen Parnaik had demolished the case that was sought to be built by Gen Kayani that *both* India and Pakistan need to withdraw from Siachen! He was only reiterating what successive Army Chiefs and Northern Army Commanders have stated.

Over the past three decades, the Indian Army ably supported by the Indian Air Force has mastered the treacherous mountains, and has evolved a high altitude doctrine that is the envy of the world. In the process, the Indian military has shed blood, made enormous sacrifices and braved the elements. No wonder, the military leadership has told the political executive time and again that it is against any withdrawal from the Saltoro ridge and Siachen glacier.

As we have seen, at the heart of the problem is the interpretation of the 1949 Karachi and 1972 Simla agreements by both sides. During both these negotiations, India and Pakistan demarcated their borders only up to Point NJ 9842. This includes the 772 km Ceasefire Line in 1949, now known as the LoC or Line-of-Control. It was stated in the agreements that the border would run "thence north" from map grid reference NJ 9842.

The Cease-Fire Agreement was signed in Karachi by top military representatives of India and Pakistan and the UN Military Observer Group. The purpose of the Karachi meeting (July 18 to 27) was to establish "a ceasefire line in the State of J&K" in pursuance of Part I of the key UN resolution of 13 August, 1948 that prescribed a ceasefire.

Present at the Karachi Conference were members of the Truce Committee of the UN Commission for India and Pakistan, Hernando Semper of Colombia (Chairman), William L.S. Williams (U.S), Lt-Gen Maurice Delvoie, Military Adviser; and Miguel A. Martin (Legal Adviser). Pakistan was represented by Maj. Gen W.J. Cawthorn, Maj. **264** GenNazir Ahmad, Brigadier Sher Khan and a couple of observers.

Representing India were Lt. Gen S.M Shrinagesh, Maj. Gen K.S. Thimayya and Brigadier Sam Manekshaw, with H.M Patel and Vishnu Sahay as observers.

The Karachi Agreement delineated the entire CFL, demarcating over 740 km on the ground. With the CFL increasingly running through high mountains and glaciated areas as it traversed north, it often followed a directional path in the absence of clear landmarks. Thus, finally, "Chalunka (on the Shyok River), Khor, thence North to the glaciers," passing through grid reference NJ 9842. The segment beyond NJ 9842 was by mutual agreement not demarcated on the ground, being a highly elevated, glaciated, unexplored and unpopulated region that had not witnessed any fighting. A plebiscite was soon to follow and the matter, it was assumed, would then be settled.

The delineation of the northern-most segment of the CFL was, however, unambiguous: NJ 9842, "thence north to the glaciers". If every one of 30 or more earlier directional commands were meticulously followed in tracing the CFL, there was no reason whatsoever for any departure from this norm in the case of the very last command. "Thence north", could only mean due north to wherever the boundary of J&K state lay. The very next section crucially directed that "the ceasefire line described above" be drawn "so as to eliminate any no man's land". Therefore, the Line, whether delineated or demarcated could in no way be left hanging in the air.

The Cease Fire Line was ratified by both sides. Twenty-three years later, it was revalidated as the Line of Control by the Suchetgarh Agreement of December 1972, in the wake of the Shimla Agreement between Prime Minister Indira Gandhi and Zulfikar Ali Bhutto. Both sides also agreed with the LoC, and the military gains made by either side in J&K in the 1971 war. Thus, in the Kargil-Siachen sector, all territorial gains went entirely to India which acquired the Turtuk salient comprising five villages (Chalunka, Thang, Tyakshi, Pharol and Turtok) just south and west of NJ 9842. This modest but important military acquisition, provided India an additional territorial bulwark against hostile cartographic or physical claims on Siachen.

While India interprets this to mean due north (along the ridge line, as is the international convention), leading to the northern tip of the Saltoro ridge known as Indira Col, Pakistan claims that the line should run northeast towards the Karakoram Pass which leads into Tibet. **265**

As many officers who have served on the glacier and in the Northern Command have pointed out time and again, occupation of the Saltoro and Siachen provides a buffer for Ladakh and in military parlance, the much needed depth for important mountain passes that are gateways to Ladakh and onto Kashmir.

There are however, a number of 'experts' who argue that it is futile to hold on to the positions on the Saltoro ridgeline, because they are important only tactically and have no strategic significance. As one Indian Army officer has written: "They are obviously unaware of the prevailing conditions in Siachen. If ever there was a tactical gain that was instrumental in providing exponential dividend to a strategic cause, this is the one."

Through innovation, hard work and sustained efforts to improve the situation, the Indian Army has established such a strong, and controlling position that it enjoys overwhelming operational and psychological superiority in Siachen. It would be folly to give up the advantage.

Self-proclaimed analysts have put forward arguments in favour of demilitarising Siachen citing the high human and material costs that the Indian military has to pay. Let us examine the costs. Between 1984 and 2007, Parliament was told that 884 Indian soldiers were killed and 13,022 wounded. That makes it an average of 38 dead in a year and 550 plus wounded. But, the figures don't reflect the fact that since the ceasefire agreement between India and Pakistan went into effect in 2003, battle casualties are down to zero. Even weather casualties are now down to a single digit on an average, in a year. This is a sea change from the first two decades of the conflict when weather and battle casualties both were high.

Financially, India has reportedly spent over Rs 8,000 crores since 1984 on *Operation Meghdoot*. The recurring costs today are pegged at about Rs 365 crores. This is no financial burden for a military that has an annual budget of Rs 2, 24,000 crore or about US 38 billion dollars (2014).

Infrastructure in the Siachen sector has developed over the years. Pipelines for kerosene and water have been laid, and better facilities have been organised in every sphere of activity. Therefore, the expenditure incurred now is more in the form of maintenance and regular improvements. Over the years, improvements in living conditions, health facilities and communications have reduced the attrition rate significantly. Today, financial and human costs for *Operation Meghdoot* are sustainable.

So why is there fresh clamour for demilitarising Siachen? More importantly, can it be done? Several experts have weighed in on the issue, and as in every other issue concerning India and Pakistan, opinion is divided right down the middle.

De-militarisation by itself is a process that consists of several logical steps: ceasefire, authentication, demarcation, withdrawal, re-deployment and verification. This concept, everyone agrees, is the best possible solution. So why is there no forward movement?

The primary cause of disconnect is the sequence of the process of de-militarisation. India insists on authentication of current troops' position as the first step. The Pakistanis want Indian troops to withdraw to pre-1972 positions before any further discussions can take place.

Then there is the question of trust.

What if the agreement is flouted and positions occupied by the Pakistan Army? The level of mistrust between India and Pakistan in general, and the Indian and Pakistani Security Forces in particular is deep-rooted, and cannot be overturned so easily.

Yet there are many 'peaceniks' who propose a unilateral withdrawal from Siachen, among them military officers who professed to be hawks while in service, but who turned doves when out of it.

Several diplomats and analysts have said India must recognise Pakistan's compulsions and offer a face-saving formula, so that the agreement on Siachen does not look like a defeat for the Pakistani Army. This is utter nonsense. If Pakistan wants demilitarisation of Saltoro-Siachen, it must first accept the fact that Pakistani Army troops are NOWHERE NEAR THE SIACHEN GLACIER.

More pragmatic military leaders like Lt Gen Nanavatty have suggested a practical formula. He says: "India's approach towards a final settlement should be based on demilitarisation of the limited and well-defined mutually agreed prescribed area." Essential steps for this, he says, begin with a political agreement followed by a formal ceasefire, delimitation, demarcation, disengagement, redeployment and verification.

The bottom-line, according to General Nanavatty, is that any peaceful resolution of Indo-Pakistan disputes is possible only when the two countries cease to view each other as military adversaries.

Officially too, India and Pakistan continue to hold dialogue over Siachen. Between 1986 and 2012, 13 rounds of talks have been held. Twice, past reports suggest, both countries came close to an agreement, but political considerations rather than military compulsions prevented any final breakthrough. As Gen Raghavan said a decade ago: "The assumption that demilitarisation is being hampered by military obduracy is, of course a misplaced one. The record of negotiations (between 1986 and 2003) on Siachen is evidence enough of the political problems in bringing about demilitarisation."

Not much has changed since then.

After the last round (held in Rawalpindi in June 2012), the bland joint statement at the end of the two day talks shows how little progress has been made on the Siachen issue. The statement said:

- The Defence Secretary level talks between Pakistan and India on Siachen were held at the Ministry of Defence, Rawalpindi from 11 – 12 June 2012. The Pakistan delegation was headed by Ms. Nargis Sethi, Secretary Defence. The Indian delegation was headed by Mr. Shashi Kant Sharma, Defence Secretary of India.
- The Defence Secretary of India called on the Minister for Defence Syed Naveed Qamar.
- The talks were held in a cordial and friendly atmosphere. Both sides reaffirmed their resolve to make serious, sustained and result oriented efforts for seeking an amicable resolution of Siachen. It was agreed to continue dialogue on Siachen in keeping with the desire of the leaders of both countries for early resolution of all outstanding issues. Both sides acknowledged that the ceasefire was holding since 2003.
- It was agreed that the next round of talks on Siachen will be held in New Delhi on mutually convenient dates, to be fixed through diplomatic channels.

The civilian leadership in India has so far backed the military's stand despite Prime Minister Manmohan Singh's avowed wish to make Siachen a "mountain of peace." However, giving up a dominant military position on Siachen without iron-clad guarantees would be a fool's errand, especially in view of the enormous sacrifices and hardships that Indian soldiers have braved in these past three decades to defend Siachen and keep the Indian flag flying.

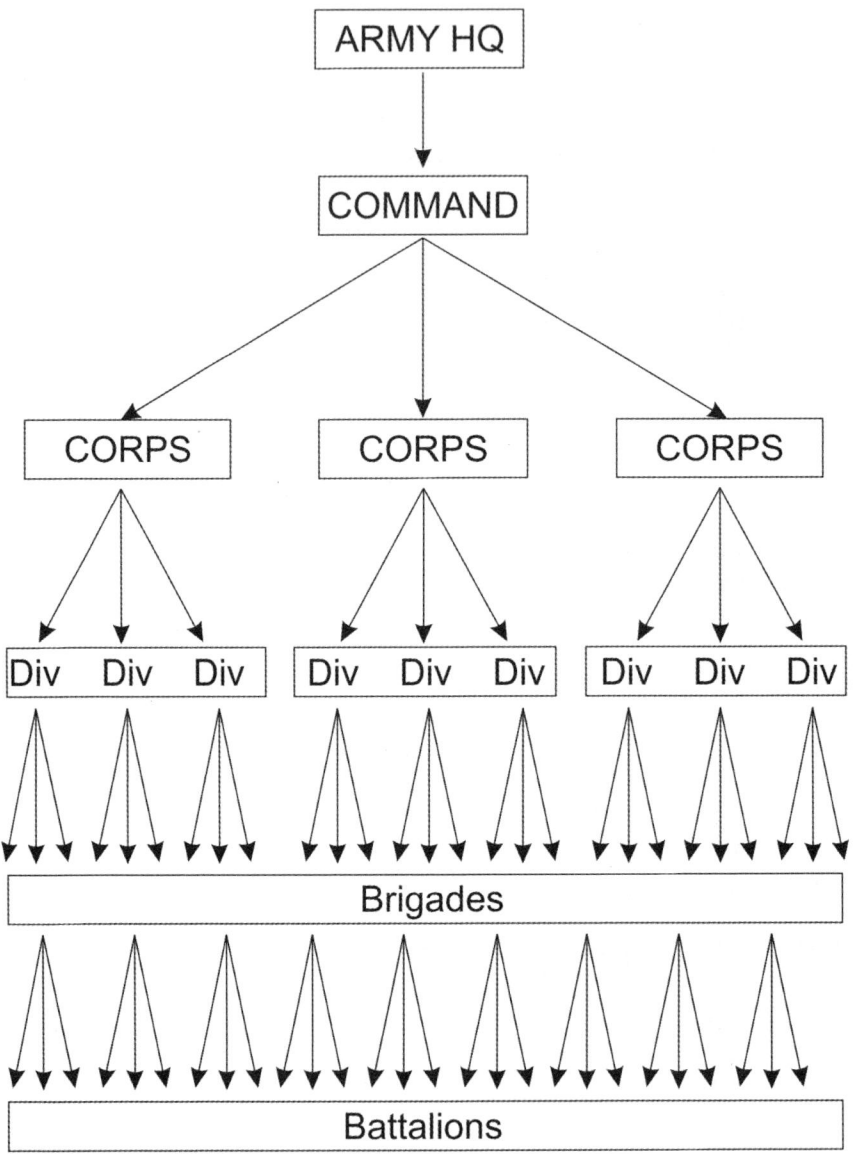

Note: 4-5 companies make one battalion.

Commanders: Siachen Brigade

 BRIG VN CHANNA, AVSM, VSM**
Commander, 26 Sector, Nov 82 to Oct 84
(Retd as Brig)

 BRIG JAL MASTER, PVSM, VSM
01 Mar 85 to 26 Feb 87
(Retd as Brig)

 BRIG CS NUGYAL, UYSM
27 Feb 87 to 17 Oct 88
(Retd as Maj Gen)

 BRIG RK Nanavatty, UYSM
18 Oct 88 to 22 Nov 90
(Retd as Lt Gen)

 BRIG AB MASIH, UYSM
23 Nov 90 to 26 Dec 91
(Retd as Lt Gen)

 BRIG VK JETLEY, UYSM
27 Dec 91 to 13 Oct 93
(Retd as Lt Gen)

 BRIG TEJ PATHAK, YSM**
14 Oct 93 to 25 Dec 95
(Retd as Lt Gen)

 BRIG KS RANDHIR SINGH, UYSM, SM
26 Dec 95 to 09 Dec 97
(Retd as Maj Gen)

 BRIG PC KATOCH, UYSM, SC
10 Dec 97 to 23 Dec 99
(Retd as Lt Gen)

BRIG RS JAMWAL
24 DEC 99 TO 14 OCT 2000
(Retd as Lt Gen)

BRIG ASHOK DUGGAL,YSM,VSM
31 Oct 00 to 19 Oct 01
(Retd as Maj Gen)

BRIG S K SINGH
20 Oct 01 to 03 Sep 03
(Retd as Lt Gen)

BRIG HPS BEDI
04 Sep 03 to 28 Mar 05
(Retd as Brig)

BRIG OM PRAKASH, SM
29 Mar 05 to 09 Dec 06
(Serving Lt Gen)

BRIG KG KRISHNA, VSM
10 DEC 06 TO 12 JUN 08
(Serving Maj Gen)

BRIG AVINASH SINGH
13 JUN 08 TO 08 NOV 09
(Serving Maj Gen)

BRIG PARAMJIT SINGH, SM
09 NOV 09 TO 23 FEB 11
(Serving Brig)

BRIG RS BHADAURIA
22 FEB 11 TO 01 MAY 11
(Serving Brig)

BRIG SK RAO
02 MAY 11 TO 31 OCT 12
(Serving Brig)

BRIG KP SINGH
01 NOV 12 -Till date
(Present Commander)

Glossary

ADIZ	:	Air Defence Information Zone
Ali Brangsa	:	Temporary camp
AMC	:	Army Medical Corps
CAS	:	Chief of Air Staff
CFL	:	Ceasefire Line, the line between India and Pakistan in J&K between 1949-1972
CO	:	Commanding Officer
COAS	:	Chief of the Army Staff
Depsang	:	Flat Open space
DGMI	:	Director General Military Intelligence
DGMO	:	Director General Military Operations
HACO	:	High Altitude Cerebral Oedema
HAPO	:	High Altitude Pulmonary Oedema
HAWS	:	India's High Altitude Warfare School
Hepter, Chopper	:	Helicopters
ISI	:	Inter-Services Intelligence, Pakistan's spy agency
Izzat	:	Prestige
JCO	:	Junior Commissioned Officer
Karakoram	:	Place of black gravel
Khalsar	:	Village at the floor
La	:	Pass
Ladakh	:	Land of high passes
Leh	:	Plateau
LoC	:	Line of control, the line between India and Pakistan in J&K since 1972

NLI	:	Northern Light Infantry, Pakistan
PoK	:	Pakistan Occupied Kashmir
Pullu	:	Temporary Shelter
R&AW	:	Research and Analysis Wing, India' external Intelligence agency
RAP	:	Regimental aid post
Sasoma	:	New earth
Sia Kangri	:	Peak
Sitrep	:	Situation Report